THE HIP-HOP GENERATION
FIGHTS BACK

THE HIP-HOP GENERATION
FIGHTS BACK

YOUTH, ACTIVISM, AND POST–CIVIL RIGHTS POLITICS

ANDREANA CLAY

NEW YORK UNIVERSITY PRESS
New York *and* London

NEW YORK UNIVERSITY PRESS
New York and London
www.nyupress.org

References to Internet websites (URLs) were accurate at the time of writing. Neither the author nor New York University Press is responsible for URLs that may have expired or changed since the manuscript was prepared.

Library of Congress Cataloging-in-Publication Data
Clay, Andreana.
The hip-hop generation fights back : youth, activism, and post-civil rights politics / Andreana Clay.
p. cm.
Includes bibliographical references and index.
ISBN 978-0-8147-1716-5 (cl : alk. paper)
ISBN 978-0-8147-1717-2 (pb : alk. paper)
ISBN 978-0-8147-2395-1 (ebook)
ISBN 978-0-8147-6374-2 (ebook)
1. Youth — United States — Social conditions — 21st century. 2. Youth — United States — Social life and customs — 21st century. 3. Youth — Political activity — United States. 4. Social movements — United States — History — 21st century. 5. Hip-hop. I. Title.
HQ796.C5943 2012
305.2350973 — dc23   2011052261

New York University Press books are printed on acid-free paper, and their binding materials are chosen for strength and durability. We strive to use environmentally responsible suppliers and materials to the greatest extent possible in publishing our books.

Manufactured in the United States of America
c 10 9 8 7 6 5 4 3 2 1
p 10 9 8 7 6 5 4 3 2 1

CONTENTS

★ ▼ ★

ACKNOWLEDGMENTS

The completion of this book has been a long and rewarding process, much of which has been collaborative. I have been nurtured and sustained by community, in all forms. From my first introduction to the two organizations and the youth I write about here to the writing groups that encouraged me through the final push, I have many people to thank. I am indebted to the youth that I met through my research and activism who allowed me to me hang out in their spaces, gave me extra time to ask them invasive questions, and communicate the stories that have shaped not only this book but my perception of and commitment to Oakland, California. Their organizing frameworks, creativity, and integrity has enriched my life more than they know. Thank you for the work you have done and continue to do.

John Hall, Laura Grindstaff, Belinda Robnett, and Herman Gray supported, encouraged, and advised me as a doctoral student. As a group, they never questioned my work with youth of color and the interdisciplinary frames I used to explain my research. Belinda, in particular, has answered numerous emails, had lengthy discussions about social movements and activism, and provided mentorship to me as a junior scholar and woman of color since that time. I also must thank Ilene Kalish and Aiden Amos at NYU Press, who encouraged me every step of the way as I wrote, rewrote, put forth new ideas, and changed things, including deadlines. Ilene, in particular, has been supportive of my work for many years prior to my coming to NYU, which has meant a lot. The enthusiasm and critical feedback of the anonymous reviewers also helped me make important decisions about this book.

My colleagues at San Francisco State University have also been a steady source of support. Each member of the Department of Sociology has encouraged my work by reading chapters, using my work in their courses, setting up dialogue around youth, culture, and social movements, and providing me with an academic home. Jessica Fields and Ed McCaughan, whose work on youth and cultural movements has informed and nurtured my own, have provided some of the most support in the form of ongoing conversations, formal and informal, about these topics, and they remind me about the importance of being a scholar activist. They have also become my good friends. Other friend-colleagues, like Chris Bettinger and Allen LeBlanc have accompanied me to the nearby mall for some much needed shopping therapy. Outside of Sociology, past and present colleagues on campus, like Nancy Mirabal, Tiffany Willoughby-Herard, Dawn-Elissa Fischer, and Catrióna Esquibel have also provided immense support, feedback, and friendship in this endeavor. Juan Hernandez and Felicia Gardner provided invaluable research assistance, feedback, and conversation. And Joel Kassiola, in the dean's office in Behavioral and Social Sciences also provided financial and academic support at San Francisco State in the form of academic release time and summer support. Finally, research funding from UC Regents, San Francisco State University, and the César Chávez Institute has provided additional financial support at various stages in the research and writing process.

Perhaps most important is the amazing community of friends/family that has been there for me through every stage of this process. I would not have been able to complete any of this work without them. I received writing feedback through various writing groups and one-on-ones with Anna Muraco, Clare Stacey, Nadine Naber, Darshan Elena Campos, Ana Maurine Lara, Nancy Mirabal, Maylei Blackwell, Marcia Ochoa, Luz Calvo, Catrióna Esquibel, Dana Wright, Tamara Roberts, Tiffany Willoughby-Herard, Mako Fitts, and Dawn-Elissa Fischer, which kept me going in some of my hardest times as a scholar. Much of this community has also provided me with the solid friendship necessary to engage in and complete this work. Each person read chapters and "coached" me through conversation and created a strong woman of color community for me in the academy. Maylei Blackwell and I added writing partners to our friend/family relationship and talked every week during the last year of revisions. Her feedback and encouragement pushed me in places I didn't know were possible, and it has made me a better writer and scholar. Nancy Mirabal and Anna Muraco allowed me to call them whenever necessary, literally, or leave messages about particular chapters and/or "freak outs." They also have added stomach-busting laughter like I've never experienced when I needed it most. Tiffany Willoughby-Herard is one of the best cheerleaders (for lack of a better word) I've ever encountered, and Mako Fitts has been my girl/ scholar/friend in all things hip-hop, youth, and activism—"you girl." Finally, Marcia Ochoa has been a dear friend who has challenged me to remember that I can push the interdisciplinary line even more (not to mention, surf!).

Other friends/family have made up the community that has nurtured me as a person, scholar, writer, activist, and friend: Kris Woolery, Veronica Terriquez, Kimberly Aceves, and Kanwarpal Dhaliwal are some of the women of color activists that inspired me to do this work in the first place, and have also provided friendship and community since. Laura Fitch, Jaime Jenett, Cedric Brown, Holly Anderson, Cheri Mims, Reid Davis, and Micia Mosely have been the close friends and family that a queer woman of color needs to remind me that I always have a space to go whenever I need some deep, deep love (and sometimes bacon). I also want to thank Melanie Cervantes for her solidarity around youth, activism, and culture, and for contributing the cover art for this book. Finally, Joan Benoit has brought a tremendous amount of love and stability (not to mention reading chapters) to my life and this process as my partner. She has made it, if not easier, much, much sweeter. Thank you sweetie, for providing such an important physical and ideological space for me to come home to. I love you so much.

Finally, I have to thank my parents, grandparents, brothers, sisters, aunts, uncles, and cousins for always encouraging me even when I have trouble explaining exactly what it is that I do. My mother, Cecelia Riley, has never doubted me, a working poor Black girl, since I left home for college and a "new life" more than twenty years ago. She is my number one fan. The cards, emails, phone conversations, visits, and hugs remind me of the strong people I come from. Similarly, my father, Walter Clay's, love, pride, and support is overwhelming and, along with his obsession with the WNBA, helps me remember that this work is important. My grandmothers, Alma Clay and Eliza Ege, may she rest in peace, also provide continual inspiration and love as I take on bigger and bigger challenges in my life. Eliza Ege, in raising me, shaped my life and the woman I am in ways she'll never know. I dedicate this book to her.

1

YOUTH
Crisis, Rebellion, and Identity

Whenever I think of an activist, I think of Tupac.
—Xochitl, 14

As a teenager, I read *Nelson Mandela: the Man and the Movement*, by Mary Bensen.[1] I was mesmerized by the story of his life as an activist: how he joined the African National Congress (ANC), developed a military branch of the organization, was indicted and spent twenty-seven years in prison, separated from his wife, family, and friends—all in the name of freedom. I remember looking up to him as someone who gave up his life for "the cause" of ending apartheid in South Africa. His commitment was similar to that of the U.S. civil rights leaders I admired at the time, such as Martin Luther King Jr. and Malcolm X. Although Mandela was still in prison when I read his inspiring story of activism, I was convinced that the struggle and hardship he endured would guarantee a free South Africa.

A few years later, as an undergraduate, I read *A Taste of Power* by Elaine Brown. As I read Brown's autobiography—which told the story of her childhood in Philadelphia, how she became a Black Panther Party member, and later the first chairwoman of the party—I felt the same sense of inspiration and awe as I had when I read Mandela's story. Both of these leaders were activists involved in "the struggle," fighting against inequality to improve their lives and those of the people in their communities. In both cases, I was also taken with the fact that these leaders are Black people, like me. As a young activist, I tried to live in their image.

Inspired by Brown's work, I became interested in the debates about affirmative action in California. In 1995 Ward Connerly, an African American businessman and University of California Regent was just beginning his campaign, Proposition 209, to end preferences based on race, sex, and national origin in university admissions. As an undergraduate, I received scholarships targeted at "minorities," and recognized the importance of education in providing access to social resources. I was concerned that Black youth and other youth of color's opportunities to succeed would be further limited if such civil rights policies as affirmative action came under attack. Contemporary struggles such as Prop. 209 reminded me of the tenuous nature of the gains made by Brown, Martin Luther King Jr., Ella Baker, and other civil rights activists. I was interested in the ways teenagers and young adults through-out California organized against Prop. 209. I wondered who would lead their struggle. Would a charismatic leader like King emerge? Or had the social context shifted so that an "individual leader" was no longer necessary? These questions, along with my initial inter-est in social change as a teenager, propelled my research on youth activism in California.

Since the 1980s, state actions intensifying attacks on affirma-tive action, the war on drugs, and laws against gang activity have left an indelible imprint on the hip-hop generation. For instance, in California, adult voters chose to enact policies like Prop. 209, the California Civil Rights Initiative, which resulted in the end of affirmative action in universities and the workplace, and Prop. 21, the Gang Violence and Prevention Act, which made it possible to prosecute teenagers as adults in the criminal justice system. These policies have contributed to decreased enrollments on college campuses like the University of California and a rise in incarcera-tion rates among Black and Latino youth. In response to these con-temporary circumstances, youth of color have been organizing in their communities, particularly in their high schools. In the last decade, youth empowerment organizations, like the two I examine here, have also emerged throughout the country to mobilize, train, and empower youth.

Troubled Youth: Studies of Deviance and Resistance

Current academic and popular constructions of youth of color portray them as gang affiliated, "troubled," and potentially dangerous. From early work undertaken by the Chicago School in the United States and the Centre for Contemporary Cultural Studies in Great Britain to more recent inquiries, sociological representations of youth culture have tended to focus on "deviant" behavior. By focusing on gangs or the consumption of fashion, music, and the media, scholars have pointed to a crisis among youth, particularly youth of color and working class youth.[2] Recent attacks on affirmative action, increases in police brutality and racial profiling, and new anti-youth legislation have exacerbated this sense of crisis, urgency, and hopelessness among critics, community activists, scholars, and the youth themselves.[3]

Social movement representations of youth suggest that young people have always been at the center of political activism and social change. Youth have been characterized as the backbone of the civil rights, feminist, antiwar, and gay and lesbian liberation movements.[4] However, little ethnographic research has been conducted on youth activism outside of these movements. Moreover, the "youth" in these movements are primarily college-aged. Little research has been conducted on adolescence as a significant identity from which to frame social justice organizing.[5] New social movement scholars have long focused on the importance of identity to social movement activism. For instance, previous research indicates that preexisting identities are an important determinant of social movement participation.[6] Others suggest that movement participation and identities are shaped by the sociohistorical contexts in which movements emerge.[7] In the following chapters, I examine how the current backlash against civil rights has impacted the activism and identities of teenagers of color.

Recognizing that contemporary forms of activism may not fit neatly into previous social justice models, sociologists have begun to compare and contrast contemporary youth activism with sixties activism. For instance, the sociologist and former Students for a

Democratic Society (SDS) president Todd Gitlin's recent book *Letters to a Young Activist* tackles this issue directly. In particular, Gitlin questions how youth can organize in an era when popular (and academic) discourse identifies the 1960s as the pinnacle of social movement activism. In one letter, "On the Burden of History, or Several Warped Ways of Looking at the Sixties," Gitlin asks:

> How can you not feel preempted, diminished even by your parents and teachers sitting around the proverbial campfire retelling (not for the first time) their antiwar stories? The afterglow threatens to steal your sense of uniqueness—an especially bracing propensity in a land that relishes the feeling of getting born again at the drop of an advertising campaign. Nothing you can do about your date of birth, after all. So you're trapped. The sixties (like parents) are useful but also oppressive. What would you do without them? What can you do with them?[8]

I attempt to answer Gitlin's questions by looking at the ways in which youth of color organize in light of the "burden" of the sixties. This book focuses on youth, identity, and social change at the beginning of the twenty-first century. Specifically, I focus on activism and the development of collective and individual political identities and organizing strategies among teenagers in Oakland, California. Moving beyond Gitlin's discussion of age, I ask: How do dominant representations of activism, which reflect previous social movements and struggles, inform how youth of color, members of the "hip-hop generation" participate in social change processes?[9] Further, because power exists and operates in dispersed and diffused ways, how is youth activism affected by the activism of previous social movements as well as the current backlash against civil rights? Finally, how does this participation, combined with dominant representations of activism, inform their political and activist identities? In addition to analyzing the dominant representations of activism, or what I refer to as the "idealized cultural image" of activism, I examine how youth activists organize and participate in social change in an era when people may in fact be "getting born again at the drop of an advertising campaign," as Gitlin suggests, but also when this country is experiencing a backlash against civil rights laws.

The Duality of Civil Rights

Other scholars have written about the post–civil rights movement creating a *dual* experience, which has shaped youth of color identity since that time. For instance, journalist and activist Bakari Kitwana highlights the duality of the persistence of racial segregation and discrimination in the wake of civil rights gains, which has contributed to a current crisis for hip-hop generationers (Kitwana 2002). The incongruity of the gains in civil liberties accompanied by continued racism, sexism, and heterosexism constitutes a cognitive and communal crisis for youth. In the face of this crisis, youth of color have employed several different strategies to create collective and individual identities. In *Black Picket Fences*, Mary Pattillo-McCoy suggests that middle-class Black youth experience a dual identity because of the negotiation of two worlds: racial marginality and high socioeconomic status. This negotiation makes Black middle-class youth distinct from their white middle-class counterparts as, despite their economic gains and benefits, racial segregation ensures they live in close proximity to poor and working-class youth, contributing to a bifurcated experience. As a result, Pattillo-McCoy observed while conducting an interview with a middle-class African American that "he . . . had a different manner of speaking with his friends from college and his friends from the neighborhood gang."[10] For instance, when he is with his friends he used "Black English," while at school and at home he uses a more standard English. This practice, which Pattillo-McCoy describes as "code-switching," is necessary for youth of color who may have to balance civil rights gains like upward class mobility and access with the values and practices of the street. This balancing act is indicative of a historical moment where diverse strategies are necessary to address oppression and opportunity.

The term "post–civil rights" has been broadly used to refer to significant shifts in structural and individual realities for people of color (particularly youth) since the civil rights movement.[11] Scholars point out that teenagers of color grow up in an important historical moment. At the same time that youth of color have presumably benefited from desegregated schools and antidiscrimination laws, recent state policies have increasingly restricted youth agency. For example, the establishment of "super jails" for youth, police surveillance of suspected gang members, and the prosecution of juveniles as adults all impact members of the hip-hop, or post–civil rights, generation. For instance, people of color have been granted certain rights as citizens of the United States, but we are still informed and targeted by the changing power structures: the rise in the prison industrial complex, increased surveillance of youth, and de-industrialization. I use the term hip-hop generation similarly in this book: while there have been gains with regards to civil rights for white women and people of color, the post–civil rights moment is a time ripe with contradiction: Take, for instance, the globalization of hip-hop culture, which was started by Black and Puerto Rican youth in the Bronx and has now become a worldwide phenomenon. In the United States, mainstream representations of hip-hop are almost exclusively of Black men. From Jay-Z to Lil Wayne, the predominant images splayed across the screen are African American men. Yet, the rates of incarceration for African American men outside (and sometimes inside) of the realm of hip-hop remain among the highest of all groups. Similarly, while there have been increases in LGBTQ (lesbian, gay, bisexual, transgender, queer) visibility with more and more celebrities coming out as queer, same-sex marriage is legal in several states (though not at the federal level); at the same time LGBTQ youth are four times more likely than their straight counterparts to commit suicide. LGBTQ youth of color also seem to experience high rates of violence, attack, and murder.[12] These contradictions define the post–civil rights generation.

I don't mean to suggest that there weren't contradictions during the civil rights era; certainly there were contradictions during the African American civil rights movement: students were mobilizing the vote among poor African Americans in the South, challenging and overturning state laws, at the same time that these same activists were being surveilled, attacked, imprisoned, and murdered. One key difference is that today's youth activists, in addition to the contradictions that are currently present, are also expected to organize *in the shadow* of previous social movement activists. More importantly, this organizing happens in the midst of the mass commodification of activist images and documentary (and fictional) retellings of these movements. For instance, the documentary *Eyes on the Prize* is a staple in American high schools, as are other films that, together, contribute to a collective understanding of social movement organizing, 1960s style, in American memory. These images were present in both sites that I studied, either as posters in the public high schools where youth organized or in the offices where they worked. This legacy is also written into the politically conscious hip-hop that youth listen to. Songs like "Propaganda," by Dead Prez, artists the youth reference, pay homage to the legacy of the Black Panther Party. As they state, "thirty-one years ago, I woulda been a Panther. They killed Huey 'cause they knew that he had the answer. The views that you see in the news is propaganda." Overall, these words serve as reminders of the social movements that preceded them as well as motivation for the youth's own organizing.

Artists like Dead Prez also make a direct link between previous social movement actors and youth organizers today, who, they suggest, have been told lies by the media, the government, and their schools. Given the pervasiveness of this dual experience for youth, particularly for youth of color, one might expect a unified, collective action against such oppression. However, U.S. public discourse has not yet recognized a large-scale social movement. The absence of a recognizable social movement may be linked to the largely diffused and dispersed ways that power and oppression operate today. Power is decentralized, often creating what Michel Foucault calls an "invisible enemy."[13] The implication is that true resistance and change have been rendered impossible because power is no longer centrally located or visible. Other scholars have written about how recent civil rights gains have created a contemporary context where the invisible enemy is still quite powerful.[14] However, I suggest that rather than being invisible, the deployment of state and ideological power is *masked* by an apparent increase in social and political rights. At the same time, though, this power has become increasingly visible in the lives of youth of color. While "positive" strides may have been made in areas, like racial desegregation in schools and neighborhoods, gentrification, a decline in wages, attacks on affirmative action, continued "tracking" in public schools, and an increase in hate crimes continue to shape the experience of youth.[15] Since 1996, five states, including California, have passed voter-bans on affirmative action. In cities like Oakland, where this study takes place, the decline and restructuring of the shipping industry and the rising costs of housing has significantly shaped the migration of communities of color out of the San Francisco Bay Area into regions farther East.[16] This economic and political landscape informs the social location and experience of youth of color.

Some youth embrace hip-hop culture, music, and performance to articulate their ideologies and create political identities, as this genre most accurately reflects the lives, language, and rhythms of youth of color, particularly in urban areas.[17] Both youth of color and white youth have turned to hip-hop culture and other forms of performance to understand and create community with one another.[18] As George Lipsitz (1994) suggests, youth use hip-hop culture to "bring a community into being. . . map[ping] out real and imagined relations between people that speak to the realities of displacement, disillusion, and despair" (Lipsitz 1994, 36). In the late twentieth century, the hip-hop industry began addressing the important connection between youth, identity, and hip-hop culture. Conferences brought together hip-hop artists, producers, writers, and young people to discuss the political possibilities of hip-hop music. This forging of community was so successful that the hip-hop mogul and co-founder of Def Jam Recordings, Russell Simmons, founded the Hip-Hop Summit Action Network (HSAN) in 2001. Since that time, HSAN's primary strategy has been focused on mobilizing the "hip-hop vote."[19] In 2003, the National Hip-Hop Political Convention was founded by hip-hop activists to create a political agenda for and encourage civic engagement among the hip-hop generation.

With the explosion of a global youth market (especially American hip-hop culture) and the "marketing of cool," teenagers have assumed a powerful role as consumers. For youth activists, this is particularly relevant because they are organizing in an era where teenagers of color simultaneously embody the identities of powerful global consumers of these images and social threats. For example, "urban" youth of color are routinely targeted by police for suspected gang membership or other criminal activity, solely based on their specific age, race, class, gender status, and social location.[20] Simultaneously, the marketing of "cool" and mass commodity consumption has been extended to radical activism. Commodity fetishism, as Marx described it, has taken on a new role in relationship to "radical" and "revolutionary" thought.[21] The *peculiar social character* of commodities is especially pronounced in the objectification of the political words, images, and leaders of 1960s social movements, which have been recuperated into consumable objects.[22]

Tools for Social Justice: Constructing Ideal Activists in Popular Culture

Each political generation has its own definitions of what it means to be an activist. For some, Martin Luther King Jr., Fannie Lou Hamer, and other leaders of the 1950s civil rights movement embody activism. Others strive to emulate Huey Newton, Dolores Huerta, Yuri Kochiyama, and other 1960s icons. Regardless of the actual person or figure, an activist is typically identified as an individual who stands up for what she or he believes in and fights for social justice. Since the 1960s, people have been inundated with images of what an activist looks like (and the spirits he embodies) through the commodification of the words and actions of such individuals as Malcolm X, Angela Davis, and Che Guevara. Snippets of their lives have been truncated for consumption in history books, biographies, popular music, T-shirts, and bumper stickers. Magazines like *UTNE Reader* regularly feature articles that focus on contemporary figures who embody the spirit of these historic "visionaries." In all of these venues, what I call an "idealized cultural image" of social and political activism has been embedded in the collective U.S. cultural imagination.

Popular discourse typically focus on individuals, often social movements leaders, that characterize social movement activism. Images of individuals like Angela Davis, Martin Luther King Jr., and Malcolm X have been commodified as the epitome of those who fought to challenge oppression. The "great individual" has been reinforced by the commercialization of these figures in popular culture. Their images have been immortalized in our collective cultural memory through Angela Davis T-shirts, Martin Luther King Jr. posters, or a bumper sticker of Malcolm X's call to action, "By Any Means Necessary." In effect, these cultural products serve not only as visual representations of previous social protest and activism but also as the model that all other activism is based. I seek to understand how we can fully understand contemporary forms of activism when the ideal is based on the historiography of these individuals and movements. How do people, especially teenagers of color, organize and participate in social change when the names and images of these leaders often stand in for the masses of social movement participants and, sometimes, for the movements themselves?

In a special issue of *UTNE Reader*, which focused on "visionaries under thirty," the hip-hop activist and author William Upski Wimsatt—himself labeled a thirty-year-old visionary—expresses a similar concern. He asks, "Where are the activists of the twenty-first century? Where is the next Martin Luther King Jr.? The next Dalai Lama? Gloria Steinem?"[23] While these are important figures and individuals who, as Wimsatt suggests, "burst onto the scene and took action" for peace and equality, Wimsatt reinforces the idealized cultural image of activism by identifying these figures as people to emulate. While it may be necessary to have visible role models, taken out of context and immortalized in commodified objects, these images become the very *essence* of what it means to be an activist, in effect overshadowing not only the work of contemporary activists, as I examine here, but also the monumentally historic impact of previous social movements. This happens not only in the naming of political leaders as

A t-shirt featuring an idealized image of an activist,
Angela Davis.

visionaries but most importantly in the use and distribution of their
political images and uncomplicated summaries of their beliefs.

The use of the idealized cultural image in popular culture often
works to erase the actual struggles of the leaders at the same time
that it helps to shape a historical and cultural understanding of a
particular social movement. Angela Davis poignantly refers to this
process as it relates to the commodification of her own image, activism, and political imprisonment for her associations with the Black
Panther Party and Communist Party. For instance, in her analysis
of a *Vibe* magazine fashion spread titled "FREE ANGELA," where
women sported Afros, wore black leather, and held their hands up
in fists, Davis argues that this marketing image erases the political
importance of her activism and mistreatment:

This is the most blatant example of the way the particular history
of my legal case is emptied of all content so that it can serve as a
commodified backdrop for advertising. The way in which this docu-

ment provided a historical pretext for something akin to a reign of terror for countless young Black women is effectively erased by its use as a prop for selling clothes and promoting a seventies fashion nostalgia. What is also lost in this nostalgic surrogate for historical memory . . . is the activist involvement of vast numbers of Black women in movements that are now represented with even greater masculinist contours than they actually exhibited at the time.[24]

Davis acknowledges how an event of media commodification effectively minimizes the oppression she experienced and the activism in which she engaged. More importantly, the use of her image also ignores the struggles of other Black women involved in the social protests of the 1960s. Moreover, the commodification of activist images, such as the "FREE ANGELA" spread, ignores the organizing and activism in which women are involved today. Ultimately, these images of activism have become embedded in our cultural memory, often superseding other definitions of protest and social change.

Sydney Tarrow suggests that protest movements and activism are grounded in the history of society, becoming part of our permanent "repertoires of contention."[25] Embedded in these models of what it means to be an activist are shared understandings of social change. These repertoires determine the types of activism the media pays attention to, how and which types of activism are portrayed in history books, and how activists construct their own identities. The idealized cultural image of activism has become part of these shared repertoires of contention, immortalized in popular culture memorabilia. For contemporary youth activists, one of the more important aspects of the mass production of activist images is the role these images play in the social construction and shared understanding of activism.

Marita Sturken refers to such shared understanding as cultural memory or, memory that is a shared blend of history, culture, popular culture, and political meaning. This collective memory is often created in the process of constructing a national identity around particular events, especially traumatic events.[26] For instance, artifacts like the Vietnam War memorial and the AIDS quilt serve to remind the larger public of the Vietnam War and the AIDS epidemic. Furthermore, films and other representations of these events often stand in for the actual events for people who weren't involved in the war or who do not know anyone who has died of AIDS.[27] In effect, representational objects contribute to a collective sense of national identity, citizenship, and community. Sturken states:

> When Americans watch events of "national" importance—the Persian Gulf War, the Anita Hill/Clarence Thomas hearings, the explosion of the *Challenger*—on television, they perceive themselves to be part of a national audience regardless of their individual political views or cultural background. Citizenship can thus be enacted through live television.[28]

Lipsitz also suggests that through mass media images, collective memory becomes, "a crucial constituent of individual and group identity in the modern world."[29] These images, like the images of Angela Davis, minimize the struggles of the antiwar movement and AIDS activism in an effort to create a national identity in relationship to these events.

While the idealized cultural image of activism overshadows contemporary activism, it also has the potential to downplay the activism of generations past, as Davis suggests. For example, the public display of a particular activist can also communicate political and social ideology. Wearing a T-shirt with an image of Martin Luther King Jr. may be an indication of a teenager's belief in nonviolent protest. In this instance, the person wearing the T-shirt becomes linked with the ideology of the activist displayed—merging the decades between the work of someone like Fannie Lou Hamer and the experiences of the youth today. As Sturken reminds us, within this process of remembering—the construction of a cultural memory—there is also a process of *forgetting* that takes place. As a culture, we commodify activist images, and in so doing we often forget the struggles of the people involved in a particular incident or movement. Public figures such as Malcolm X and Angela Davis have become abstract, almost perfect images of what it means to be an activist, standing in for the ultimate representation of social and political change in the United States.

The youth in this study were well aware of the idealized image of activism and who constitutes an activist. For instance, Frida, a-seventeen-year-old Latina participant at Multicultural Alliance (hereafter MA), clearly articulated the idealized cultural image of an activist and her own relationship to it when I asked her if she thought of herself as an activist:

> I don't like that word because it's so stereotyped. Like in the media, what I've seen in the media is that an activist is someone who speaks with a banner and a piece of paper and is demanding something. And an activist is so much more than that, like talking to someone you don't know, like telling your sister something different. Like you don't have to be screaming and this and that. I mean, I do that too, but I don't really like that word.

In this quote, Frida clearly references the idealized cultural image of activism by first naming the media as a player in the construction of what an "activist" is. Given the shared cultural images of leaders like Martin Luther King Jr. and movements like that of the Farm Workers, it is no surprise Frida has internalized this image of activism. However, she also states that although she does participate in this type of activism, her own definition includes specific mechanisms, or tools, that are available to her as a young Latina.

While, as Gitlin states, the idealized cultural image of (sixties) activism burdens contemporary youth activism, it is also important to acknowledge that for many civil rights activists the "dream" has been met on a number of levels and the *struggle* itself is over. Popular discourse suggests that the main project for the social movements of the 1960s and 1970s has been reached. The Civil Rights Act was passed in 1964, the Voting Rights Act in 1965. Organizations like the Student Nonviolent Coordinating Committee (SNCC), the National Organization for Women (NOW), and others focused on equality as the overriding goal for "the movement." While I do not suggest that racism (sexism, heterosexism, and classism) and discrimination no longer shapes people's lives, the civil rights movement and other social movements of the 1960s, as many of us have understood it, were primarily organized in opposition to a series of state and federal laws. As Robin D. G. Kelley argues, "(l)ocal and national campaigns waged by the Southern Christian Leadership Conference (SCLC), the Congress on Racial Equality (CORE), the Student Nonviolent Coordinating Committee (SNCC), to name only the big three, fought for citizenship, the right to vote, and desegregation, and succeeded in getting the federal government to pass the Civil Rights Act and the Voting Rights Act."[30] Significantly, these groups organized around a shared experience of the denial of civil rights to protest the racist policies of the American political system. Ultimately, this organization drew upon and reflected a collective identity. As Michael Omi and Howard Winant suggest,

> Racial change is the product of the interaction of racially based social movements and the racial state. . . . In the postwar period, minority movements, led by the black movement, radically changed the dominant racial ideology . . . [these] movements create collective identity . . . by offering their adherents a different view of themselves and their world; different, that is from the characteristic worldviews and self-concepts of the social order, which the movements are challenging.[31]

While some have critiqued the civil rights, women's, and the gay and lesbian movement as "identity politics," the collective identities that emerge out of social movements organized around identity, I argue, have since defined what it means to be Black, female, gay, or lesbian for a younger generation of activists. It is difficult to imagine or understand what it means to be African American, Chicano/a, or gay without taking into account the social movements organized around those identities. More importantly, the experience of being involved in social movements has the potential to impact the rest of the activist's individual life. As one volunteer explained when referencing her experience in Freedom Summer, "'It was simply the most important experience of my life. It really set me on a course in my life that I'm still on.'"[32]

Ultimately, social movement participation and activism can shapes one's individual and collective sense of identity as well as her or his life goals. However, the legacies of the civil rights movement, feminist movement, and the gay and lesbian movement of the 1960s, 1970s, and 1980s continue to influence the strategies, role models, and individual identities of today's social movement activists. It is important to note that youth also identify with *new* role models who reflect their generation and the possibilities for organizing in this particular historical moment. For instance, as Xochitl's opening quote suggests, the rapper Tupac Shakur is the person she identifies as an activist. When I asked her why, she pointed to his ability to "keep it real":

> Yeah, because a lot of times, like Tupac gets a lot of stuff because he disrespects women and all that stuff, but in order to get yourself heard you need to speak on people's level and then once you're on top, you can get your voice heard. He did a lot of songs that weren't about bitches and hoes and all that. But he had to go through that for his voice to be heard. But he never forgets about that, even when he was up there, he never forgot.

Keeping it real (or, as DJ Kool Herc says, keeping it right[33]) and speaking on people's level is a common theme in the contemporary youth movement and a key component in their activist "tool kit."[34] Hip-hop, like consciousness-raising tools in the feminist movement, gay and lesbian movement, and the civil rights movement, has been attacked by adults because of the misogynist, sexist, homophobic, and sometimes violent content.[35] In spite of this (and sometimes very much because of it), the culture remains significant for teenagers of color as they organize around social justice issues in their local communities. This is one of the intergenerational dynamics I address in my examination of two nonprofit organizations in Oakland, California.

Studying Youth in Action: Two Nonprofits

Oakland is an interesting site for studying youth activism because it is both ripe with political history—for example, the Black Panther Party organized here, and the San Francisco Bay Area was the site of many student antiwar protests and demands for Ethnic Studies programs in the sixties—and it is an urban area that has been plagued with a high crime and murder rate amid growing racial and economic disparities. At the same time, student organizing in opposition to Props. 187 and 209 sparked a youth movement that drew attention to the experiences of post–civil-rights youth. Since that time, several nonprofit organizations have been established to address the needs of urban youth of color in the Bay Area. These organizations range from youth recreational centers to social justice organizations, from educational and community centers and boys' and girls' clubs to poetry slam training grounds. Youth from different socioeconomic, racial, sexual-orientation, and gender statuses participate in these organizations primarily after school and on weekends. Between October 2000 and June 2002, I worked with two such organizations—Teen Justice (hereafter TJ) and Multicultural Alliance (MA).[36] I volunteered as a mentor and research evaluator for TJ from October 2000 to June 2001. In August 2001, I began working as a program coordinator at MA, where I assisted in training youth to lead anti-oppression or, popular education, workshops for other youth.

Teen Justice was founded in 1996 in response to several race riots between Blacks and Asians in Oakland public schools. In an effort to combat the violence, TJ focuses on developing multiracial leadership and student organizing in their community and on high school campuses. As a volunteer at TJ, I worked with the leadership team at Bayview High School. Multicultural Alliance, a smaller nonprofit, was founded in 1998 out of the founder's desire to generate a deeper understanding of and appreciation for cross-cultural/cross-community organizing among youth. Similar to TJ, MA worked with young people to develop youth leaders who assumed a central role in fighting oppression in their communities and among their peers. The primary tool for creating this society free from oppression is teaching youth to facilitate anti-oppression workshops with other youth in Oakland.

As a researcher in these settings, I engaged in participant observation by taking field notes and conducting informal interviews with youth and staff members at each organization. In particular, I studied two processes. At TJ I focused on the development of a youth center at Bayview High. At MA, I focused on the development and execution of anti-oppression workshops with other youth. I decided on these events to gain a deeper understanding of the ways in which youth of color engage in social activism. I used participant observation to understand and explain how youth of color make sense of themselves and their society through activism. I sought to achieve this understanding through "virtual or actual participation in social situations, through real or constructed dialogue between participant and observer, or what [social scientists] call the hermeneutic dimension of social science."[37] In what follows, I engage in this hermeneutic or explanatory process by linking theory and data. Specifically, I situate my ethnographic study of youth activism in relation to previous research on youth culture and social movements.

Although participant observation provides the main empirical basis for examining youth activism in Oakland, another primary source of data collection for this study comes from in-depth interviews I conducted with twenty-one youth participants from TJ and MA.[38] I interviewed the majority of youth with whom I worked closely at both organizations, including members of the organizing/leadership team at TJ and the primary workshop facilitators at MA. I also conducted formal interviews with key staff members at each organization, as well as informal interviews with other adults in the scene, who often played key roles in supporting and assisting in the leadership of the youth in this study.[39] I conducted interviews until I felt I had reached a "saturation" point, that moment at which the interviews ceased to provide any new information.[40] For interviews in both organizations, I relied on my initial contacts and a purposive, snowball sample to obtain participants. By employing multiple methods, I provide an in-depth description of the case of youth activism at the beginning of the twenty-first century. More-over, these methods allow the youth themselves to provide their own definitions of activism.

What Are We Fighting For

The burden of sixties activism, as Gitlin describes it, is present both in academia and popular culture. One important factor in the study of social movement activism is the sociohistorical context in which it emerges. In chapter 2, I use ethnographic data to explain how the geographic, racial, and economic landscape of metropolitan cities like Oakland influences the lives and organizing frames of the poor and working-class youth of color. Specifically, I discuss importance of the local setting and scene for youth activism. Because of ongoing economic and racial segregation in Oakland, I also examine how different California voter ballot propositions like 187 and 209 have influenced local strategies to remediate problems in the lives of youth of color. In particular, I look at several laws that established the specific financial support for TJ and MA at the time of this study. More importantly, these local initiatives reflect larger, national initiatives that have targeted affirmative action programs, vilified undocumented immigrants, and increased the criminalization of "deviant" youth of color. Overall, I construct a genealogy and social history of the origins of youth activism in the post–civil rights era by providing an in-depth examination of the framing strategies, missions, influence, and assessment of the outcomes of the overall programs of Teen Justice and Multicultural Alliance.

Chapter 3 builds on chapter 2 by examining not only how youth organize in the aftermath of civil rights gains and losses but also how they navigate racial and ethnic, gender, and sexuality boundaries in the twenty-first century. In particular, I describe how multiracial youth activists identify with specific social categories and build coalitions with one another across these lines. This information is crucial at a time when youth of color continue to be constructed as deviant in popular culture, and are treated as such by policymakers, educators, and parents—a moment I describe as *violent*, most notable in the social abandonment of urban youth of color. Youth at TJ and MA integrate their experiences with the structures of racism, classism, and ageism into their organizing strategies. Finally, I explore how youth construct these frameworks at the same time that the youth activists themselves were traversing the violence in their neighborhoods, home lives, and schools.

I begin chapter 4 by examining how youth incorporate hip-hop culture into their organizing strategies inside and outside of their work at TJ and MA. Popular culture, and hip-hop in particular, has been an important source for mobilizing youth around social injustices in the Bay Area. Youth at both organizations identified hip-hop as an important social justice tool, not just for their individual motivation and understanding of their social location but also as an important source for mobilizing other youth. Overall, I look at how youth, who incorporate hip hop into their organizing, become cultural workers who educate others about their lives as youth in the post–civil rights era.

In addition to identifying as members of the hip-hop generation, many of the youth identified as gay, lesbian, bisexual, or queer. All of the youth at MA, regardless of sexual orientation, made homophobia a key frame in their social, cultural, and political work in peer-led, anti-oppression workshops. I examine how youth activists negotiated across racial/ethnic, gender, and sexual orientation lines to make heterosexism and homophobia a central frame in their organizing activities. In chapter 5, I also examine how popular discourses based on a predominantly white Lesbian, Gay, Bisexual, Transgender, and Queer (LGBTQ) Movement (via same-sex marriage debates and television shows like *Will and Grace*) shape queer identity and activism among queer youth of color, while simultaneously excluding them from this movement. This impact is even more pronounced with firmly established, national school-based organizations like the Gay/Straight Alliance (GSAs) and other gay and lesbian youth organizations that specifically service LGBTQ youth. Finally, I also consider how homophobia based in bias at school, in their families, and among other youth activists impacts the youth of color in this study and their relationship to queer identity and community.

In chapter 6, I explore whether and how the youth think of themselves as activists. Specifically, I explore whether their definitions of activist align with social movement theories and popular cultural representations of activism, both of which are largely understood in relationship to the idealized cultural image of activism. Overall, I ask the questions, "Given larger cultural understanding of activism and social change, is their organizing work activism?" and "How do their own understandings of activism and their role in social change rewrite dominant repertoires of activism?"

I conclude this study in chapter 7 by outlining a theory of youth activism and its implications upon future sociological and movement understandings of social change. I also explore how these efforts affect understandings of disenfranchised, urban youth in the post–civil rights era. Specifically, how do the strategies of organizing at the local level, the use of popular culture to mobilize others, and popular understandings of the term "activism" combine to affect the predominant understandings of youth, social movements, and activism?

2

KEEP YOUR EYES ON THE PRIZE
The Contemporary Struggle

At almost any point along Skyline Boulevard in Oakland, you can see the San Francisco Bay, the Bay Bridge, and on clear days the Golden Gate Bridge. To the west, the beaches on the island of Alameda and the Port of Oakland spill into the Bay. Directly below, the rest of the city of Oakland looks alive. In contrast to the peace and quiet of this vantage point known as "the hills," "the flats" are bustling in the distance—cars move along slowly through the city streets, much as they do on the freeways full of commuters. Up here, the city sleeps; a person could easily drive through this area and not even see some of the houses tucked behind large oak and redwood trees. "Hidden Driveway" signs alert fellow drivers that residents will be exiting their dwellings to mingle with the rest of the city's inhabitants. As you drive down the snakelike, hilly roads back to the city, it feels as if you're driving through a park. Tall redwood, oak, and fir trees line the streets and the median, with few if any sidewalks for foot traffic. Meanwhile, the Bay is almost always in view and Mount Tamalpais sits in the distance. You may see one or two joggers or pass another driver on the road, but for the most part it feels as if you are far, far away from anything resembling a city.

This feeling of escape was exactly what the developers had in mind when they started building this area at the beginning of the twentieth century. Middle- and working-class whites were encouraged to move their families into the refuge of the hills.[1] As Oakland's population began to diversify, the desire for distance from the "noise" of the city also increased. One of the initial selling points of the hills was the promise that a homeowner would experience "nothing but beautiful homes and gardens around him—no intrusion of business, no apartment houses, no double houses or flats, no spite fences, no freak houses, no shacks, no private garages allowed to be places where they will spoil his outlook, no unsightly feature of any sort."[2] This promise remains today: you must travel several miles, into the city proper, to see any businesses or apartment buildings.

Many of Oakland's working-class families moved out of the hills long ago and now live in the area between the hills and the flats known as the "foothills." As you continue to drive down Skyline and turn onto Redwood Road, the houses are closer to the street and neighborhoods begin to take shape. Still primarily stable working class and middle class, this area has more of a "new" family presence: tire swings on trees, home renovations in progress, basketball hoops in the driveway, and bicycles scattered on lawns. Not only are the houses closer to the street, they're painted bright shades of blue, yellow, mauve, and pale green. The view of the Bay is not as expansive, but the feeling of safety and escape persists. Large trees protect front yards from the sun, while lemon, orange, and jasmine trees bloom throughout the area. The houses also seem more inviting than in the hills; window curtains are pulled back, allowing neighbors to peek in at the fireplaces, rocking chairs, and freshly polished dining room tables.

As you drive even further down the winding street, Redwood Road becomes Thirty-fifth Avenue, eventually intersecting with MacArthur Boulevard. The neighborhood continues to shift: streets become narrow and crowded with coffee shops, gas stations, grocery stores, fast-food restaurants, and beauty salons competing for space along the stretch known as the Laurel district. Residential neighborhoods begin to fade into the background. Nondescript apartment buildings take the place of houses on these busy streets and a multiethnic mix of people dart in and around cars trying to cross the street. After school, Black, Latino, and Asian youth cluster around bus stops waiting to take long bus rides to distances east and west.

Even though the streets are busy and alive with people, the flats to which many of these youth travel have an isolated and deserted feel to them. Rusted, broken-down cars are firmly planted in front of small houses that are still painted blues, pinks, and greens, but the paint has faded and chipped and curtains are pulled tightly behind barred windows. Police cars are regular fixtures in these neighborhoods. All the while, no matter where you are in the flats, the hills are in plain view.

As a researcher in Oakland, I became very familiar with the flats (and the hills/flats divide), particularly in East and West Oakland. Most of the youth in this study live and work here. For instance, the youth who worked at TJ were bused from their neighborhoods to schools in the hills, where they also organized. Multicultural Alliance youth led all of their anti-oppression workshops in the flats. For some of these youth, the economic and racial divide was a key part of their political formation. For instance, Conrad, an eighteen-year-old Black youth from TJ speaks to the race, class, and political divides between people who live in the hills and the flats, where he lives:

> I mean like white folk that come from I don't know, Walnut Creek [a small city outside of Oakland], and they come down on Sundays to go to the rallies, you know what I'm saying, and they really don't know. Like, you can leave that rally, you know what I'm saying, and go back to the hills, and do your compost heap thing. I don't have a back yard for a compost heap, you know what I'm saying, I *don't* have, so, you know I do without all of the time, but I am surrounded by people who are *so* [sarcastically] active but they can't really feel me, you know what I'm saying?

As Conrad's statement implies, the Oakland hills and surrounding areas like Walnut Creek continue to be perceived and experienced as a site for escape, whereas the flats, where Conrad lives, is a place where people "do without." At the same time, he also astutely evokes the political history of Oakland, a city where outsiders come to "go to rallies." This social and political landscape ultimately shapes his racial and political formations as a young Black teenager who does not have the "luxury" of leaving behind the area where he lives, works, and organizes.

The racial/ethnic and socioeconomic split between the hills and the flats in Oakland began in the early part of the twentieth century. At the time, the city was undergoing industrial expansion, with the growth of railroad and shipbuilding industries, and an increase of people moving into the city for work. The 1906 San Francisco earthquake also contributed significantly to a housing boom. In just five years, between 1918 and 1923, there was a 900 percent increase in the number of houses built in the hills close to Berkeley.[3] This growth continued throughout the 1920s, with the optimism fueled by workers' wealth and the ability of working families to buy homes. The majority of buyers in this area were white, in contrast to the growing Black communities in West Oakland and the Asian communities downtown.[4] Racism's influence on the structure of the city was evident in "limitation of ownership" clauses enacted by real estate agents selling houses in the hills. Some leaflets like "The Protection of Rockridge Affords" were explicitly racist: "it is probably unnecessary to mention that no one of African or Mongolian descent will ever be allowed to own a lot in Rockridge or even rent any house that may be built there."[5] Today, informal policies still influence residential patterns in neighborhoods throughout the city. Although people of color have moved into the hills in increasing numbers over the years, and areas in downtown and West Oakland have been gentrified through white and middle-class ownership, the city remains largely racially and economically segregated.

The economic and racial segregation present in Oakland has influenced tensions between the working and middle classes, and between people of color and whites, throughout Oakland's history. These divisions are central to the everyday lives of the youth in this study. The flats are where most of the youth live, while many of them go to school in the hills. For instance, TJ members, like Conrad, spent forty hours or more per week at Bayview High School, which is located in the hills. Bayview, like many of the houses in the area, is tucked behind the trees and sits high up on a hill, far from the street. In fact, there is a stoplight set up specifically for entrance into the school, making it seem more like an intrusion in the quiet neighborhood rather than an public institution of learning.

Bayview High School is known as one of the better public high schools in Oakland. According to the youth with whom I talked, students who attend Bayview have a better chance of enrolling in a four-year college or university. This may be related in part to Bayview's teachers, many of whom are committed to mentoring students. For instance, Mr. Thomas, an English teacher and faculty sponsor of Teen Justice, went to Bayview as a teenager and began teaching there, he told me, to "give back" to its predominantly Black, Latino, and Asian population. Ms. Shepard, an openly gay teacher also mentored many of the straight and queer students of color at the school. However, Griselda, the adult coordinator who worked with the youth at TJ, told me that, despite Bayview's reputation, few students who actually live in the hills go there, opting instead for private schools in and outside of Oakland. Moreover, 90 percent of the school's population is bused in from the flats.

In contrast to Bayview, Washington High school, where I worked with MA, doesn't look much like a school at all, looking instead like one of the empty warehouses that clutter the area where it is located.[6] I almost drove right past it the first time we visited with some of the students because it faded so easily into the background. The school is about two blocks long, and dark; it is an exhaust-stained brick building surrounded by a fence with a black iron gate. Across the street, older men sit outside apartment buildings and mechanics shops, drinking beer and talking. Whereas Bayview is regarded as one of the best public schools in the area, Washington is one of the worst; I was frequently told by some of the youth that it has the "bad" kids and teachers. For instance, before I attended one of the workshops at the school, youth at MA lamented for weeks about how they were going to have to go to Washington where all "those crazy fools" went to school. I found this statement interesting because all of the youth with whom I worked at MA and TJ grew up in the flats. Achilles, Lana, Patti, David, Jose, and Shabee all lived in the neighborhoods surrounding Washington High. The racial and economic segregation that shaped Washington High and the students they mocked also contributed to the social conditions of their neighborhoods.

Growing Up in the Flats

Most of the youth in this study live in the flats of East and West Oak-land, which resemble typical "ghettos" or "inner cities" in the United States.[7] In 2006 the murder rate in Oakland reached its highest rate ever (145), with the majority of the activity occurring in these two areas. The youth were not immune to the violence in their neighbor-hoods. During this study, there were several shootings that affected the youth. One afternoon a handful of teenagers were shot at a local Taco Bell where Teen Justice participants waited for the bus on their way to and from Bayview. For weeks, youth at both organizations were buzzing about whether they knew anyone who was wounded, and expressed gratitude that it wasn't one of them. Other times these experiences affected their ability to make it to work or school. For instance, one day Shabee, a sixteen-year-old Black intern at MA, called in sick because her boyfriend had beaten her up on her way to school. She, along with her parents, had obtained a restraining order against him because he had been violent in the past. Ignoring the restraint on that day he was waiting for her in her front yard as she left for school.

In addition to interpersonal violence, "turf" violence also occurred between East and West Oakland. On another occasion, I was sitting in the MA office with Achilles, an eighteen-year-old African American male, and greeted him by asking about his weekend. He answered nonchalantly, "It was okay. My sister got shot." Two days earlier, his sister went with friends to a drag race in West Oakland. Upon learning that some of the people gathered to watch the race were from East Oakland—where Achilles' family lives—people from West Oakland began shooting into the crowd. Achilles' sister was shot in the arm and had to stay in the hospital overnight.

On another occasion, the violence spilled over directly into the youths' ability to prepare for upcoming workshops. Donelle, a fif-teen-year-old Black participant at MA, also experienced violence on a regular basis. At the time of this study, he was using the organi-zation as a "safe haven" after school. One day while he was in the office, his troubles reached a boiling point, which I recorded in my fieldnotes:

> There were five of us sitting in the office. Patti, Lana, Clark and I were practicing some icebreakers for an upcoming workshop. Donelle was sitting in the corner of the room, surfing the Internet. He had been hanging out at Multicultural Alliance for several weeks in the afternoons. Although he wasn't "officially" working as an intern for the organization, he was invited to hang out and accompany youth on workshops as well as pick up odd jobs around the office. While the interns and I were preparing, he received a series of calls on his pager and picked up the phone to return the calls. The interns and I were in the middle of an icebreaker, "the rope" [a names exercise] when Donelle, who was standing in the next room, began yelling into the phone, "Oh yeah, well if you comin' after me, I'm gonna knife you," and slammed the phone down. The other youth in the room stopped in their tracks and stared at me and one another in disbelief. We sat in silence for a moment and, finally, Patti turned to me as the only adult in the room and said, "I think you need to intervene here."

After this incident, I pulled Donelle aside while the other youth continued to run through the exercises. As I tried to calm him down, he explained to me that he had had a "misunderstanding" with the person on the phone several weeks before and had been hanging out at MA so he wouldn't have to confront him. During the course of our conversation he also told me he saw one of his friends get shot as they both walked out of a grocery store when he was thirteen. He held his friend and watched the blood run out of his chest as he died. It wasn't clear if the two incidents were connected, but I knew that because of the violence Donelle experienced in his neighborhood and at school, his mother had moved him and his brother to Richmond, a city outside of Oakland, several months earlier.

The struggles of growing up in East and West Oakland that Donelle and others faced, also affected the youth at Teen Justice. Once, when I inquired why Eduardo, an eighteen-year-old Xicano,[8] didn't show up for work, Griselda told me he had run away from home because he was fighting with his mom. He surfaced several days later. On another day, Griselda and I gave Charles, a fifteen-year-old African American, a ride home and dropped him off at his grandmother's house. When I asked if he lived with her, Griselda said no, but that he was staying with her temporarily because his mother and father were addicted to crack. She also told me that before Conrad joined TJ, he sold marijuana briefly as a primary source of income and was struggling to stay in school. Trisha told me that she also struggled and "started doing drugs and stuff—smoking weed with my friends and not going to class" when she first started at Bayview. Another member, Jose, a fourteen-year-old Mexican American, was actively being recruited by a neighborhood gang before he became involved with TJ. He has since dropped out of school.

The realities the youth in this study experience at home, at school, and in their neighborhood reflect the duality of the post–civil rights era: they grow up in an era where they can benefit from going to one of the better public schools in the city, but they continue to be exposed to violence, drugs, and poverty. These experiences affect not only the everyday well-being of the youth in this study, but also the political opportunities that are available to them.

Oakland Fund for Children and Youth: Building Resilient Youth

In California, the post–civil rights backlash is reflected in statewide propositions like 187, 209, and 21.[9] These propositions specifically target and impact youth of color, including the ones in this study. The City of Oakland has responded to this backlash in several ways. One of the most effective responses occurred in 1996, when Oakland voters passed Measure K, a law that specifically addressed the needs of the city's youth. Also known as Kids First! Oakland Fund for Youth, Measure K was established in response to the violence between Black and recently immigrated Asian communities post-propositions 187 and 209. Concerned with the welfare of Black and

Asian youth in Oakland, Measure K was aimed at "help[ing] youth become healthy, productive and honorable adults."[10] Specifically, this amendment to the City Charter established the Oakland Fund for Children and Youth (OFCY), which set aside 2.5 percent of the city's unrestricted General Purpose Fund to support "direct services to children and youth, less than 21 years of age."[11] OFCY funded Teen Justice and Multicultural Alliance as "youth empowerment" organizations.

OFCY's definition of youth empowerment aims to instill democratic principles, which dictate that "good citizens" participate in society. The expectation is that by learning principles of respect and responsibility, youth will engage in pro-social rather than anti-social behavior. As the OFCY vision statement declares,

> Anti-social behavior of youth can stem from a lack of respect for others and for community values. Such disrespect is more likely to be demonstrated by those who are alienated from the benefits of community membership or who are themselves subjected to disrespect. Youth who feel a lack of respect and cut off from meaningful participation in mainstream society are more likely to have little respect for society, its laws, and its values. . . .The success of OFCY programs will depend on the community's capacity to teach youth to respect themselves and others. Youth need to be assisted so that they may see a future and role for themselves in society.[12]

As this statement suggests, OFCY's commitment to positive youth development reflects a larger, national agenda that understands civic participation as aligned with democratic principles and practice. By learning how to respect themselves and others, individuals become better citizens. Presumably, this citizenship will encourage them to obey laws, participate in democratic processes, and engage in civic responsibility. Reminiscent of Gramsci's theory of civil society, OFCY relies on the youth organizations it funds to encourage and train youth to participate in civic duties, respect the laws of society, and to take charge of their communities as adults.[13] In order to become upstanding, law-abiding adults, individuals need to learn particular values and behaviors as teenagers, which is what organizations like TJ and MA are encouraged to instill in their participants.

OFCY also expects funded organizations to provide Oakland youth with opportunities to grow socially, emotionally, morally, and spiritually. According to OFCY philosophy, growth in these areas will protect youth from the violence and other "environmental threats" in Oakland. Funded organizations are expected not only to provide mentorship and a positive environment but also provide opportunities for youth to positively participate in their community. As OFCY evaluation team member Bonnie Bernard states, "long-term studies of positive youth development in the face of environmental threat, stress, and risk succinctly identify . . . caring relationships, high expectation messages, and opportunities for participation and contribution as important principles in the development of positive youth."[14] Referred to as "protective factors," these principles have been linked to the development of "resilience," or the ability to "rebound from adversity and achieve healthy development and successful learning."[15]

In addition to developing problem-solving skills, which encouraged youth to cope with the challenges in their lives, youth involved in OFCY-sponsored programs were expected to demonstrate "emotional intelligence" and an ability to learn from their mistakes. Overall, youth were encouraged to complete their programs with an ability to

> develop a sense of one's identity and to act independently and exert some control over his or her environment by developing a sense of independence, internal locus of control, sense of power, self-esteem, self discipline, refusal skills, conflict resolution, anger management, and impulse control [and to] develop a "sense of autonomy, purpose and future."[16]

Program administrators believed teenagers who possess these social assets have a better chance of "navigating" risk factors—like drugs, guns, gangs, and violence—found in their communities. By participating in programs like TJ and MA, they argued, Oakland youth would be able "to walk through the 'risk factor mine field without stepping on the mines.'"[17] In sum, OFCY's overall goal is twofold: First, the organization wants young people to survive the "risk factors" in their communities; second, they want to train youth to become *responsible* adults who participate in civil society.

OFCY's commitment to positive youth development reflects a national agenda to clarify youths' civic duties. For instance, National 4-H, which claims to serve 6 million youth in the United States, bases it's understanding of positive youth development squarely within a civic engagement/civil society framework. Two of the main "mission mandates" focus on citizenship and healthy living, combining democratic principles and participation with developing the "physical, mental and emotion health of our nation's youth so they may lead healthy and productive lives into adulthood."[18] "Healthy" and "productive" lives, in this instance, mirrors democratic ideals masked, in Gramscian terms, through the state's position as "night-watchman—i.e., of a coercive organization which will safeguard the development of the continually proliferating elements of regulated society."[19] In other words, teenagers will participate in necessary, structured activities to ensure civil society engagement, with little regard for their experience as youth.

Recent examinations of civic engagement and democracy among teenagers also focus on "volunteer" activities as a site for entrance into civil society. Teenagers are often encouraged to participate in after-school and volunteer activities as a way to encourage future political participation, enhance college application processes, and instill a sense of self-worth. Volunteer organizations vary in their definition and can begin in childhood and often include organizations such as the Girls Scouts, Boy Scouts, and Little League sports. Some of these organizations originate and are affiliated with the schools that youth attend, or are already included as part of the school infrastructure itself. The importance of after-school activities in regards to youth involvement in voluntary associations and civic engagement is made especially clear in Daniel McFarland' and Reuben Thomas's study of voluntary associations and youth civic engagement.[20] Using quantitative data to study school-related activities, parental engagement, and other social networks, these authors found that those organizations where youth were encouraged and trained in the areas of public speaking, vocal, dance, and instrument training, enhance and encourage future civic engagement and political participation among youth. As this, and other recent studies suggest, voluntary and after-school activities have a significant impact on the leadership potential of youth. Sociologist Amy Best also concluded that even innocuous events, such as the senior prom, are important sites for communicating civic responsibilities, democracy, and political ideology among youth.[21]

Among teenagers, scholars have also begun to study more traditional forms of youth and leadership development as a way to understand youth civic engagement. Moving away from volunteer and after-school activities, youth leadership organizations set out to train the youth to assume leadership roles in their communities, often on par with adults.[22] These organizations vary from being youth-led organizations to organizations led by adult allies who train the youth as organizers. The overall assumption in these organizations is that youth are as deeply and equally invested in the well-being of their communities as adults, who are often positioned as leaders.[23] The topics of the organizations vary, ranging from educational change, art, speech and debate, and spoken-word poetry. In each case, the overall goal is to engage and support the youth as leaders in their community, able to make decisions for the "good of all." Specifically, these organizations seek to (1) have youth and adults work together as allies; (2) provide youth with leadership capabilities that will be sustained over time; and (3) create opportunities for the youth to understand and incorporate their own experiences into their organization's strategies. These were also the goals of both TJ and MA, but with significantly different strategies than OFCY.

Unity and Diversity: Empowering Generation Next

Teen Justice and Multicultural Alliance are similar in their visions of instilling youth with the appropriate tools for social change, but they differ in their approaches. I explore the ways these approaches differ, paying particular attention to their fundamental variations in addressing institutional and interpersonal change. For example, TJ's vision of youth development is centered on challenging institutional structures, like racism, in local schools and neighborhoods, while MA is centered on addressing how individuals have internalized the oppression they have experienced and can use that as a basis for social change.

Teen Justice: Unity is Power

Teen Justice (TJ) was founded in 1996 as a "community-based response to increased interracial conflicts and violence in [Oakland] school communities."[24] In the aftermath of Proposition 187 and Proposition 209, parents, teachers, and mental health workers reported an increase in interracial conflict among Blacks, Asians, and Latinos throughout the city. In response, social justice activists came together to create TJ, a project designed to develop multiracial student teams to lead school-based violence prevention efforts at five East Bay high schools. All of the founders, ranging from a civil rights lawyer to a former Black Panther member, were self-described activists. They combined their expertise and experience to initiate change and forge alliances with other groups in the community.

According to the mission statement, the primary goal of TJ is to create an environment where students' perspectives are validated. Specifically, the organization is committed to training youth to be "resilient community leaders and organizers who stand up for the rights of all oppressed communities."[25] Central to this goal are the tasks of building alliances across race, gender, and age lines, and ensuring healthy, just communities in Oakland. Moving beyond the goals of OFCY and civic engagement, TJ is committed to building strong youth leaders who not only "walk through the risk factor land mine" of their communities but also are trained to combat the land mines of racism, educational inequities, and poverty in their neighborhoods and schools. And, as youth like Naseem state, TJ also instills a real sense of social change in youth, beyond their immediate location:

The change [is] that every little thing that Teen Justice does, it's gonna produce some change for somebody. . . like lately I've been thinking "Why am I here?" and "Why am I doing Teen Justice?" and like I wanna change—not just Bayview and not just Oakland, I wanna be able to change like the whole world and like, cliché, make it a better place and that's probably one of the main reason that I keep going 'cause like if I stop, who else is gonna do my job?

The main project of TJ is focused on organizing leadership teams in Oakland and other East Bay high schools. Each team consists of one adult coordinator and between five and ten core student members. Teams set up at each high school address racism and other forms of inequality that affect the overall learning environment. Team leaders spearhead school reform campaigns and work with teachers, staff, other student organizations, city council members, and school board officials to create institutional change in their schools.

I was introduced to the leadership team at Bayview High School through Griselda, the adult site coordinator. Like other staff, she was in her early twenties and had been working at TJ for a little more than a year when we met. Griselda is a short, thin Latina with long hair who dresses in vintage skirts and knee-high boots. Her enthusiasm for social movement organizing is contagious. Combined with her generous smiles and laughter, this enthusiasm attracts youth to the organization. Upon meeting Griselda, I too developed huge affection for her, which fueled our working relationship. When we first met for coffee she told me she began working as a research evaluator with TJ while she was completing her master's degree, and was later hired as a full-time staff member. She then invited me to come and sit in on the leadership meetings to get a feel for the organization and meet some of the youth.

I went to Bayview High on a warm October day to attend my first meeting with TJ members. I arrived on campus to meet with the leadership team just as school was letting out for the day and the busses were filling up with students.[26] As I made my way from the parking lot to the classroom where we were meeting, I was startled by the number of youth crammed onto the buses. Black and brown faces stared out at me as more and more students piled into the bus as it started up and left campus. I later learned that for most of the youth, the bus is the only way on and off campus, which often interferes with their ability to participate in after-school activities such as track and football as well as academic and social clubs. The inability to participate in these after-school activities was a constant source of tension between the school's primarily Black, Latino, and Asian population and the majority white neighbors who lived in around the school.

When I walked into the classroom where the leadership meetings were held, Griselda and eight or so youth were milling about, getting ready to start the meeting. As we moved our desks into a circle and sat down to begin the meeting, I introduced myself as a graduate student who was "interested in writing a book on youth activism." Then the students went around and introduced themselves. There were seasoned members like David, Conrad, and Eduardo, who had been involved in the organization since they were freshmen; Conrad and Eduardo were seniors, and David, a mixed-race Chinese/Laotian youth, was a junior.[27] Most members, like Naseem—a mixed-race Persian/African American sophomore, were recruited through the Teen Justice training program that targeted eighth graders the summer before their freshman year of high school. During this eight-week program, youth participate in anti-oppression exercises and gain organizational skills from both youth and adult staff members. By the time I met Naseem, she had emerged as one of the leaders of the team. She used this status to recruit her friends and sister into the organization. One of her friends, Trisha, a Latina sophomore, also recruited her two sisters, Xochitl, a freshman (who was also the president of Bayview's Gay/Straight Alliance), and Monica, a senior. Other students, like Jose and Rico, both freshmen, and Charles, a Black sophomore, were voted in by the leadership team.[28]

After my initial meeting with the Bayview chapter of TJ, I began observing the planning strategies of one of their youth-led, school-reform campaigns. Immediately following the chapter's establishment at Bayview High, members of the leadership team became involved in struggles to improve their school environment. As David suggested, "There is no week where you just don't have anything on the agenda. There is always a problem that you have to solve or that you have to change and that you have to contribute to, and that's what Teen Justice is all about." As I studied the organization, I found his words to be true. For instance, when I began volunteering with the leadership team, they were just finishing up a disciplinary action campaign where they worked with students and teachers to address inequality in the classroom. Prior to the disciplinary campaign, TJ also successfully led efforts to reduce student suspensions at Bayview.

One of the largest, student-led campaigns TJ executed was the establishment of youth centers on Oakland high school campuses. The Youth Center campaign was launched as a proposal to create youth-positive spaces at schools throughout the Bay Area. As Griselda told me, the primary purpose of the youth center was to "facilitate better coordination of existing services at school[s] and provide access to students who need it." I worked with Bayview's leadership team as they planned the youth center process at Bayview High. After conducting a survey with over five hundred "ethnically diverse" students,[29] TJ staff and student members concluded that some of the problems that Bayview students face include depression, insufficient health care, institutional and interpersonal violence, and poor educational opportunities. Many of the students surveyed, including members of the leadership team, felt the youth center would provide them with people who cared about student needs. As Monica explained to me, "We don't have anyone that wants to help us. The youth center will provide [us with] folks that want to do it."

Other proposed goals for the center were to have TJ members gain leadership skills; increase self-esteem, civic engagement, a sense of community service and responsibility; and acquire "a deep understanding of what is possible through the collective power of positive youth."[30] Perhaps more importantly, TJ sought to create a youth center that would serve as a safe haven for youth by providing services before, during, and after school. These services included providing individual access to mental and physical health services, improving academic performance, and offering opportunities for positive youth development. Once these initial goals were in place, members of TJ began garnering support from administrators, other students, and faculty on campus, as well as from city council and school officials in the city. In January 2001, representatives from each of these groups began meeting on a monthly basis on the Bayview High school campus. I attended these meetings, as well as the preparatory leadership meetings, in an effort to understand the strategies TJ youth used in their alliances with the school, the community, and their adult allies. These efforts culminated in a media conference in April, where youth exhibited their leadership in the process.

On the day of the conference, the superintendent of schools, to whom the youth had written letters asking for support, was in attendance, along with several candidates who were running for city council. I walked into the library where the meetings were held and was struck by how small the room was. Indeed, it had been a long time since I'd been in a high school library. In the middle of the room, there were six medium-sized tables, each with four or five chairs. The area was enclosed with chest-high bookcases packed with books. I recognized some of the titles as I took my usual place at one of the tables: *Charlotte's Web*, *Little Women*, and *The Autobiography of Malcolm X*. On the other side of the bookcases were smaller, round tables, with a row of computers in the back of the room. The walls of the library consisted of several larger bookcases with books on most of the shelves, except for the one shelf in the front of the room that held magazines like *Latina* and *Essence* behind plastic sheaths. Posters above the bookshelves encouraged students to "fall into a book" and featured famous people: the rapper LL Cool J smiling with an open book; the actor Edward James Olmos looking over his glasses as he read lines from a text, and the basketball superstar Magic Johnson giving a "thumbs up" as he read.

One of the two big, heavy doors at the front of the room was open and people began filling the room. Naseem, Griselda, and Eduardo stood in a corner of the room looking over a pile of petitions the youth had begun collecting from students at Bayview. A podium was placed on one of the tables at the front of the room for the various speakers in support of as well as opposition to the center. All of the people associated with TJ, myself included, were dressed in the Teen Justice T-shirts, displaying a quote from the civil rights activist Fannie Lou Hamer. At the door, as people filed in, several students handed them red armbands with the word "Unity" spelled out Spanish, English, and Vietnamese.

When it was time for the meeting to convene, Griselda tried to get everyone's attention so we could begin and introduced David, a junior at TJ, who would lead the meeting and introduce the various speakers. At the previous leadership meeting, David and Griselda had been selected by the rest of the members to be the main facilitator that afternoon. David stood at the podium and introduced the first speaker, Phillip Robinson, a member of the school board. Mr. Robinson, an African American man in his mid- to late forties, stood in the front of the room with a drum. He wore a long purple and yellow dashiki with a matching cap, glasses, and dark pants. He explained that in addition to being a school board member, he was also quite active in his church, which was based on African principles. He suggested we start the day with a blessing to honor our collective ancestors and ask for their blessing on the collaborative endeavors of the school. He squatted and began beating on a drum and chanting, upon which his son, a Bayview High school sophomore, joined him at the front of the room. This seemed to be part and parcel for the type of activities that happened in Oakland: I had been to several events outside of the organization where African drumming was a key part of the ceremony.

Once Mr. Robinson finished, David thanked him for his blessing and then introduced the next speaker, his best friend, Eduardo. Eduardo, like David, was dressed in the standard male youth TJ uniform I became accustomed to over the course of my research: TJ T-shirt, jeans and sneakers. However, unlike David and some of the other young men, Eduardo seemed aged beyond his years. He was short and stocky underneath his baggy clothes and walked like he worked in manual labor: a little hunched over in the shoulders. His face also looked a bit weathered, his hair pulled back exposing the red tone in his cheeks, and the lack of smile lines, as I rarely saw him smile in the first year that I worked with him at TJ. Along with his physical demeanor, he was quieter than the other youth and a bit more stand-offish. Even though I visited the TJ leadership meetings on a weekly basis during the school year, it took me a full year before he hugged and acknowledged me as did some of the other students. It was at this time that he also agreed to be interviewed.

Eduardo was also a little more studied in his approach to organizing, often citing Malcolm X and others in his discussions of activism, or wearing a Che Guevara T-shirt. And, on the days that I would come into the TJ office to meet with Griselda, he was there, writing letters to representatives for various youth-led campaigns. Yet, at the same time, I would "catch" him being the eighteen-year-old that he was, rapping along to the sexually suggestive lyrics of Ludacris on our rides home from school, or throwing up East Oakland "faux gang signs" in photographs. Eduardo stood up near the podium and explained that the purpose of the collaboration was in the spirit of "the village" and each one of us taking care of our own. In other words, he explained, it takes everyone to provide the best for students at Bayview High and that's why we were gathered there that day. He then talked a little bit about the efforts in the collaborative process thus far. In particular, he acknowledged the participation of the different members of the community—including policymakers, teachers, students, parents, and neighbors, most of whom were present—who were involved in the monthly meetings. He then gave the microphone to Naseem, whose role was to demonstrate the first step in the collaborative process, mobilizing other youth. Naseem approached the microphone with the same mixture of enthusiasm and shyness that I had observed in the past. She was one of the most visible leaders in the organization because she was the one who passed out the clipboard of petitions as various events, which she held up as she told us about her efforts. She was as serious in her efforts as Eduardo, but seemed much more like a young teen; she giggled with her friends during meetings, tied her curly ponytail back with pink ribbons and barrettes and, as a tall (5 × 10 or 5 × 11) and large girl, seemed insecure about her frame. She often pulled her T-shirts down over her waist when she stood up to speak.

When she stepped up to the podium, she presented a clipboard full of yellowed petitions that TJ had begun collecting in the fall, in support of the center. The members had solicited other students, community members, and parents to sign the petition. Once Naseem sat down, others lined up to pledge their support for the center. Each of them had an allotted time of two minutes to demonstrate how they were going to participate in the collaborative process. Among the first supporters was the superintendent, who took off his tie—which made several adults in the room laugh, asking him if he was really going to give up what looked like an expensive tie—as a demonstration of his commitment to enter the process as a human being, not just an administrator. He also said that he was willing to do the dirty work necessary to build the center. Apparently, he meant this as a purely metaphorical gesture, as he presented TJ with a check for ten thousand dollars. Next, one of the city council candidates, an African American man in his mid-forties, pledged his support. In the planning stages of the meeting, the students had mentioned their interest in him and his potential as a supportive member because of his previous work with labor unions in Oakland. He alluded to this work by bringing in a hammer as a symbol of his commitment to building not only the center but also the relationships in the room. This seemed to impress the youth most of all, as other candidates talked little about the specifics of the center, instead focusing on the commitments they pledged to the Oakland community as a whole.

The last person to speak was Frank, a member from the neighborhood task force. Some of the youth around me snickered as he came up to the podium. I, too, was skeptical of what type of commitment he would pledge. Frank was an older white man, in his sixties and retired, who was the neighborhood representative. He didn't hide his feelings about the youth who attended Bayview; in one meeting he referred to them as similar to "sewage waste." Teen Justice members often pointed out that he drove a Mercedes and lived in the neighborhood around the school. Frank was one of the strongest opponents to the youth center, citing after-school crime and loitering as reasons not to have youth hanging around the school. In previous meetings, he had suggested that the security would need to be tightened to watch the youth after school. When he stepped up to the podium, true to form, he said "I don't have anything to offer except conversation and a willingness to make sure the center was a place we *all* can be happy with."

Lauren, who founded the organization, commented that the purpose of the collaborative was exactly "what had begun this afternoon and it will, indeed, take a village to build this center." She wiped her eyes as she added, "And it's not a small significance that the process included all of the different groups in the room. We cross age, race, and class lines in our commitment to build this center for the youth."

Then Conrad read a poem in which he expressed the importance of education, growing up in Oakland, and making change in the community. The members of the audience applauded when he finished, seeming to wake up a bit in response to his reading. He and David then asked us to form a circle around the bookshelves as a symbol of unity. David led the group in a "unity clap," which he informed us came out of the Farm Worker movement in California. As a sign of solidarity, he explained, the farm workers would clap while working in the fields, starting out quietly and then getting louder to symbolize their power and strength in number. The members of the audience proceeded to clap, as we always did, at the end of the meetings until we reached a loud and rapid rhythm.

Griselda thanked everyone for coming and informed the press— members from local newspapers, the PBS news channel, and the high school paper—that she and several of the youth would be taking questions. As people trickled out of the meeting, Griselda, David, and Naseem answered questions about the process. I made my way out the door and met Carlos, a Mexican-Black member of the group who was smiling as we left. I asked him how he thought it went, and he said it went well and that he was especially excited about the press. One of the reporters had asked him a question about being a member of the organization, and he was hopeful he would see himself on television later that evening.

The media conference highlights an important aspect of contemporary youth activism versus "positive youth development." The youth led the process of bringing together city officials, parents, reporters, Oakland school board officials, and neighborhood officials to build an effective collaboration around organizing for the youth center. Youth also participated in a style that was also reflective of their status as teenagers: in T-shirts and jeans, using hip-hop and poetry, and leading a unity clap at the end, which signaled a relationship between previous movements and the movement today. More importantly, the youth organized against a state institution, their school, and lobbied city officials, parents, and community members in the process. However, their leadership did not end with the conference; the youth didn't passively take in the words of the adults that were gathered that day. After we debriefed the day, the youth were happy with the success of bringing people together but were also critical of some of the people gathered that day. They identified the superintendent of schools and his gesture of removing his tie as an "adult move," just there for show. His gesture, they argued, was similar to some of the other adults in the collaborative, like Frank, who didn't understand or, sometimes, take seriously their roles as organizers.

Like Teen Justice, Multicultural Alliance is interested in building youth leadership, and challenging oppression in their efforts to make the world a better place for youth, based on young people's own understanding of that reality. And, while each includes civic engagement and participation, it is *one* piece of the puzzle, unlike OFCY, which expects youth to simply avoid these realities and become better citizens. Differing slightly from TJ, MA's approach focuses on "healing" the individual and understanding how racism, sexism, and homophobia impacts their lives, prior to (and, in many ways, rather than) organizing to address structural inequalities in their communities.

Multicultural Alliance: Healing the Hurts of a Community

Multicultural Alliance is a smaller organization than Teen Justice, with only three staff members at the time of this study.[31] Ze, a white Jewish man in his early thirties, started the organization with a vision of strengthening cross-cultural/community relationships and promoting dialogue between groups. Founded in 1998, the organization is modeled after a coalition-building organization that brought together Catholics and Protestants in Northern Ireland in an effort to build skill building, service learning, and cross-community understanding. Ze was inspired by watching the program's commitment to and skill in "community building and cross community awareness and . . . bringing people in the community together and creating friendships with each other."[32] He used the tools and lessons that he gained from that experience to create the vision for Multicultural Alliance, which states:

> As we begin a new century, we are still haunted by the old demons of racism, discrimination, intolerance, ignorance, and exclusion. We live among greater diversity than at any other time in our country's history, yet a vast number of individuals, families, and communities still fail to welcome or understand the value of this diversity. And as the increase in hate crimes in this country attests, this lack of understanding is one of the core issues that threaten our society. Fortunately for us all, today's youth have powerful ideas and want to participate in finding ways to eliminate hate crimes and racism—to better the world they will be inheriting. . . .The mission of Multicultural Alliance is to use the talents and enthusiasm of these young people to strengthen cross-community interaction and foster mutual respect and understanding to build alliances and to positively impact society.

To build cross-community interaction and promote dialogue across cultures, MA combines popular education tools with training youth as anti-oppression education facilitators. After their initial training, youth are interviewed and further trained as facilitators. During the school year, the interns would visit different organizations for a total of three times. These programs included similar peer leadership programs at area high schools, girls clubs in elementary schools, and upper-division elementary school classes. As a researcher, I followed MA youth who led these workshops in

"Change Happens," a program that targets youth in after-school programs throughout Oakland.

One of the first workshops that I attended with MA was at Washington High School. Each time we discussed the plans for the day, the youth lamented having to go to the school where all the "bad" kids went. Margaret was also a bit concerned about the school's reputation and asked two of the more skilled facilitators, Patti and Lana, to lead the first workshop. Patti, an eighteen-year-old Black girl from West Oakland, was in her second year as an intern at MA. The first year, Margaret told me, Patti held back a little and didn't lead the workshops, but had emerged that summer as a strong facilitator. I met Patti as part of my introduction to the organization. On the day of the Washington workshop, she was dressed, as she normally was, in tight jeans, tennis shoes, and a turquoise T-shirt. She also wore a star-studded belt that read "Sagittarius." Her demeanor was serious and confident. She was currently applying to colleges—Occidental College and Howard University were her top choices. College was her ticket out of Oakland, a city that she had never left. She was the middle of three children and, because she had a car, was responsible for picking up her younger sister from school and taking her home, which often made her late for workshops. I never got a clear sense of where her older brother was during the time of this study; according to Margaret, Patti didn't talk about him much because he had been involved in gangs and other criminal activity. When Patti spoke, I got a sense of the responsibility and leadership that she took on outside of her job as an intern.

Lana, a fifteen-year-old Latina, was more playful than Patti and looked more like a tomboy. She was often dressed in an oversized, blue, hooded sweatshirt, baggy jeans, and tennis shoes, with a black bandana wrapped around her shoulder-length straight hair. Lana seemed more outgoing than Patti: she laughed and smiled a lot and had a more relaxed demeanor. I first met her when she interviewed for the organization, where she readily shared that her favorite band in the whole world was TLC, an all-female R&B hip-hop group. In fact, when one of the members of the trio, Lisa "Left Eye"

Lopes, died, Lana called me crying, saying she wouldn't be at work that day. Despite her playful demeanor, Lana was also a skilled and serious facilitator. When she began working as an intern, Margaret pegged her as one of the more experienced youth in the organization because she had worked on other youth leadership projects in Oakland.

When we arrived at Washington High School, Patti and Lana met briefly to discuss how to proceed with the workshop. Margaret and I also discussed what our roles would be during the ninety-minute session. As we were talking, I glanced around the hallways at the dirty, green-gray colored walls. The halls were empty and dark, with the exception of a janitor, whose uniform seemed to blend in with the walls. At first, I didn't think anyone was there for the workshop, the atmosphere seemed so quiet. However, as we got the supplies ready and moved into the classroom, the scene erupted into a flurry of noise and activity.

About twenty-four students were packed tightly into the tiny classroom. It looked evenly split between Blacks and Latinos, with slightly fewer boys than girls. Two adult women, one white and one Black, stood at the teacher's desk talking to one another. The air in the room was stuffy and hot. Two chalkboards faced each other at either end of the classroom. One wall was littered with wrinkled and torn posters and cutouts of famous American political leaders like Malcolm X, Martin Luther King Jr., Frederick Douglass, and Cesar Chavez. The walls were painted dingy beige, similar to the gray-green walls in the hallway. The fourth wall was made up of four large windows with heavy black shades, which were pulled down tight, locking out the outside world. Diane, the white adult who appeared to be in her mid-thirties and a little heavy set, walked over and introduced herself to Margaret and me. As she told us more about the students in attendance, Patti and Lana joined us. She spoke to them, "These guys [her students] are peer leaders just like you all," she said, assuring us that the students should be reasonably cooperative, but that they also knew a lot of the peer education agenda that we had planned. She glanced up at the clock above the door and whistled for the youth to together as a group. Movement escalated in the room as they pushed their chairs into a circle. Lana and Patti took their places near the chalkboard at the front of the room.

Lana started the workshop by going over the goals of the day and introducing herself and Patti to the group. She looked like she could easily be one of the youth sitting in the audience. As she talked, though it was clear that she was a leader in this situation. Her tone was relaxed and confident, and her skills as a facilitator overcame any nervousness or hesitation she had previously communicated. Many of the attendees had their heads down, not making eye contact with her. Several of them sat with the tables of their desks turned down so they could sit closer to one another. A couple of the girls sat on the tops of their desks braiding their own hair and/or their friend's while studying their neighbor's reading material. A slim Black boy whose gold teeth peeked out when he smiled draped his arm around his girlfriend, who had her head and body turned toward him and was whispering in his ear. A brown-skinned Latina, whose straight, dark hair hung down to the middle of her back, sat crossed legged in the middle of the circle, looking at her nails. A Samoan boy, who had the stocky build of a football player, sat with his headphones on. Although it wasn't clear if he was listening to music or not, he had his eyes focused intently on Lana as she talked, chewing his gum slowly as he slumped down into his chair.

Patti started off by going over a list of group agreements for the day's proceedings. At every workshop, the group would post a set of rules that the participants in the room agreed to follow throughout the workshop. Patti hung up a piece of white butcher paper, which, in colored ink, listed the group agreements including: confidentiality, respect, no interruptions when other folks are talking, honesty, and no cursing. She asked if the students in the audience agreed and had anything to add. Several youth shrugged their shoulders and shook their heads, finally agreeing with the list. Patti then moved onto the first exercise, an activity called "Values Four Square." She led the exercise and read off a list of values that included a few, introductory statements like not lying to parents, and not cheating on tests. She then moved on to heavier questions like violence in the community and teenage drinking. When she read off each particular value, the youth were supposed to move to the sign that best applied to their values, "Yes for Me," "No for Me," "Yes for Others," and "No for Others." One of the final values that day was "homosexuality," upon which the crowd scattered around the room quickly when she said it—particularly the boys—moving to the signs "No for Me," "No for Others," and a few to "Yes for Others."

As one lone girl moved toward "Yes for me," Margaret grabbed my arm and said, "C'mon let's go" as she ran from her chair toward the sign. I knew what she meant—she had mentioned that she often came out as queer in workshops if there were gay or lesbian youth in the classroom. I was a bit nervous to come out as queer myself in this classroom—it was one of my first workshops, and I wasn't feeling that familiar with the other youth and my role as both a participant and observer. Still, I followed Margaret. The girl who had been draped over her boyfriend looked at the three of us standing under the "Yes for Me" sign. "Really, Katrina?" she said to the young girl, her arms folded and forehead scrunched up. "That's nasty," one of the boys muttered, and Dianne cast a strong glare in his direction. Patti calmly interrupted, and asked us first to describe why we moved to the "Yes for Me" sign. Margaret and I briefly told our coming-out stories and how we identified as queer. The class then turned its collective gaze to Katrina, who stumbled some as she spoke.

"Oh, well I came over here because I don't call myself gay or nothin' like that," she started out, "but I don't think there's anything wrong with it, if people want to be gay, that's fine." She continued, "My mom used to be like that—you know used to be with women and so does my aunt so I don't have a problem with it."

Patti smiled, thanked her for speaking, and moved on to the other groups. Under the "No for Me" sign was a boy who thought homosexuality was nasty, along with a Latino boy who explained that he couldn't get down with two dudes getting together, but that he was "feelin' two females." Some of the girls rolled their eyes at this comment. One Black girl, dressed in a pink jumpsuit, with long braids similar to Patti's, stood under the "No for Others" sign. When it was her turn to speak, she explained that she couldn't support homosexuality because she was a Christian and the Bible said it was wrong.

Patti, looking a bit exasperated, turned to Margaret for guidance, who smiling tried to reassure her at the same time that she motioned to her watch indicating that it was almost time to stop. Patti finished up the exercise by saying that it was important to respect all opinions and values, and applauding the group for listening to each other.

We moved on to the next activity, called "Act Like a Man, Act Like a Woman," which Lana led. She asked the students to make a list of expected roles for men and women in society. She started out with stereotypes for men. The crowd rustled around a bit, eager to put out their specific thoughts. Several raised their hands, both boys and girls, and shouted out things like "Have a job," "Be strong," "Not supposed to cry," and "Be 'playas.'" Lana and Patti wrote down what each person said, or asked the room for agreement if those things were supposed to be on the list. By the end, there were two full sheets of butcher paper with lists of gender stereotypes. Some of the ones for women were "Be pretty," "Be thin," "Do housework," "Have children," and "Be emotional." Lana looked over the lists and then asked what women were called who didn't fit into this category? "Bitch!" one of the girls said.

"A dyke!" the Latino boy yelled out, tapping a friend of his on the shoulder sitting next to him. "A ho!" someone else yelled out.

As they spoke, Patti wrote up the words in red marker. I glanced over at the other adults in the room to get a sense of how they were feeling with the language. The first time we did this exercise with the participants at MA, I was surprised by the harsh words used. However, over time I had somehow become immune to the words. Diane looked a little tense, as she covered her mouth with her hand and narrowed her eyes at Margaret, myself, Lana and Patti to try and see where we were going with this exercise.

Lana continued, "Okay, so a bitch, a ho, and a dyke. What about the guys? What if you're not a playa, don't have a lot of honeys, don't have a steady job, and cry sometimes and don't hold it all in."

"You a faggot!" one of the boys yelled out. Some of the other boys in the room laughed and added "butt boy" and "sissy" to the list. One of the girls protested, saying that she liked boys who were "sensitive" and "emotional." Other girls agreed.

Diane winced and approached the boy who initially had used the word "faggot" and whispered in his ear. She later informed us that he had recently had a sister who came out to him and his family. Looking a bit exasperated, she glanced toward Margaret and me for reassurance. It did feel like the situation was a bit out of control until Patti stepped up to one of the boys who initially made the faggot comment and said, "Okay, but what if someone called you a nigger, wouldn't you be offended?"

"It depends on who it is," the boy responded," Like if my boy called me a 'Nigga', I ain't gonna take no offense."

"Yeah, but you know what I mean, what about like a white boy or something just called you a nigger one day, you wouldn't be offended and think that's wrong?" Patti said, holding her ground.

"I wouldn't care really. Besides, it's different. Because fagg—I mean," he corrected himself as he looked over in Diane's direction. "Well, being gay or whatever is different 'cause it's just different. Like they kinda' sissy-like, I mean I don't mean no disrespect!" he said, looking at Margaret and me.

His friend, a young Black boy with short dreadlocks, interrupted him and addressed Patti and Lana specifically, "Wait a minute, are you guys trying to get us to be sympathetic to homosexuals' needs 'cause that seems to be all we talking about!"

Patti explained that it was important to talk about homophobia in relation to the other types of oppression that we had been talking about as a group. Margaret interrupted, as we didn't have much time left, saying, "No, this is not necessarily about you being sympathetic to people's needs but rather to talk about how stereotypes hurt people and in particular how we're supposed to act one way as men and women and the consequences if we don't act a certain way." She looked back at Patti and Lana and nodded for them to take over again.

"Yeah, we just want to get people talking about how what kinds of stereotypes are out there and have you think about how sexism and homophobia affect us just because of what we look like or what we do or don't do, you know what I'm sayin'?" Lana said in response to the boy, but to the entire room as well. "Again, we're not here really to change your minds, but we do want you to think about how society works and stuff like that." It looked like her hesitancy had returned, but she was still holding her own. A few of the students in the room nodded, looking both exhausted from the conversation and eager to go home. Patti and Lana finished up by doing a go-around with the students asking them what they liked or didn't like about the day. Outside, after the workshop, the four of use debriefed about the workshop, Patti and Lana looking visibly exhausted. Margaret and I applauded both Patti and Lana for their facilitation, which they didn't think went very well. They were usually a little hard on themselves after a workshop, expecting more immediate change and cooperation. We then divided up into our separate cars, Margaret in hers, Patti in hers, who left quickly to pick up her little sister. Lana and I piled into my car and talked about the next workshop at an elementary school the next day.

As we have seen, MA uses popular education exercises to teach other youth the ways that racism, classism, and homophobia impact their daily interactions. Whereas OFCY focuses on simply identifying and maneuvering through the "land mines" that youth encounter, TJ and MA aim to teach youth how ideology shapes the youth's lives just as much as the neighborhoods where they live. Popular education exercises move beyond simply learning about oppression cross-culturally, but they are central to building trust and coalition among youth members. As the youth activist William Upski Wimsatt suggests, "bitter old arguments about who is most oppressed have subsided, and everyone is talking about how to build coalitions . . . we're learning to create solid alliances and friendships across the great divides." By participating in these exercises, youth activists bring older movement strategies, like consciousness raising, into their own, new framework for social change.

Conclusion

Divisions between the hills and the flats, staff and organizational goals, OFCY expectations and interpretations of youth development, and community support all influence the building of a youth movement in Oakland. Youth's participation in anti-oppression exercises, like the ones described in this chapter, is a key piece for overcoming the obstacles of their communities and adult organizations to build a larger youth movement. At the same time that youth are actively participating in their own cognitive liberation, anti-oppression work and learning about internalized oppression are also parts of a larger goal, mainly on the part of funding agencies, to "build resilient youth" in the Bay Area. Throughout this book, I explore how the youth worked with and around the goals of Teen Justice and Multicultural Alliance to make youth activism and leadership projects of their own. In this process, youth of color build coalitions with one another, participate in social change, and construct individual and collective political identities in Oakland. In the next chapter, we see how these organizations and their training as social change agents equip them with the tools to navigate social abandonment and surveillance in the post–civil rights era.

3

IT'S GONNA GET HARD
Negotiating Race and Gender in Urban Settings

It was a cycle. For years, Oakland experienced interracial and inter-ethnic violence at almost every public high school in the city. One year, at Washington High School, school coaches agreed that soccer teams could use the football field on campus to practice.[1] Unfortunately, Black and Samoan football players were not notified that the predominantly Latino soccer team would be using the field to practice that day. Once they spotted the soccer team on their "turf" and suspected rival gang members in the mix, fighting ensued, leaving one student stabbed and another seriously injured. On another day, an African American student rear-ended an Asian American student in the school parking lot, leading to a long conflict between Blacks and Asians on Bayview's campus.[2]

Sociological studies of youth and violence often center on traditional understandings of violence in American culture. For urban youth of color, these studies are particularly pronounced, mirroring the opening paragraph. For instance, recent studies conclude that violence is a normative experience for urban youth of color, regardless of gender or race, and that gang behavior is almost a necessary ritual in inner city neighborhoods.[3] Other scholars also argue for the equal examination of violence/aggression among young women, primarily Blacks and Latinas. While central to our understandings of the youth of color experience, often these examinations reinforce stereotypes of the *urban*, youth experience, which are rooted in violence. Ultimately, these understandings render youth powerless, categorized as social "problems," and both victims and perpetuators of a noncritical understanding of violence. In this chapter, I characterize violence as the institutionalized social structures of racism, sexism, classism, and homophobia (see chap. 5) that shape young people's lives in this study. In particular, I am interested in how youth understand and navigate the violence of institutionalized racism, sexism, and classism and the methods they use to address it.[4]

Coupled with this oppression is the violence this generation experiences through a social abandonment by previous generations—in local and national discourse related to youth and also a deep understanding of their experience as urban, youth of color. The organizations in this study work to address this abandonment in a very different way than organizations like OFCY, and are vigilant about creating safe spaces for youth, in the city of Oakland. In the following pages, I explore how youth activism is understood in the context of this abandonment and how young people navigate this social, political, and cultural landscape. A landscape informed by what some social movement scholars may describe as abeyance,[5] but what I contend is abandonment, marked by the social abandonment of urban youth of color.

Abandoning Youth: Violence in the Post–Civil Rights Era

In *Whitewashing Race: The Myth of a Color-blind Society*, the authors describe the post–civil rights era as a moment where a "new" racism is defined by individual or collective acts of prejudice and discrimination.[6] These acts are coupled with a general belief that the movements of the sixties and seventies "took care of all of that," so any opportunity or lack of access that people of color—particularly African Americans—endure is of their own doing. Or, as the authors suggest, members of previous social movements themselves often understand racism to be "over," and that they waged and won such a significant "fight" that any subsequent experience bears little merit:

> Instead of expressing alarm at the persistence of deeply rooted racial inequalities and searching for new ways to reach America's

egalitarian ideals, many former advocates of racial equality proclaim the civil rights movement is over and declare victory. Racism has been defeated, they tell us. If racial inequalities in income, employment, residence, and political representation persist, they say, it is not because of white racism. Rather, the problem is the behavior of people who fail to take responsibility for their own lives. If the civil rights movement has failed, they insist, it is because of the manipulative, expedient behavior of black nationalists and the civil rights establishment.[7]

In this instance, the movement discourse shifts from abeyance, or what Verta Taylor contends is "a holding process by which movements sustain themselves in nonreceptive political environments and provide continuity from one stage of mobilization to another" to abandonment.[8] One recent example of this is the "pull your pants up" debate, in which older African Americans (and non-African Americans) have chastised members of the hip-hop generation for wearing "sagging" pants. Songs, music videos, and web pages have linked this style to the denigration of the Black community in particular but also to a generation of uneducated, disrespectful, and deviant youth. More importantly, this abandonment is demonstrated in the number of city councils in cities across the United States that have moved to criminalize those who wear sagging pants for indecent exposure.[9] In California, laws like the Gang Violence and Prevention Act, or Prop. 21, is another way to characterize the abandonment of youth of color in that voters passed an initiative to prosecute youth as young as thirteen as adults in the criminal justice system. This abandonment, I argue, potentially shapes the growing intergenerational divide between young people and adults. Ultimately, urban youth of color, including youth activists, are expected to navigate this political, social, and cultural landscape on their own.

When I asked Conrad about being an activist in Oakland, he described a similar victorious tone among civil rights activists, who have moved on, abandoning contemporary social justice movements:

I get pissed at all of these like, old cats I meet, male and female who walk up to me and are like "You know, back in the sixties, you know I was at UC Berkeley. I was leading . . . I was at the rallies and the march[es]," and I go, "What happened?" [They answer] "Well, you know, I got married, I had a kid, got my picket fence." Having a kid is *more* of a reason, you know what I'm saying, to keep fighting for freedom, and it's like their excuse for giving up or something. It's stupid. But, I also know it's a lot of brothas out there who had ancestors who are under wraps, like they are hiding out, you know what I'm saying, because like at the fall of the Black Panther party, a lot of people had to go into hiding or they were going to be murdered or killed, you know.

I experienced some of the "dream is over, victory is won" attitude as well in numerous informal conversations with people about my research. For instance, I was once at an event and introduced to a former Black Panther Party member who, when I told her that I was writing a book on youth activists in Oakland, she lowered her eyes, looked at me and said, a bit sarcastically, "Well, what *is it* that they're doing?" When I told her a little bit about the anti-oppression workshops and organizing for a youth center—the two primary methods that Multicultural Alliance and Teen Justice employed—she said, "oh, uh-huh, I see" and turned around to her conversation. Other seasoned activists laughed when I explained my book, asking, "What is it a pamphlet or a worksheet or something?" Both interactions insinuated that if a movement *did* exist, which they weren't convinced did, the youth weren't doing enough.

These comments were fairly innocuous, compared with the ways that some of the youth communicated the new racism they experienced in their interactions with adults. Naseem recounted one particularly extreme interaction she had with Frank, the leader of the neighborhood association at Bayview. Frank had a history of complaining about the youth at Bayview, including the ones involved in organizing for the center, which he was opposed to. The youth often suggested that he was racist and, on this day, he seemed to confirm their beliefs.

N: I don't know if Griselda told you about the time when, when he said that—he did this analogy and he referred to the [Bayview] students as the waste?

AC: As the waste?

N: Yes, he was talking about this sewage problem that he had, and he did this analogy and the students were the waste, the sewage problem.

While Frank's example may be extreme, Bayview youth were clear about the feelings that the neighbors had about them as youth of color. As Naseem told me:

Yeah, and a lot of times with the neighbors, they talk about, they like call the football players animals, 'cause a lot of times they go down the private road 'cause that's the fastest way to get to the bus stop if there's no buses coming up to the school . . . so like people go through their like property and turf and then like they generalize, like "Oh these people did it so the whole school is like that" and [they] lie. Even though they're not talking about me, I still feel offended, because . . . like I know football players, like David, and I know he's not like that and there's students who I know that walk down that way and that's just because they're trying to get home and there's no other way to get home.

I, too, had heard the neighbors regularly cite occurrences of youth trespassing on their lawns at the monthly collaborative meetings. However, it was impossible not to walk on some of the lawns, as there were no sidewalks leading from the school to the bus stop at the corner of Thirty-fifth and MacArthur, which was approximately a three-mile walk. And, as Naseem states, many of the youth relied on the bus system to get to and from school.

In addition to the economic and racial landscape of Oakland; youth experienced racism, sexism, and classism in other ways, in spite of what popular discourse suggests is a "color-blind era." Sociologist Eduardo Bonilla-Silva states that the myth of this era is characterized by what he describes as "color-blind *racism*":

As part of this new racism, a new racial ideology has surfaced: the ideology of color-blind racism. This ideology is characterized by a focus on culture rather than biology as well as by the abstract extension of elements of liberalism to justify racial inequality. I label this new ideology as color-blind racism because this term fits better the *political* language of the post–civil rights era.[10]

Accordingly, color-blind racism is used to justify a commitment to the current racial status quo, where race and racial privilege are hierarchized. This hierarchy is characterized by "the persistence of poor housing, poor heath care, illiteracy, unemployment, family upheaval, and social problems associated with poverty and powerlessness."[11] As a slightly more nuanced and developed understanding of racism post–civil rights, Patricia Hill Collins allows for an understanding of the impact, not only of colonialism and slavery, for youth of color (primarily African American in her research) but also desegregation laws—one of the biggest victories for the civil rights movement—that directly affect youth of color. As a consequence, these youth are then the ones who

remain written off, marginalized, and largely invisible in everyday life . . . at the same time that Black American youth experience these social problems, their mass-media images tell a different story. In the 1990s, images of poor and working class Black American youth as athletes and entertainers flooded global popular culture. The actual ghettoization of poor and working-class African Americans may render them virtually invisible within suburban malls, on soccer fields, and in good public schools, yet mass media created a seemingly authentic Black American culture that glamorized poverty, drugs, violence, and hypersexuality.[12]

Like others, Collins constructs a dual reality that, ultimately, informs the contemporary experience of youth of color. Importantly, as she notes, the increasing (hyper)visibility these youth experience in popular culture, which celebrates a mythical existence while elevating primarily urban and Black youth to a superior status in the popular imagination.[13] The violence lay both in the duality of this experience, but also in the philosophy of organizations like OFCY, which was more interested in providing a space for youth to avoid the so-called land mines in their communities, rather than address the structural inequalities that continue to persist.

The youth very much set the context for the complexities of the post–civil rights landscape in their interviews as well as their everyday conversation. For instance, on a Wednesday in January, shortly after Achilles began working at MA, I found him sitting in the office. We still didn't know each other that well, so he would always slip in a question or two to try and figure out who I was and what I was about. On that day, he started to ask me questions about where I was from. I told him Missouri. "Missouri, really? Huh," he said. "Do you have any brothers or sisters?" he asked and, feeling a particular moment of disclosure, I answered, "Yes," and then told him about two of my closest siblings, a sister and a brother, whom I hadn't been in touch with in years, because of their addictions to crack cocaine. To this he replied, "Oh yeah, because you're Black." "What do you mean," I asked. He replied, "Well, you're a Black person in America, I don't know any Black people who don't know about crack."[14]

When I sat down to interview him a couple of months after this interaction, he evoked this dry wit as part of his answer to my question, "Describe what type of social change you're involved in?":

> A: The workshops are aimed at like getting rid of, or talking about homophobia, sexism, *sectarianism*, racism, [and] ageism. It's like talking to youth about diversity issues and things like that, like getting to hear their opinions and hearing where they stand on these issues. It's very interesting because you get different people's perspectives. Like if you go to Piedmont, you are going to hear that they don't like coming to Oakland and they keep their eyes straight on the road, so they don't have to look at Blacks and stuff.
>
> AC: Someone said that to you in Piedmont?
>
> A: They did not say *Black* people, but they said they keep their eyes straight ahead because they are so scared of Oakland.

While humorous in his discussion, his answer also points to not only the co-existent experience of this historical moment, where he can joke and equate anti-sectarianism with anti-racism, anti-sexism—part of a backlash against identity politics—but also understands the racism inherent in statements like, "I keep my eyes straight ahead when driving through Oakland." These conditions, coupled with the ways that crack cocaine, AIDS, unemployment, desegregation, and gentrification have shaped the neighborhoods, communities, and livelihoods of people of color in urban areas, serve as the "tool kits" youth activists assemble to navigate this terrain. The dry tone that Achilles and other youth employ to describe post–civil rights racism evokes Jose Muñoz's discussion of disidentification, in the sense that he "neither opts to assimilate within the structure nor strictly opposes it."[15] In response, individuals, particularly "minoritarian subjects" *dis*identify with dominant structures:

> disidentification is a strategy that works on and against dominant ideology. Instead of buckling under the pressures of dominant ideology (identification, assimilation) or attempting to break free of its inescapable sphere (counteridentification, utopianism), this "working on and against" is a strategy that tries to transform a cultural logic from within, always laboring to enact permanent structural change while at the same valuing the importance of local or everyday struggles of resistance.[16]

The experience of having discriminatory laws changed and oppressive practices criminalized because of previous social movement struggles, at the same time that sexism, racism, and homophobia impact the everyday lives of youth of color forces youth into a process of disidentifying, or "opting out" in many ways while they firmly plant their feet into the struggle for institutional change. The process of disidentification speaks directly to the post–civil rights era as a strategy that youth activists utilize to both embrace the tactics of previous social movements and also to critique the process of identifying those movements as *the* movement or as a stand-in of mainstream discourse. This is especially true in the struggles around education, where California voters regularly enforce the belief that youth have achieved a level playing field. Nowhere is this more evident than in the passage of Prop. 209, the statewide push to end affirmative action on college campuses and in the workplace, led by the former UC Regent Ward Connerly and backed by the then governor Pete Wilson. In their early campaigning for the voter initiative, they endorsed the measure by invoking civil rights language, notably naming it the "civil rights initiative." In several arguments for the proposition proponents cast the initiative in civil rights language:

A generation ago, we did it right. We passed civil rights laws to prohibit discrimination. But special interests hijacked the civil rights movement. Instead of equality, governments imposed quotas, preferences, and set-asides. Proposition 209 is called the California Civil Rights Initiative because it restates the historic Civil Rights Act and proclaims simply and clearly: "The state shall not discriminate against, or grant preferential treatment to, any individual or group, on the basis of race, sex, color, ethnicity or national origin in the operation of public employment, public education, or public contracting." Reverse discrimination based on race or gender is plain wrong! And two wrongs don't make a right! Today, students are being rejected from public universities because of their race. . . . Government should not discriminate. It must not give a job, a university admission, or a contract based on race or sex. Government must judge all people equally, without discrimination! Government cannot work against discrimination if government itself discriminates. Proposition 209 will stop the terrible programs which are dividing our people and tearing us apart. People naturally feel resentment when the less qualified are preferred. We are all Americans. It's time to bring us together under a single standard of equal treatment under the law. . . . Government agencies throughout California spend millions of your tax dollars for costly bureaucracies to administer racial and gender discrimination that masquerade as "affirmative action." . . . the better choice: help only those who need help! We are individuals! Not every white person is advantaged. And not every "minority" is disadvantaged. Real "affirmative action" originally meant no discrimination and sought to provide opportunity. That's why Proposition 209 prohibits discrimination and preferences and allows any program that does not discriminate, or prefer, because of race or sex, to continue. The only honest and effective way to address inequality of opportunity is by making sure that *all* California children are provided with the tools to compete in our society. And then let them succeed on a fair, color-blind, race-blind, gender-blind basis. . . . Vote for fairness . . . not favoritism![17]

This statement, like Prop. 209 itself, is laden with civil rights and anti-discriminatory language, much like the title of the proposition itself. The argument, an addendum to the attorney general's official preparation of the bill, argues that the state should not discriminate against anyone based on race and gender preferences—echoing direct language from the Civil Rights Act passed in 1964, which, among other things, ended discrimination in public sites and outlawed segregation in public schools. Invoking this language represents the violent discourse of the post–civil rights era: using the emancipatory language of civil rights to evoke equality at the same time silencing the inequality that exists. Although there were mass student protests against Prop. 209, on both high school and college campuses throughout the state, California voters ultimately passed the bill in a 54 to 46 percent vote. The aftermath of this has significantly shaped the ways that youth activists experience one of the most important sites in their lives: education.

They Schools Don't Teach Us[18]

The youth in this study reflected on the inequities of their educational system, some comparing it to the prison industrial complex, on a regular basis. School heavily structures teenagers' lives: it is the place where they spend a significant amount of their waking hours, create and maintain relationships, and participate in extracurricular activities. For the youth in this study, it was also the primary site to organize for social change: either at Bayview High for Teen Justice youth, or various elementary and secondary schools for Multicultural Alliance interns. For instance, Courtney, a sophomore at UC Berkeley and an intern at MA, addressed the educational system directly in her discussion of social change:

> You just have to really start from the bottom up and that, that's also giving more money to education and not to prisons, it's about, um, just not giving up on people because of like where they're at or some things that they're doing 'cause that's when, it just becomes, that's when it seems really hopeless because you just give up, and just looking under the table they're not, they're just like completely lost.

Similarly, other youth cited their own experiences in the classroom as part of this "forgotten," or "lost" group, who are often overlooked in the educational system. For instance, formal and informal tracking along race and class lines in public schools was an experience several of the youth cited as motivation for their own activism. As Achilles states:

> At school, I don't know, I was placed in the "ugly kids class," or "Black Biology" by a counselor, and Black Biology is basically a biology class where you don't learn anything, and it does not count for college credit. It is just to get you to graduate high school, and I did not know that. They just said, "You are in Biology," and I was like, "Biology is awfully Black," you know. These are the people that don't come to school, come on now. Then, finally, I talked to my Black teacher and he was like, "You don't want to be in this class, you are too smart for this class. Get in Advanced Biology." I was like "Oh, thank you," and then you know, I notice that when classes get whiter, you know, they all righter.

Here Achilles suggests that he was tracked into a class that was predominantly Black because of his racial background, without being tested. Although his Black teacher noticed the error, he also reinforced the tracking system by identifying him as "too smart" for the class. Neither was able to address the structural inequalities that set up the different experiences of Black students in their school. Achilles' experience speaks to the post-integration reality that many youth of color face: although movements for civil rights were often squarely focused on education, urban students of color are often treated like they are unable to succeed, regardless of academic merit. As Collins observes, "despite the 1954 *Brown v. Board of Education* decision . . . large numbers of working-class and poor African American children remain warehoused in poorly funded, deteriorating, racially segregated inner-city schools. Regardless of *individual merit*, these children as a *class* of children are seen as lacking merit and unworthy of public support and are treated as second-class citizens."[19] This status was central to their motivation as social movement actors.

In addition to Achilles, several youth that I interviewed told me how racism in their schools reinforced their passion for social change, For instance, Trisha told me about a similar experience to Achilles' "Black Biology" class in her discussion of how she experiences racism:

> There's a teacher [at Bayview] that grades—like 60 percent of her grade is based on class participation but she didn't call on me, she never called on me, so I complained to one of my teachers Ms. Shepard, you know Ms. Shepard right? I complained to her and then Mrs. Smith went to talk to her and she's like, "I mean, well what's the point?" She's like, "I don't really call on Latina or African American females. . . . They're gonna get pregnant and drop out anyways, so what's the point?"

She experienced this attitude with other teachers and classes as well, for instance, it wasn't until a mentor at her school informed her that there were Algebra classes being offered, which she could enroll in. However, once in the classes, she described feeling isolated as the only Latina in a class that was predominantly white and "Asian":

I mean, it's not any kind of Asian, you don't see any Pacific Islanders in AP class. You don't see any Pacific Islanders in Math Analysis, like you see Chinese and maybe Vietnamese, but it's like it has a lot to do with race and who they're willing to keep down and who they[re] not and, like I never got offered Algebra when I was in junior high; all the Asians and all the white students were in Algebra their seventh grade year and Geometry their eighth so by the time they got here they were in Algebra Trig, or Intermediate Algebra, you know, by the time they got in high school. I never got offered— the lady I was working with for the discipline committee, she was like "Well you're very smart, why aren't you in Algebra?" I was like "They never—I didn't know they offered it here," you know? And so she got me enrolled in Algebra and that's the only reason I got Algebra in junior high. But, whenever [it] got offered, they never went into my class and said "Oh, you guys wanna take Algebra?" That was never an option. The schools believe that if you're gonna, if you're already making it, you're gonna make it and if you're not making it you're just screwed and you know "forget you" and it just so happens to be like everybody in math analysis and AP classes are like white and Asian and you know . . . like wanting to keep you down has a lot to do with race.

Trisha, and many of the youth, made clear connections between their experience and the racism of the administration at both her high school and junior high. She disidentifies with this moment by identifying and critiquing educational practices of keeping people down because of race.

Eduardo's experience mirrored both Achilles' and Trisha's when he arrived at Bayview, where he was placed, almost immediately, into an ESL (English as a Second Language) class. Knowing Eduardo was born in Mexico but moved here when he was three, I asked about his high school placement in this class. He replied:

You know to tell you the truth I didn't know. And then my mom thought it was a good idea, you know. She was, like, "Oh you know its going to help you out and this and that" but, at the same time, I

saw my friends doing other things, like, reading stuff and, like, writing, you know, mini-essays and stuff like that—things that I didn't
end up doing til, like, senior year. So, how did that help me out?
Now that I think about it, how did that help me out in the long run?

When I asked if his first language was English, he answered:

No, it was Spanish. But at the same time when I went in there and
started to do the work my teacher—I forgot her name—she was
like, "You don't belong here. You don't belong here. You can leave,
you should leave, and you should get out of here." And I stayed there
for about a semester . . . and like I missed out on a lot of things,
like, art and music that were given out of those programs and I only
had a semester of that throughout middle school. And, um, things
like that, you know, um, just going, being outside and, um, and,
and seeing like [how] my other friends would be placed in Math 1,
Math A and a lot of the classes were, you know, mainly filled with
people of color . . . but that didn't get really overt until I got to high
school where like, you know, there where like I saw that the middle
class, you know, middle/upper class both of color and white, mostly
white, were in those classes.

Like Trisha, Eduardo is critical of the system that assumed he
should be in ESL classes. And even though he "opted out" of the system by staying in the class for semester, despite his teacher's urging
for him to get out, it provided him with a particular vantage point
that directly informed his strategies to address educational inequalities:

And like now I'm working with Spanish Speaking Council and now
actually helping set up a tutoring program for students who are not
in school who want to get back in school, or, students who are in
school but are not doing anything . . . the so-called knuckleheads
of high school. Or the loud mouths. Even the good students, you
know. Just bringing in different things, like, working with the arts
and, 'cause a lot times I see that, like, a lot of Raza youth, like, they

get put away from that. They get put away from the arts. That's what silenced me for so long. And this faulty ass education system that we have, you know?

The "faulty ass" education system that Eduardo refers to in Oakland has a 52 percent dropout rate, with over 5 percent of students dropping out in a single year, and 22 percent over a four-year period.[20] Other youth were also motivated by the California educational system. As Donelle told me:

D: There's a lot of things I want to make a difference in, like mainly the schools. . . . In my opinion, about this whole school board in California? I think it's kind of messed up how they do us because they make youth just wanna give up. I mean they say they want students to push themselves, but really, you gonna want to make them give up because at one point they gonna find it's too hard 'cause I know there's a little thing going around talking about, "it's gonna get hard."

AC: What do you mean it's gonna get hard?

D: Like some people might can't do it 'cause for the people who know they ain't gonna make it but they try, you know at one point they're gonna say "Forget it," and they just gonna give up. And then now, ok like now it's like youth is the biggest issue 'cause now we got police officers and brutality and gettin' people killed and all that. And then we got this jail thing that happened and now they talking about you can't graduate unless you know where you going. So, I'm like "That's kind of messed up." Why— they say we the next generation—but, then again they make us give up on ourselves and they try to kill us off. So, I'm like, you guys make this big thing like "we should do good in school" and then there are some schools where the teachers don't pay attention. Like, at McClymonds the teachers they kinda—they say, you know even though they're the smaller schools . . . and it should be like a private school, but a lot of people say that since that school doesn't have a lot of people, the teachers should be able to work more better with the students, but it's not like that. And, it's kinda hard 'cause the teachers be off track with the students who [are] not tryin' to learn. And they just get all distracted and leave the students off to run around. Some of the teachers, I'm not sayin' all of them do, but that messes with people's academics and that gets people all frustrated and they get mad.

The frustrations that youth experience in high school didn't seem to change once they entered and/or prepared for college. For instance, when I asked Xochitl what her experience with racism was like, her answer was directly centered on post-secondary education, which she was far from, as a freshman:

Like I went to college night, it's for juniors and seniors, but I'm always trying to get ahead.[21] And, I want to go to UC Davis, so I went to the table to look at stuff for the veterinary school and there was this guy there and he's this white guy and I was like "I heard that you all have a really good Veterinary school can you tell me what it's like?" And he was like, "Well, yeah we do, but you might not want to get in anyway, because it's too hard for people like you to get into." And this guy came, this white boy, came and he gave it to him. I don't experience [that] too much but when I do have stuff like that happen, I just go off in my head.

Even though Xochitl self-prepared to go to college by attending this college fair, she was rejected because of her race, class (and gender) status. Like the teachers that Trisha interacted with, the recruiter from UC Davis didn't think she, as a young Latina, was "the right kind of person" to get into college.

Once she was in college, Courtney encountered racism in the misinformation that she received from a student instructor at UC Berkeley:

c: My GSI [Graduate Student Instructor] was horrible, like, I ended up writing a letter to the class and distributing it, saying, "Why?" 'Cause anytime I would start to bring up racial issues it would be brought back to class [economic status] and then she would feel it was necessary to bring up points, like, "You guys should see what you guys are writing about, African Americans. 'Cause we need to recognize that like 50 percent of African Americans are middle class."

AC: "50 percent?," I asked, thinking this was a high number. She agreed.

C: Yea *50 percent* of African Americans are middle class, and I'm just like, whether or not that's true and you're just pulling this out of your—yeah, it's just like why do you feel the need to bring that up when we are trying to discuss these issues, just so it's like "Okay there's this sunny side over here," so we don't have to feel so bad about this, we don't have to focus on the bad stuff. [I'm] like, "What are you doing here?" She came from the History department and she was the only one that wasn't like as strong [as the other GSIs were] so she didn't even understand the whole struggle of keeping Ethnic Studies, and like the whole strike that was going on just a few years ago. But, that was just so annoying to me, 'cause it's like you find this space, like, within my major—I'm like Ethnic Studies all right—that I'm going to find what I'm looking for, but the professor was awesome, Takaki, he just, [was] really great, she just ruined it all.

Perhaps directly related to the aftermath of Prop. 209, Courtney's GSI steered discussions about African Americans away from race and racism, and provided false information about the numbers of African Americans who have entered the middle class. All of the experiences that youth encountered in their educational institutions reflect the abandonment that currently structures their experience. The post–civil rights era is characterized by the experience of "lost" youth, as Patricia Hill Collins points out, which is reflected in the stories of Eduardo's placement in ESL classes when he didn't need to be, Donnelle's experience with teachers who didn't care (and are often overworked, underpaid, and improperly trained), and the lack of real discussions of the structural inequalities that the youth are trained to address. In effect they are overlooked and forgotten about, at the same time that, as *urban* youth of color, their movements are also heavily scrutinized and surveilled.

The Streets Is Watchin' Me

The youth articulate a sense of abandonment by different institutional structures—the educational systems into which they are tracked, the criminal justice system, which always looms, but also in everyday conversations about "bad neighborhoods," or the "ghetto," which inevitably implicate their particular raced, classed, and gendered bodies, as Achilles' earlier statement about Piedmont suggests. I argue that at the same time that this functions as abandonment, it also acts a type of surveillance, in the Foucauldian sense of the term, that operates through the processes of abandonment and social distancing. Youth articulated this surveillance in their conversations with me, but there were also direct discussions of surveillance in their organizing strategies. I observed this in a discussion about security at the Youth Center during one of the collaborative meetings with Teen Justice:

> Several representatives from Teen Justice, the neighborhood coalition, the facilities team, and Bayview High were gathered to discuss the location of the youth center on campus. Because previous meetings had been fairly tense between youth and some of the neighborhood representatives, Griselda hired a facilitator, Cherry, to lead the conversation. However, this day was no different, during the meeting the conversation shifted from building location to safety and security on campus. Frank stated that he couldn't agree to the proposed location of the center (the southeast corner of campus) because of increased crime. "We've had major problems along that fence line." Frank's status as a "blocker" was firmly established and although they looked exasperated, the youth were used to his stance: Naseem quickly spoke up, saying "Actually the fence is close to the place where students can get dropped off, making it really accessible for students. Plus, it's well lit and easily accessible to support staff." Her answer was an effort to shut him down, but he didn't

take the bait. Instead he countered with, "If we had it in the northeast corner of campus, the neighbors could serve as the 'eyes' for the center." Again, Naseem chimed in, "The northeast corner is not conducive to students because they can't park there, that's a faculty parking lot." Steve, a math teacher at Bayview also added that the northeast side of campus was "difficult" because it is out of reach of the current security system on campus, a pan and tilt camera. "Yes, but that camera isn't always in use because it must be manually operated, so a lot of times, no one is there to supervise," Frank said. Charles, who was sitting in the corner, added "there's also a camera on top of the auditorium, which watches students come into campus, some teachers have volunteered to operate that." Frank shook his head, adding, "the neighbors have made suggestions to school officials for years and none of them have been realized." I looked at the clock, which Eduardo was also watching as he intervened, saying that a special committee would be setup to deal with surveillance issues, so as to alleviate concerns. Cherry took that as her cue and shifted topics.

The discussion of security and surveillance of youth on campus was illuminating on a number of levels. First, Steve's description of the pan-and-tilt camera on campus sounded like a direct descendant of Bentham's panopticon, which Foucault describes at length in his discussion of surveillance. Second, I was struck by how no one questioned the existence of the cameras on campus and in relationship to the Center. The youth seemed to be immune or numb to the presence of a camera, albeit one that didn't work on a regular basis. Like Foucault's description, the pan-and-tilt camera was something the youth were aware of and, working or not, reinforced the ever-present "totally seen, without ever seeing" experience for youth.[22] This allowed them to be controlled, always assuming they were being watched, with discipline inscribed on (and in) their bodies and actions. In this, and other ways, "power had to be given the instrument of permanent, exhaustive, omnipresent surveillance, capable of making all visible, as long as it could itself remain invisible.[23] This permanent surveillance and implicit distrust of the largely youth of color population represents the social abandonment that marks the urban youth of color experience.

The prescribed monitoring at the school was translated into their everyday lives. For instance, I asked each youth a series of questions related to discrimination and, in most instances, was given answers that related directly to their status as youth of color living in the Bay Area. For instance, when I asked Achilles if he had ever been discriminated he answered, straight-faced, "No." He then laughed and said, "I mean yeah, of course, yeah." He then elaborated:

> Well, I was in this porno shop on Castro, and like I walked in or whatever, and then you know, the Black guy, I am thinking, "He's Black, he's working here, [and] he's looking at me like harder than the white guy," like "Are you gonna buy that, are you gonna steal it, do you have a gun?" You know, just looking at me like, okay, and people have been like, you know, "Are you gonna buy this, and . . . I mean, it happens all of the time. I try to tune it out, but it happens all of the time.

In his usual dry and sarcastic tone, it was often difficult to tell when Achilles was being serious and when he was trying to unnerve me. In this instance, although he uses a porno shop in the Castro to situate his experiences of surveillance as an urban, youth of color, it did resonate with other stories that youth shared when I asked them about their experiences with discrimination. For instance, Trisha talked about being in upscale neighborhoods in Oakland:

> I think the only time where racism was really like against me was— oh actually there was twice: one time I was walking by Montclair[24] in the hills and—but not the commercial area—my friend lived around there and a cop stopped us and asked us where we were going and all this other stuff and he drove us down to the bottom of the [hill], like down to Thirty-fifth and Macarthur where we belonged because we were—it was me, two other Latinas and two African Americans and one Asian and he assumed we didn't belong

there and he drove us to the bottom of the hill. I thought that was weird, like that was *harsh.*

When I asked Naseem the same question, she also equated being discriminated against with store surveillance. When I asked her if she had ever experienced discrimination, she answered,

> Not to my face—oh, there was this one time, with me and my sister—we went to the mall and we went to this candy store and we were getting candy and there were like these three other like white, blond, girls with blue eyes and the guy was following us for the whole time and that's the only time that I can think of that it's happened to my face, but there's always times when you're discriminated [against], especially being a youth of color.

Naseem's distinction of being discriminated against "to her face," and all the other times is an important one in the discussion of surveillance and youth of color—even when it is unnoticeable to them, they are aware that it's happening all the time, it's something they expect, And, as Xochitl points out, everyone has the ability to watch youth, "like a faceless gaze that transformed the whole social body into a field of perception."[25] She recounted:

> When you go to stores, expensive stores, and there are a whole bunch of white people and it's not the fact that we are young because there are other young white people in the store, but we always seem to be the ones that get followed and the thing is like "Oh, it's a white person following you," but it's not even that, sometimes it's an Asian person or something. And it's like, "Okay why do they have to follow you?" And they don't even try to hide it, like every five seconds they're like "Oh, do you need help?"

The monitoring of youth in department stores was something I was familiar with and experienced personally as a young (and younger looking) woman of color, but also something I observed routinely as a researcher. The first instance was on a trip with MA to a Los Angeles museum. I was chaperoning with Margaret and Ze and about twenty youth involved with the summer program. Before we went inside the museum for a civil rights history tour, several of us stopped at the gas station across the street to get a soda. I was standing outside the station when one of the youth ran out of the store and up to Margaret, explaining that they were being denied entrance. Looking up, I noticed that there was a crowd of youth standing outside the gas station, talking with one of the employees. As we approached, I heard him explaining that, "We don't allow more than four youth in the store at one time, we're too small." "You can't do that, that's not fair" one of the youth explained.

Margaret approached the man, asking him what the problem was. He repeated his statement that they didn't allow teenagers to enter the store in large numbers as a general rule because of theft. Margaret agreed with the youth, stating that he wasn't allowed to do this, but eventually shepherded the youth out of the store and over to museum, telling them, "Let's just not shop here, we can get sodas somewhere else." To which the older man shrugged and went back inside.

I too was surprised at this occurrence, never having experienced this confrontation. However, throughout the course of my research, particularly driving youth around to various workshops, I noted several Oakland stores—candy stores, stationary stores, clothing stores—that displayed signs highlighting the number of teenagers that could enter simultaneously—four at a time, two at a time, etc. This type of monitoring and surveillance embodies the post–civil rights ideology of expecting young people to succeed, but at the same time we fail to trust them and, more importantly, we *fear* them.

Thug Life: Hating or Fearing Black Men

Educational policy, media representations of urban youth of color, and everyday experiences significantly shaped how the youth in this study articulated and, more importantly, internalized oppression. In this section, I juxtapose two conversations—one with Te and one with Conrad—who communicated the effects of the contemporary landscape and their process of disidentification as African American boys, soon to be men. For instance, Te, a nineteen-year-old, articulates this in his discussion of how he navigates being a young Black man in his everyday life. Like Courtney, Te was one of the founding interns at MA and was a skilled facilitator. He took up a lot of space when he entered a room, mostly because his size: he was about 6'1" and between 250 and 300 lbs. Unlike Achilles, who was of a smaller frame and with a dry sense of humor that he enacted almost immediately in different situations, Te was much quieter and more reserved in everyday settings. I noted when I first met him that his quiet demeanor, size, and race might intimidate some of the youth, based on racist stereotypes of Black men. He was incredibly sweet, and like many of the other youth, after you hung out with him for a while, he opened up, joked, smiled frequently, and reached out to others. I observed this tone in several workshops with elementary-aged youth, boys and girls, who immediately responded to his playful nature.

During our interview, I asked Te what he did to "kick it" (hang out) with his friends. In his answer, he told me of the ways that he and friends sometimes sit around and talk about oppression, which he taught others about regularly at MA but, as he suggests, is an activity that is rarely associated with young men of color:

It be so funny, though, 'cause you really wouldn't think like five, six males would be in the room talking about racism, or homophobia, and things like that . . . and I used to sometimes just like stop and, like be in the middle of conversation and I be like, "Do you know what we're doing right now?" you know. Like this isn't supposed to be happening [he laughs], but it happens, and it trips me out when it happens, so I know it trips other people out.

He paused, thinking, and I asked him why it shouldn't be happening, or why it tripped people out, and he answered, quickly, "'cause you're male, Black, everything in society, you know. These are not, not issues—you don't talk to, talk about outside of groups like Multicultural Alliance."

As Te suggests, the expectation is that men, particularly young Black men, are not expected to critically examine racism or other forms of oppression, so much so that even when he does, despite his work with MA, he is often caught off guard. When I asked him if he was able to engage in similar discussions with all of his friends and members of his family, his answer revealed both his inability to talk with his parents about what he does—not uncommon among teenagers—but also a deeper exploration of how expectations around Black manhood impact those conversations:

> They don't see me like that. Um, a lot of my friends don't see me doin' stuff like this 'cause they're like "You're not, you're not that type of person to be doin' stuff like that." 'Cause I'm like very short-tempered when I get mad and very violent sometimes so it's like they don't see me. It's like, "You? Not your crazy ass. You're loud and obnoxious and cuss people out all the [time] and want to fight everybody like you crazy and you trying to help somebody" [laughs]. . . . They know, I'm like, "There's more than one side to me," you know. Like there isn't only one side they know both sides, everybody [has] seen a little of both sides of me. They just trip out on me.

In the short time that I had known Te, I had only seen and heard *one* side of him. In the hours that I had hung out with him, observing his work in and outside of the office, I had never seen him angry, or anything but his "work self," preparing for or facilitating workshops. I wasn't surprised that there was more than one side to him, as a teenager (or anyone else, for that matter), but I was intrigued. I asked him to clarify what he meant, asking if he got into fights. He responded by shifting in his seat a bit, smiling:

> T: Who me? About what? [pause] I'm just, I'm crazy, I'm just, I got a short temper, I don't—I expect to be respected by everybody and I expect to be right and I expect to do things the way I want to do things and that gets me in trouble 'cause then I get hurt easily by people. I get hurt especially if I trust you then I get hurt easily then

I hurt you back. Or I don't really care about, I don't care about how other people, uh, I mean this is my own community mostly, like, I don't care about 'cause it's like growing up with survival of the fittest and everything in a community where you gotta be the biggest and baddest to survive so I adopted that, like, at sometimes I be tryin' to get away from it 'cause it gets me in trouble getting in a lot of positions I don't want to be in. But then part of me thrives on being there, so it's like, that fills me and it feels good when I'm in a situation like that or—I don't know, it's weird.

AC: But do you feel comfortable telling me what kinds of situations are you talking about?

T: I mean, I mean I been in situations where I felt like the only way I was going to handle the situation was I had to kill somebody and we had weapons [and] we were going looking for the people and we were going to kill them if we found them, like that, stuff like that. Situations where I got jumped by eight people and over stupid stuff or even like somebody like my best friend 'cause just somebody pulled a gun out on them something like that and we'd go look for them and that was like last week we had to go find them and stuff like that and I was [like], "Alright lets go do it." I mean I never think like, "No Te, you going to school and you gonna be—" but its like I can't abandon my friends 'cause when it comes, when it was time when what I was going through they'd be the ones I call for. And a part of me don't really care like, uh, I can't say there, I'm scared, I was scared, I'm like, but people are always thinking like, *"he's not scared,"* like my friends, *"he's not scared,"* but I know, but I'm more scared than you, I'm more scared than them and I think I use that fear, you know like when a dog is backed up in the corner and they just attack, I use that a lot. Now when I go in a situation and I'm like terrified and I don't want to be there I just do what's natural. I think I'm more scared of myself and what I do, then actually the people that uh, instead of what I make the people do to me if I don't be quiet or *if I don't, what I do.* Its crazy, but uh I'm not in it as much as I used to [be]. So, that's like when I was new to Multicultural Alliance everything just happens, no responsibilities more having people look at me different and its

like, dang c'mon Te you can do this its, you know, so [it] takes a
little time or a lot of time to get myself in trouble. That's why if you
give somebody like a youth that's in trouble and they get responsibility and they got people that are actually counting on them in
another way, in a different way, but not really putting pressure on
them but just counting on them—it's kinda hard [because] they
still probably going to get in a lot of that trouble 'cause that's
where they goin' that's where they live unless you going to move
them out from where they from. Of course, they still going to get
in some mess, but they think more about other people.

Te's comments speak directly to the process of code-switching
that Pattillo-McCoy and others describe for post–civil rights youth.
As a youth activist, Te has to contend with the realities of the duality of his life: his work with MA (and as a college student) and the
expectations placed upon him as a young Black male, out with his
friends. Thus, pointing to the reality that is always present for urban
Black males, a particular experience that has been argued by others
as definitive of the "Nigga" experience—one that is shaped by the
particular post-industrial, post–civil rights abandonment allowing for a judgment and racism not only by white Americans, but by
African Americans as well.[26] His discussion also evokes images of
the differences between the Southern Christian Leadership Conference (SCLC) and the Black Panther Party, and the descriptions of
Black manhood and activism in expectations of "institutionalized
charisma" among members of SCLC versus the livelihood of the
"brothers on the block" necessary for Black Panther Party membership.[27] While the two organizations existed simultaneously, the
change in political agenda that they signaled also marked the demise
of the *idealized* civil rights movement as we know it. Te's discussion
symbolizes this demise in the distinction of the two models: you can
either be an educated Black man, or an urban thug. Ultimately, in
the words of Dead Prez, it is essential for youth activists to be "revolutionary but gangsta" in their straddling of the two identities.

Conrad also evoked a sense of nihilism in his discussion of being
a young Black man combating racism—the most important social

justice issue to him—as an activist.[28] His statements were similar to Te's discussion but focused on the collective, rather than individual, effects of institutionalized racism.

> To do away with racism is not to do away with white people calling us niggers, you know what I'm saying? To do away with racism is to do away with racists, [or] like policies, that are implemented that bring us down, you know what I'm saying? I can deal with the name, I can't deal with the state of [the] name, you know what I'm saying? What being a nigger is.

Conrad leaned back in his chair, ready to launch into it, so I asked, "What is it?"

> Well, it's two sided. One side of being a nigger is, I think people say, like "nigger," to give pain to you . . . like to be condescending. And people use nigger to [say] you know, "I'm not A nigger, I am THE Nigga, you know what I'm saying? Like, pain is love, so Nigga is love, you [say] "I love you, Nigga," which is stupid. Like I am not at all justifying them . . . and uh, like I never see Asians go "What's up ching-chong? Or white folks, "What's up peckerwood/cracker, come on let's go have a pilgrimage . . . you pilgrim, or Mexicans go "Hey, wetback, let's roll." But, we go "What's up, Nigga?" Or you know what else I see in the workplace? All of these so-called Blacks [who say], "I used to be radical in the sixties," right? [And then say] like, "You know that's how Black folks is. We [say]—"Niggas is just like that," then when they have an issue with their white boss, they lean at me and go, "You know she's messing with me because I'm Black." So, we whisper "Black, Black, Black," but we yell "Nigga, Nigga," you know what I'm saying? It's so ignorant. So, to step away from other people of color and to follow with Black folks is that . . . we have enough enemies and we become our own enemies. You can go to Chinatown—there's no "'Blacktown," you know what I'm saying? It's like, it's such an individual space. That is why I never see like an Asian crackhead. Because there is a family basis . . . like my brother just got done doing nine years in the pen . . . another

brother, he produces the news in Fresno, for like the #1 news station out there. And, he is married and he has a home, and he is younger than my brother that went to the pen. But, in a Black family that is an individualist-based, you know what I'm saying, and this is what my mother says, but not what my father says, my father has seven kids, but, on an individualist-based Black family, you do your thing, and you do yours, and I will do mine. So, you can have Leroy and Tasha who go off to school, you know what I'm saying, and then you could have Jermaine and Ne Ne who go to jail, and they be from the same parents, it's a very individualist base, whereas white folks, you know what I'm saying, Chad goes to college and then he works for Sniberholt, Inc., and his name is Chad Sniberholt, and Chad Sniberholt's great-grandfather founded some oppressive-assed company that is making money. You know what? I give it to white folks, well not white folks, but white Corporate America, it's their brilliance in sticking together, you know what I'm saying? It's sick, but it's brilliant.

The use of the word "Nigga" by members of the hip-hop generation has been debated by rappers, pastors, journalists, and celebrities like Mos Def, Oprah Winfrey and Bill Cosby—further exposing the distance between the two generations. Conrad's words capture this debate at the same time that he characterizes it as a uniquely African American experience—not because Black people have reappropriated the word (as is often the argument) and, therefore, taken the power out of it—but because it symbolizes how the Black experience has a distinct, solitary nature, defined by nihilism and individualism. As West suggests, this "lived experience of coping with a life of horrifying meaninglessness, hopelessness, and (most important) lovelessness" characterizes the contradictory nature of the post–civil rights moment in which we call one another and accept words like "Nigga", at the same time that "ex-sixties activists" accuse their white bosses of racism and distance themselves from "Niggas." The detriment of this class and race based divide, is similar to comedian Chris Rock's stand-up routine in which he makes a clear distinction between Black people, whom he loves, and Niggas, whom he hates:

Now we've got a lot of things, a lot of racism in the world right now
Who's more racist? Black people or white people?
Black people. . . . You know why? 'cause we hate Black people too
Everything white people don't like about black people
Black people *really* don't like about black people
There some shit goin' on with black people right now
There's like a civil war goin' on with black people
And there's two sides . . .
There's Black people and there's Niggas
And Niggas have got to go
Every time Black people wanna have a good time
Ignorant ass Niggas fuck it up
Can't do shit without some ignorant ass Nigga fuckin it up
Can't do nothin'
Can't keep a disco open more than 3 weeks
Grand opening, grand closing
Can't go to a movie the first week it comes out
Why? 'cause Niggas are shooting at the screen
What kind of ignorant shit is that?
Hey this is a good movie, this is so good I gotta bust a cap in here
Hey I love Black people, but I hate Niggas
Boy I wish they'd let me join the Ku Klux Klan
Shit, I'd do a drive-by from here to Brooklyn
I'm tired of Niggas man
You can't have shit when you around Niggas.

Like Conrad, Rock's commentary points directly to the distancing and abandonment by previous generations of the post–civil rights generation. While Rock and the audience members who applauded loudly at his show (*Bring the Pain*, where this skit was first performed live) are members of the post–civil rights generation, they uphold a permeating ideology inside and outside of the Black community, that there are "those" Black people, Niggas, and then the respectable African Americans. Conrad's statement differs from Rock's, which no doubt is comedic but also representative of a collective sentiment, President Obama referenced Rock's routine in his election campaign. Conrad is also clear in his disidentification, that this divide is a consequence of the abandonment that characterizes the post–civil rights era. For instance, unlike Rock, he points to adults that call out racism in the workplace, but who don't apply that same logic to their own feelings about youth who may use the word "Nigga," rather marking themselves as different. This distinction further ignores the ways that "Nigga speaks to a collective identity shaped by class consciousness, the character of inner-city space, police repression, poverty, and the constant threat of intraracial violence,"[29] highlighting post-civil rights abandonment.

Watching Back: Challenging Interpersonal and Institutionalized Oppression

To address the negative conditioning that youth faced, Multicultural Alliance and Teen Justice staff led anti-oppression exercises as part of the youth's training. Staff at MA built their philosophy and practice of youth empowerment on this training, while TJ focused more broadly on institutionalized inequalities with frequent trainings to address personal experience with oppression. Generally, these trainings took place during a six-week-long summer program and also during quarterly day-long retreats. I sat in on one of these quarterly trainings, which focused on stereotypes. On that particular day, members from all five area schools were gathered as part of a weekend retreat. For the stereotypes exercise, the youth and adult staff broke up into four groups, according to racial background—Black, Asian, Latino, and Mixed-Race. In each of these groups, an adult staff member led a discussion about racism and people of color. I sat in with the African American staff and students for the twenty-minute breakout session. Once the groups finished, everyone came back together, and a designated youth member whom we chose during the session led the discussion of her/his racial/ethnic group. During the reports back, one youth from each group had to summarize the issues they had addressed. In their responses, they made the connection between the stereotypes that each group faced and how they often internalize these stereotypes. For instance, two girls—one Asian, the other Black—presented the stereotypes that their group came up with:

Mai, a junior, stood up as a representative for the Asian group. She wore a brightly colored dress and spoke in a quick and excited tone; anxious to make sure we understood the importance what she saying. The group's sheet of butcher paper, which was covered with words from corner to corner, was pasted behind her.

"Okay, y'all we had a hecka' bunch to say as you can see." She smiled and threw her hands out in front of her, as she talked, much like a rapper, pointing to no one in particular, using her gestures to enunciate the words as she spoke.

"Okay, so we put a lot stuff up here like some of the stereotypes are that we only eat rice, that we just got off the boat—that's a big one—that we don't speak English, that we smell, that we want to be other people, you know that we don't want to be Asian. Like, some people think that just because I talk like this and say 'yo' and what's up and stuff like that that I'm trying to be Black. Oh, and then the last one is that we all drive Hondas." Mai finished, everyone applauded, and she sat down. Jill, a Black sophomore, stood up as the representative for the African American group.

"Okay, y'all," Jill started, she was a little more subdued and laid back in her presentation, wearing a zip up hoodie and jeans, "Here's what we came up with: some of the stereotypes are that the girls are hoes or bitches who just want to get pregnant and spend money." She used her finger as a pointer as she went down the list, "all of the men are in prison or on parole, we get pulled over by the police a lot because they think we're criminals, we don't have a culture and think we're all a bunch of thugs, we're lazy, we're stupid, we only eat chicken and greens and soul food and stuff." She paused as if reflecting on what she had just said and then continued, "Some of the things that we've internalized or whatever are that light skinned Black people are better, that we have to process our hair and not keep it natural, that we're thugs, and that the best way to get ahead is to have money and be "bling-blingin'" it and stuff. That's about it, I guess," she said and sat down. Again, the room erupted in applause and Griselda stood up to close out the session.

Similar to the youth at MA, youth at TJ learned how oppressive stereotypes shaped their racial/ethnic identity. These exercises, aimed not just at getting youth to understand the difference between reality and stereotypes of each group but also how people of color have internalized racism (sexism and classism). As Griselda told me later, once the youth recognize the negative conditioning that they have experienced as individuals, they will be better equipped to organize others for larger social change.

These tactics also prepared Courtney for her organizing outside of MA, particularly as a college student at UC Berkeley, where she and other Black students participated in a "blackout" to challenge the changing racial landscape on UC campuses:

> c: We had a blackout, um demonstration in the Spring of last year, just to kinda stand up, 'cause we were, there had just been like a printing of, "Ten Reasons Why Reparations Are Unconstitutional," like, some guy paid for that and then there was just a lot of bad stuff following that, that just, it created a very, um, unwelcoming environment for the Black students, and so we decided to do this blackout demonstration; we dressed in black, we had bandanas covering—that's actually a minor thing—bandanas covering our faces and . . . after going into classrooms and just standing there silent in the back room for maybe five or ten minutes, then we went to Sproul and, went across Sather Gate from 12-1, just like standing there, and that was pretty powerful. I was really glad I did that, and I definitely did that because I felt it was very necessary that we do establish a presence because it, we were just being like run over, and I wasn't feeling all that welcomed, and I was feeling disappointed, initially disappointed 'cause it was my first year there and I just didn't see the diversity that I thought I was going to, so.

AC: What kind of response did you get from doing that?

c: One guy walking by yelled "fuck diversity." But then we had a lot of other students that sat down and, um, raised their fists in the air with us, in acknowledgment, and, it was a good mixed response, but even now, I'll hear people, [say] like "Oh, you were, you were part of that black out?" I said "Yeah, I did," and they said "That was really cool," and they just, they thought it was a really powerful thing, because we weren't out there protesting or yelling, like a lot of other groups can do, and people just get annoyed by that, we just stood there, it was just our silent presence so.

Importantly, Courtney's statements highlight the importance of different strategies for post–civil rights youth—strategies that people won't "get annoyed by." While it's clear to her, as earlier quotes suggest, that racism does in fact exist—the unwelcoming atmosphere for Black youth, the misinformation she received from her instructors—she, along with fellow students, employed strategies that addressed their experience in a public manner.

For Eduardo, his strategies for addressing oppression were rooted in building solidarity in his community:

You know, like, the whole concept . . . of you being my other me and like you know, just saying, you know, like, you are my other half kinda thing, you know. Whatever happens to you happens to me, you know. Like kinda building solidarity and, like, and like getting a sense of life. Unification among people of color. And like pushing that all the time. . . . And, like, or to go to, like, a slam, to like other slams and having someone that just comes up to you and say, or when you, or we went to a school in West Oakland, McClymonds, and said the streets are like a movie, you know, and then he goes, what are you talking about, well, and then, our streets are the movies. Or like, or like, doing a cycle of violence workshop and a young man saying that, "Shit, I just went through that,"[or] "Shit, I just got pulled over by the police," or "Shit, my friend just died and his girlfriend's pregnant and she's been wanting to kill herself and, and, and," Like, when you, when you see, like, the connection between that, the students and the community, and what you're performing or what you're saying then you know that you're going in the right direction. When you don't have to say the next piece because someone already said it to you because they say, exactly that's what happens, then that's you know that its something. The small changes are being created.

Conclusion

The youth in this study face particular obstacles because they are young people, teenagers, so their time is heavily structured, monitored, and scrutinized overall. Also, a large part of their organizing happens at their (or others) educational institutions because that is where they spend the most of their time and is an important site for organizing other youth. For youth of color, this is especially important; not only are there not that many places for them to congregate outside of school, their movements as youth of color are often heavily surveilled in popular culture, in their families, and at school. For instance, laws determine when and where young people can congregate, at what times, and how many is too many (Prop. 21) This not only affects their organizing but also their understanding of their social location and life chances as young people of color.

I examine this as a crisis among urban youth of color, similar to Cornel West's discussion of crisis in the Black community, where he discusses the social abandonment of poor African Americans by their middle-class counterparts and which is reflected in the commentary of Chris Rock. In the post–civil rights era, adults have abandoned urban youth of color out of fear: a fear of the young Black male body, as Te and Conrad describe; the fear of the young Latina (pregnant) body, as both Xochitl and Trisha speak to; and, ultimately, a fear of the collective organization of youth, as the discussion of surveillance cameras and the Youth Center demonstrates.

What this means in terms of defining youth activism is twofold: first, youth must navigate that landscape, one in which individuals do not define their experience as racism, sexism, heterosexism, and classism, and that adults in their everyday settings often contend that "things are alright." Second, youth of color are expected to be thankful for the opportunities that previous generations fought for. While these experiences shape their everyday landscape, youth also find ways to organize and challenge the abandonment they face. In the next two chapters, I explore the successes and limitations of organizing around culture and identity in the post–civil rights era.

4

HIP-HOP FOR THE SOUL
Kickin' Reality in the Local Scene

I'm like Che Guevara with bling on, I'm complex.
—Jay-Z
I'm a hip-hop head. I listen to rap. I'm a Black boy from the ghetto.
—Conrad
[With] a lot of the hip-hop and the poetry and stuff, you can convey
a message. And if you can get that message out to people, you can't
change the whole world, but you can start by a little piece.
—Xochitl

On a surprisingly warm day in March, I attended a "Youth Solidarity" event at Bayview High School, sponsored by Teen Justice. The Youth Solidarity week was an annual event that Teen Justice organized on school campuses, which focused on raising awareness about various social justice issues. This year, David took a lead role in organizing the event, with a specific focus on garnering support for the youth center. I arrived at Bayview at noon, during lunch. It was a beautiful day, which was more evident as I met up with Griselda and the others on the senior quad. In this particular spot, it looked more like the campuses of California schools that I had seen in the movies: green grass against a backdrop of light blue skies and a view of the city off in the distance. Griselda, Jose, and Trisha were already sitting on a small hill, making "Solidarity" armbands to hand out to folks that were gathered outside. The armbands were made with red cloth and black lettering, similar to their banner, and written in different languages: Spanish, Vietnamese, and English. When I asked David, who smiled and gave me a hug when he saw me, what the purpose of the armbands were he told me, "We like to hand out the armbands as a symbol of unity between the different folks here." As I looked through the crowd gathered on the quad, several people had the band wrapped around their upper arms.

The event seemed pretty low-key; I wasn't sure what was happening next as students gathered and ate their lunches. Griselda motioned to David, who was sitting with his leadership class, to indicate that the guest speakers had arrived. I looked over in the direction she was motioning and noticed two African American men, dressed much like some of the youth that day: baggy pants and T-shirts, but a little more colorful than the standard white T-shirts that most of the boys wore on campus. In addition to the microphone one of them had in his hand, they stood out not only because of their age but because one of the men wore his hair in long dreadlocks and the other was wearing a newsboy cap. David went up to them, shook their hands, and then directed them to the middle of the quad. As they moved closer, I recognized them as Rashid Omari and Brutha Los, from the local hip-hop group, Company of Prophets.

"Hey y'all," David said, speaking into the mic, a few people turned their heads. "My name is David and I'm part of Teen Justice and this is our Youth Solidarity week. Today, we're organizing for a youth center on campus so we can address stuff that's going on, like violence, in our schools." He seemed a little nervous, I wasn't sure if it was the setting—he seemed more comfortable in front of adults—or the fact that people were milling about, not looking at him directly.

He continued, "Right now, I want to introduce Company of Prophets who are going to perform a few songs for us." He handed the mic over to Brutha Los, who addressed the crowd. "Yeah, what's up Bayview High School, we are Company of Prophets and we're here with Teen Justice to talk about your schools." They then went into a rap about public schools, which reminded me of "They schools," by Dead Prez, but in a cleaned-up version, departing from "they schools don't teach us shit." As they performed, I noticed more people immediately gathered around them nodding their heads in seeming agreement with their words.[1]

I was impressed that the youth were able to secure a popular, political, hip-hop group, who were central to the Seattle WTO (World

Trade Organization) protests in 1999. As Company of Prophets performed three fairly quick songs, I watched them motivate the crowd
in a way that David, as a solitary speaker minutes earlier, couldn't
do. I had seen them perform at several different events around
town and would describe them as a politically conscious group who
talked about the different realities of living in Oakland and in the
United States: poverty, police surveillance and brutality and, on this
particular day, the school system. It was certainly a cleaner version
of their regular lineup; they didn't curse but focused on what they
were asked to do: get the crowd hyped. It was difficult to follow their
exact words from where I was sitting, but the chorus of "where my
freedom fighters at?" that they chanted over and over at the end of
their set resonated with the students on the lawn as people stopped
to stand and watch: girls and boys equally, participating in a call-
and-response manner. All the while, I watched Naseem dart in and
out of the crowd petition-stuffed clipboard in hand, armband on her
arm, collecting signatures for the youth center.

Scholars, activists, and hip-hop artists themselves have analyzed the relationship between hip-hop culture, youth, and social
change. Hip-hop music often acts as a base for social protest
among today's youth,[2] in much the same ways that rhythm and
blues, early rock and roll, and folk music did for youth activists
in the 1960s.[3] Music has been a useful organizing tool for social
and political protest because it reflects the lifestyles and values
of youth. For example, in the 1960s antiwar movement, activists
reinvented traditional folk music as an authentic political force.
As Ron Eyermen and Scott Baretta's work suggests, activists interpreted folk music "as a depository of the 'people' or the 'folk'. . .
providing an alternative to manufactured, mass-mediated forms of
cultural expression."[4] Youth activists in this study interpreted hip-
hop in much the same way, as an authentic youth culture, even in
its most commercialized forms. Hip-hop has been a particularly
important site for youth of color to understand and define themselves and their experiences. Moreover, hip-hop can be a powerful
tool in communicating to an outside audience what it means to be
a youth of color in this particular historical moment.[5]

Almost immediately upon its movement into the mainstream, hip-hop, rappers in particular, have received criticism because of what some describe as a "minstrelization" of the genre, which has come to define the music.[6] In this chapter, I explore how youth use hip-hop music and culture in their activism on their high school campuses, in their everyday settings, and at the organizations they work with, in spite of this critique. I also examine how youth take on the role of cultural workers by using hip-hop to intervene in dominant under-standings of youth culture, resistance, and identity.[7] At the same time that I examine the larger social justice potential of hip-hop music for youth, I also explore how hip-hop music assists in the development of a political consciousness among individual youth activists.

During this study, I attended hip-hop poetry slams, talked with youth individually about hip-hop music and culture, and observed youth using rap music as a political organizing tool with other youth around school-based social justice campaigns, highlighting racial profiling by police, and as a consciousness-raising tool infused with narratives of inequality. In the following pages, I bring those settings and conversations to the table in an effort to understand the important relationship between culture, social movements, and identity. Overall, I aim to make several arguments: First, hip-hop is an important cultural art form for youth at this particular historical moment. Second, hip-hop culture is a significant tool in organizing other youth for social and political change in their local communities. Third, hip-hop is often an important part of the individual formation of a political consciousness among youth of color involved in activism, enabling them to address and combat racism and other forms of inequality. Finally, I argue that youth of color incorporate hip-hop into their developing political consciousness at the same time that they critique the contradictory aspects of hip-hop music and culture.

Performance, Culture, and Social Change

Culture and performance has long been central to social movement culture, discourse, and protest.[8] For instance, theater, music, and poetry have all been important tools of previous social movement organizing and activism. From Teatro Campesino to ACT UP (the AIDS Coalition to Unleash Power), culture has played a significant role in activism and social change. Scholarship on new social movements and activism points to performance as an important strategy for intervention into collective and individual understandings of oppression.[9] Sociologists like Gary Alan Fine and Anne Kane have studied the use and creation of culture in social and political movements. For instance, in Fine's essay "Public Narration and Group Culture," he discusses how culture, particularly discourse and performance, often emerges from and becomes a resource for a particular movement and its members. Specifically, consciousness raising during the feminist movement was both a marker of and a resource for the women who participated in the movement, which helped create group solidarity. As Fine's work demonstrates, using personal experiences to articulate the politics of the feminist movement was central to the consciousness-raising groups in the movement. In effect, a culture was created and boundaries maintained through this narrative practice.

Stephen Duncombe, a longtime political activist and scholar, departs from the study of social movements and culture, turning his focus on resistance and everyday life. He states that "cultural resistance can provide a sort of 'free space' for developing ideas and practices . . . and resources for resistance. And as culture is usually something shared, it becomes a focal point around which to build a community"[10] Similarly, I argue that hip-hop is one narrative that youth utilize to create community. Youth activists use hip-hop music and culture in their organizing efforts because it is accessible to them, and also because it is a reflection of their everyday lives and experience, something that other youth can identify with. This is particularly true of teenagers, members of the hip-hop generation, who, because of their birth date, are also overwhelmingly associated with the "MTV generation."[11] Music, television, and film have become important sites for identity construction, community representation, and political action in the post–civil rights era, especially for youth. As Stuart Hall observes in his discussion of Black popular culture, popular culture is often a site for self-discovery and realization:

> Popular culture, commodified and stereotyped as it often is, is not at all, as we sometimes think of it, the arena where we find out who we really are, the truth of our experience. . . . It is where we discover and play with identifications of ourselves, where we are imagined, where we are represented, not only to the audiences out there that do not get the message, but to ourselves for the first time.[12]

Despite the increasing commodification of popular cultures like hip-hop, it remains an important tool of cultural expression for oppressed groups. In this case, popular culture is a place for youth to identify, imagine themselves, and build coalitions. As Paul Gilroy suggests, hip-hop, specifically rap music, creates a "text of freedom" for youth of color in a time of increasing civil rights backlash, disillusionment, and despair.[13] For many youth, individual artists are central to creating this text.

Tupac: Rose, Thug, or Hitler?

One rapper who has had a lasting impact on the political formation and identity of youth of color is Tupac Shakur. Several of the youth in this study identified Shakur as an important, if not the *most* important rapper to emerge in hip-hop's short history, because of his ability to mix the everyday realities of growing up urban and of color with larger social justice issues. In short, he could "keep it right." This is evident in songs like "Changes," where Tupac talks about how he has been targeted by racial profiling, police brutality, the war on drugs, and growing up in poverty:

> Cops give a damn about a negro
> pull the trigger kill a Nigga he's a hero
> It ain't a secret don't conceal the fact
> the penitentiary's packed, and it's filled with blacks...
> And still I see no changes

> can't a brother get a little peace
> It's war on the streets & a war in the Middle East
> Instead of a war on poverty they got a war on drugs
> so the police can bother me.[14]

In these lyrics, Tupac articulates how racism structures his everyday experiences of police brutality, the prison industrial complex, the influx of crack cocaine in Black communities, gun violence, and war. Lyrics like these have established him, in both popular and academic discourse as "the supreme symbol of his generation."[15] In *Holler if You Hear Me: Searching for Tupac*, Michael Eric Dyson claims that Tupac's honesty secured his place as one of the most respected rappers in hip-hop. Based on interviews with Tupac's mother, friends close to him, and other Black public figures, Dyson also concluded that

> Tupac may be the most influential rapper to have lived. His voice rings through our cultural landscape and hovers over our spirits with formidable intensity. . . . He narrated his life as a road map to suffering, wrenching a brutal victory from the ghetto he so loved, and the fame and fortune that both blessed and cursed him. As the supreme symbol of his generation, he embodied its reckless, audacious liberties and its ominous hopelessness.[16]

Many of the youth I interviewed agreed with Dyson's praise of Tupac and his important contributions not only to the genre but also to the hip-hop generation. At the same time, they also understood his position as one that was useful in mobilizing others. For instance, Xochitl's statement at the beginning of chapter 1, "When I think of an activist, I think of Tupac," is indicative of the melding of the social justice and hip-hop worlds, especially the importance of hip-hop as an activist tool. Others also named Tupac as a figure who was synonymous with "conscious" hip-hop. For instance, when I asked David what he liked about hip-hop, he distinguished Tupac from other mainstream artists, "I am not saying that the artists that I listen to are like all revolutionary and . . . are activists, but I do listen to like Tupac, of course, and I read his book *The Rose that Grew from the Concrete.*" Donnelle's discussion was similar, placing Tupac in a category above other rappers, someone that you automatically listen to not only as an activist but as a young man of color, "Yeah, basically, I like G-Dog and, not really P Diddy but Nas, and Mos Def, he's good, like Tupac." Te, however, expressed the most enthusiasm for Tupac, calling him the "greatest rapper of all time," a title that was widely contested among his friends:

> He's the biggest to me. And my roommate, my mama, and everybody else; we get in arguments over that. We sat in college—half a college was arguing who's the best rapper of all time? Half a college was. And I was like, "Damn I didn't know it was that damn important to everybody," but it is. Like we sit on the stoop and be like thirty people—people want to fight over this—over who's best rapper of all time. Like, friends want to fight each other over this. 'Cause, like, mine is, it's like, Tupac is the best 'cause he brought so much emotion—he can make you cry, laugh, kill somebody all in one song, and it just make you think deeply about everything. You know it's like how Hitler is one of the best speakers of all time? What he said isn't all that cool, but if you could evoke that emotion and get people—you just gotta get as many as possible. . . . Not too many people going to do that. . . . And that's like any piece of great music makes you feel something and he did that.

Together, these comments suggest that rappers like Tupac (Nas, Biggie, and Lauryn Hill were also cited) have taken on a significant role in the lives of youth. As Bakari Kitwana and others have suggested, in this era, role models, like politics, have shifted. While there is much to unpack about the link that Te makes between Hitler and Tupac, his comment indicates the important position that Tupac has assumed in the lives of young people of color. In direct contrast to popular discussions of the thug status of hip-hop, like those rooted in the visions of sagging pants and the ills of hip-hop, youth are increasingly looking to charismatic hip-hop performers as leaders and/or role models for social change.[17]

In *The Hip Hop Wars: What We Talk About When We Talk About Hip Hop—and Why It Matters*, Tricia Rose argues that role models, particularly those in Black music, are important "agents for changes, not just models for the status quo."[18] More importantly, she acknowledges that while hip-hop is in a current crisis, rappers, like Tupac, often combine personal and political issues in their songs, which draw in youth. Several youth referenced lyrics by Tupac and other artists that directly reflected their lives, their values, and overall experience. For instance, Trisha cited Dead Prez—themselves fans of Tupac—as important artists in her social justice work:

> I like the Dead Prez CD, the one where, I don't know the name of it, but it talks about like the schools and like, it starts "They schools can't teach us shit, my people need freedom. We're trying to get all that we can get. All my high school's teachers can . . . "[19]—[laughs] yea, that, I like that song. I think that it really talks about like what we're trying to do right now with the Youth Center. . . . Like it talks about how like in his high school he never like, it wasn't really work 'cause he never learned like anything that like had to do with his type and never learned anything that, that related to his existence in this world and how, how like it never prepared you for the real world, it never prepared him for the real world and it just kept him down.

Donelle also talked about Tupac's specific relevance and impact on the Black community. When I asked why he liked Tupac, he answered:

> 'Cause he talks about the community and the type of stuff that happens in the Black community. And, you know, what happens when you go down the wrong track and what they were doing when they were hustling and what made them change. And that's it. . . . Well, Tupac is from Oakland and his mom was a Black Panther and all

that and he was one of the people that was really brutalized by the police and watched people get shot.[20]

While many rappers have been accused of and called out for their exaggerations of their lifestyles—both real and imagined—I couldn't help but remember the conversations I had had with Donelle about his own experience of watching a friend get shot, of going down "the wrong track" and having his mother move them out of Oakland so that he could avoid the "dangers" in his neighborhood. Te also described how Tupac's words encouraged him to reflect on his actions.

> It could be, just something that's deep. I used to play out, like, *The Rose That Grew From Concrete*, like, uh, you know that *The Rose That Grew From Concrete* that, uh, Tupac wrote? It's a poetry book. He was doing some concert in Oakland and sung a lot of the songs and I was like, I looked at that and I said and I thought about "Man, my community, *my* community is like that." And I was like, "Man, I don't want to be like that, like, one of those [who] abandons, like, one of them [songs] was talking about you could go buy your gold, you could buy your gold chain and gold teeth and get a new pair a Jordans every week but you can't buy your own baby some Pampers, *uh*. Like that is how it make you [be] like, "Nah, I ain't going to do that. Like I ain't going to do that. I better *not* do that. So it's a lot of stuff, its like I'm just gonna go, and—is there a lot of music that make people just go [and] try to change the whole universe with like, with one song? Like "Oh shit I gotta change the world!" It makes you think . . . about shit you never thought about and you never really considered.

Conscious hip-hop often reflects the contradictions inherent in the overcommodification of hip-hop music, at the same time it relies on that status as an entryway to affect change. As these quotes suggest, this is true of artists like Tupac. And as Rose continues:

> Tupac Shakur understood this dynamic and worried about how his attempt to tell compelling stories to and for an already exist-

ing criminally involved subculture might encourage other kids to join the fold—or at least to emulate the style and attitude associated with it . . . as reflected in his statement in the film *Tupac: Resurrection.* . . . When he said that it might make thug life "look glorious to the guy that doesn't live that life," he acknowledges how his celebrity made thug life "cool."[21]

For Eduardo, it was this thug identity that was central to his decision to use Tupac to organize other youth:

Like homies and homegirls and people who are into that kind of life, they like Tupac. They can connect to him, right. So, I listen to Tupac . . . because it's true, I mean, the worries, you know . . . he portrayed them so well even if he wasn't all the way like that, you know, he portrayed it so well, like, that's the greatest fucking artist of all time because he performs for you, all the time. He could take that revolutionary role and put it on, he can take that, "Yeah I'm down, I'm a thug," or "Yeah I'm a soldier" role, you know. . . . And I can say, "Have you heard this song by Tupac where he talks about him getting chased by the police and how they got money for war but can't feed the poor?" And it's a reference that I can use to get folks to think about other stuff 'cause they're not at the point where they're going to read Wallerstein or Malcolm X even, you know? So, little examples that you can use to get them reading that stuff and thinking about stuff in different ways. Hip-hop is a tool. It's a big fat tool.

As Eduardo suggests, hip-hop is a successful tool in organizing other youth precisely because it is an authentic culture that "homies and homegirls" listen to. By talking to youth about an artist like Tupac, Eduardo is able to connect with other youth. Because youth may not respond to Malcolm X, (not to mention Immanuel Wallerstein) as Eduardo suggests, he uses Tupac's thug identity to talk about issues in their community. In her study of the use of popular culture in the Chicano nationalist movement of the 1960s, Rosalinda Fregoso demonstrates how student activists in the Chicano movement "affirmed repressed identities" by including the Pachuco (urban street youth), the pinto (ex-convict), and the Aztec warrior as central to Chicano liberation. Incorporating these identities into the political activism of the Chicano movement opened up a space for alternative representations of identity and activism:

> The social and political context of the Chicano movement opened up a discursive space for the formulation of alternative representations of Chicano/a cultural identity. Cultural workers nurtured by the political activism of the Chicano Movement rejected the assimilationist thrust of previous generations of Mexican Americans. Rather than conforming intellectuals affirmed precisely the identity that the dominant order had positioned as the Other.[22]

As cultural workers, youth in this study use hip-hop, including "thug" images, to organize other youth. Because of his ability to traverse both activism and thug life, Tupac fit into youth's organizing frame. This practice has also been central to more mainstream, democratic processes. For instance, Russell Simmons, co-founder of Def Jam records, has been central in organizing the "hip-hop vote" in recent presidential elections, while Sean "Diddy" Combs launched his citizen change campaign with the slogan "Vote or Die" to heighten awareness about the lack of registered voters in the hip-hop generation. These tactics are in addition to the grassroots organizing efforts on behalf of the National Hip-Hop Convention, which organized the first hip-hop gathering and youth summit in 2004, the second in 2006. Youth at Multicultural Alliance and Teen Justice also individually and collectively incorporated hip-hop into their organizing.

"It's Bigger Than Hip-Hop": Pop Culture as an Organizing Strategy

Hip-hop was a key organizing strategy for youth at Teen Justice and Multicultural Alliance. Youth used it sustain their own activism as well as to organize and educate others. For instance, Courtney listened to Neo Soul and hip-hop artists while organizing a particular event or if she had to give a talk: "Erykah Badu and Jill Scott have really done it for me . . . it's just what I look to if I'm getting into an activist mood musically." Other youth, like Eduardo, used hip-hop to motivate themselves to do schoolwork, "when I have to write something, I listen to hip-hop. [If] we're going to have a musical, I listen to it, specifically. And when I'm doing something on Black Power I'm going to listen to Dead Prez and Talib Kweli." Using hip-hop music as an organizing tool subverts the commercialization of hip-hop music by using it to talk about poverty and police brutality—issues that affect youths' everyday lives. As Lipsitz states, hip-hop can "bring a community into being through performance."[23] Youth at Teen Justice and Multicultural Alliance use hip-hop as an organizing strategy to bring a community into being through their activism.

Several youth at Teen Justice discussed how hip-hop culture, as an *authentic* youth culture, was an important resource for organizing other youth. For instance, Naseem told me that, "People listen to hip-hop in especially urban areas. I know that a lot of people say that it brings a lot of negative tension, but most times, it's very positive and it gets people hyped up. And a lot of people in our school, our group, our community listen to hip hop music." David made a similar statement, explaining that "Hip hop is a new trend that everybody can dig. It's a thing that you can just get with. Every generation has its moment and hip-hop is the new trend that can connect with people." In these two statements, Naseem and David clearly articulate the importance of hip-hop for this generation of youth, and its potential as an organizing tool. Donelle also points out that hip-hop has moved far beyond the reaches of urban youth, and solidified it's place firmly within American culture:

Like now, like, the new millennium or whatever, mostly everything you see is like hip-hop. Slogans for Sprite have the little hip-hop song in the background and when they do shoe commercials also, they do hip-hop beats. They got Kobe Bryant doing it. It's like people get the word out if it's a hip-hop thing.

The commercialization of hip-hop is an important critique, and one that has been widely debated by scholars, hip-hop artists, and consumers. Donelle is right, the music and culture that was once maligned and is still heavily scrutinized, has moved firmly into mainstream culture: for example, in one of his speeches President Obama brushed the "dirt off his shoulder," hip-hop music provides the soundtrack for a number of video games and commercials, and hip-hop artists routinely cross over into acting in mainstream movies, television, and advertising. Still, the significance of hip-hop as an organizing tool, is one that Conrad deftly speaks to:

> I think if the movement was based in the sixties it'd be based on that type of music, you know what I'm sayin'? But right now, it's [hip-hop] just the music of our time and this revolution. Everyone is listening. And, it used to be that people thought that rappers were just Black, but I know the Black population is only between 11 and 17 percent in this country, so we ain't the only ones buyin' it.

As Conrad suggests, Black youth are not the only youth consuming hip-hop; hip-hop has long had a majority white audience, as its popularity grew (see Wimsatt 1994; Kitwana 2006; Mansbach 2005). At times, hip-hop has outsold country and rock music in the United States. Yet, the importance of hip-hop as a source of empowerment for youth of color and the reference to the genre's roots in Black and Puerto Rican communities suggests that it is an authentic site from which to organize youth of color, even as the genre becomes more and more commodified.

Turn Off the Radio

There is no question that hip-hop culture is inconsistent: sexism, misogyny, homophobia, and materialism have become synonymous with hip-hop since it became commercialized. Critics have focused on the negative aspects associated with particular rappers—Tupac included—the glorification of violence, drug use, and pimp culture in a genre aimed at young people. Hip-hop scholars have argued the importance of hip-hop's cultural influence and the negative aspects as a reflection or indictment of core American values.[24] Others have pointed to the complicated, often contradictory nature of production and consumption as it relates to the hip-hop generation's commitment to this genre. Hip-hop feminists have made one of the strongest arguments, evoking a radical women of color politic of the personal as political in their articulation of the contradictions of embracing a culture that often celebrates misogyny, sexism, violence, and self-hatred.[25]

The youth in this study were equally aware of the contradictions of hip-hop and were often critical of the genre. When we talked about it, some were defensive, as if answering to overwhelming assumptions about their unwavering, nonquestioning support. For instance, while Eduardo finds Tupac and hip-hop to be an important organizing tool, he also notes that as significant as Tupac is, he is putting on a performance—in the Goffmanian sense of the term, something that often "presents as an idealized version of the situation."[26] In this sense, the idealized version relies on exaggerations of urban youth of color's lives, which have become familiar. In contrast, for many youth, the measure of authenticity revolved around the ability of different artists to, as they state, "keep it real." As Donelle contends, for hip-hop to be useful for social change, it had to teach youth something:

> Like Mos Def and Talib Kweli, cats like that. Like they rap about how the schools are not really teaching anything—I mean, what happens when you go to school? They not teaching anything like our history. They teach a little bit, but mostly about what happened in England, Columbus and all that. And when there [are] Black students in the class, they just go on about that, but when they get transferred to all Black schools, they don't know nothing about what they teaching, and they [teachers] should know, stuff like that . . . . And also what rappers do for youth, like telling youth about school and "You do what you gotta do" and representing Black culture. An example is they sing about songs that say "Here's the Black people that make a difference."

"Keepin' it real," the overused, catchphrase of the hip-hop generation, was one of the requirements among the youth in their deter-
mination of authentic hip-hop. As Clark, a fifteen-year-old Filipino
from MA states, "Here's the thing . . . if the lyrics are really good and
if they motivate people, I really like that song." David also pointed
out the importance of "real" hip-hop when I asked him what he liked
about the culture, "I am not even sure what is like hip-hop anymore
or what they might call hip-hop, because some hip-hop music is
just—they might *call it* hip-hop, but it just is there for people to do
wrong." Lana and Conrad agreed, pointing out specific artists who
were consumed by larger audiences as the culprit between what is
real and not real hip-hop. For Lana, it also came down to a discussion of "real" music:

> Look, I appreciate what I call *real* music. I don't listen to what's on
> the radio. Like I have people who are like, "Why don't you like—I
> don't know, just real typical people you're supposed to like." Cash
> Money, for example.[27] I don't like Cash Money. Why? 'Cause all he
> talks about is how he has all these girls and money and that's not
> something I'm going to learn from. It's not something that helps
> me as a person, so why am I going to listen to it?. . . . And, they
> can say whatever they want, but messages like, ok, "I got hoes in
> different area codes?" Okay, Ludacris, how are you gonna help me
> better myself? How are your lyrics gonna influence me? And, it's
> really fake when I see something on MTV that's says [imitating a
> female high voice] "Ludacris, you've changed my life," or "Juvenile,
> from Cash Money, you've saved my life." Okay, seriously, when you
> think about it, what does Juvenile talk about? Baby got back? How
> are they helping you? Why do you like them? Because they got good
> beats? They beats is clean? They got money? They look good? What
> the fuck? Seriously, when I say I like that song, it's because it's got
> meaning and it's gonna help me and it's gonna help others.

Several girls in the study, who, as young women, often had the
fewest role models to look for in hip-hop, articulated this sentiment.
Xochitl said:

Women complain all the time about being called bitches and hoes and stuff but then they gonna come out with a song that calling themselves that. And, it's like, they don't see what they're doing. We're always fighting for women's rights, you know, for women to vote and you know, but yet you're gonna put yourself down as a woman? And, I think if people were more educated about what they were doing, they wouldn't do that.

Jasmine, a thirteen-year-old Latina from MA, also told me that for her hip-hop was more about the beats than the lyrics: "I like the music, but not the lyrics because they're sexist." Though, there were several artists like Queen Latifah that Jasmine listened to because "She's good, and she's tough. . . . Seems like she wouldn't take shit from anyone and I like her songs." Lana's discussion of the female artists she liked was similar, citing Lauryn Hill as one example of someone who motivated her, because of her model. As she states:

Like Lauryn Hill for example, is someone who is always keeping it real. The song "Doo-wop" is like, "You're not cool for not paying your child support." . . . That's true and people relate to that. I don't know, I just like music that's out there for a purpose. . . . Like, all the music I listen to, I like it for a reason. You feel me? Like, I look up to Lauryn Hill, she just keeps it real all the time and I love her so much.

The tensions between commercial, or mainstream hip-hop, and underground, or politically relevant hip-hop, have been present since the genre first hit mainstream audiences.[28] Much of this debate centers on the lack of creative, often exploitative, lyrics present in commercial hip-hop and the more social-justice oriented, empowering lyrics of the underground, or "real" hip-hop. As Q-Tip, from A Tribe Called Quest, illuminates in their 1991 release "Check the Rhime:

"Industry rule #4080,
record company people are shady,

so kids watch your back
'cause I think they smoke crack,
I don't doubt it, look at how they act.
Off to better things like a hip-hop forum,
pass me the rock and I'll storm with the crew and proper.
What'd you say Hammer? Proper.
Rap is not pop, if you call it that then stop."[29]

Referring to the popularity of the rap artist MC Hammer who used the word "proper" to indicate his dedication to Pepsi-Cola in a 1991 commercial, Q-Tip indicts the practice of using rap to sell commodities, along with the artists that participate.

Conrad picks up on this debate, citing the commercialized aspects of hip-hop that may have the potential to sabotage any underlying political message:

> I like Jay-Z, you know what I'm saying. I think a lot of times people who listen to hip-hop, like they try to stay away from [it]. You know just because your story is not all about blowing up capital state buildings and stuff . . . it's about, okay, for example, who is weak, talking about, "I want a diamond ring, bling, bling," that is not creative. Now if they put it in a creative form how they want a diamond, like Jay-Z on his one cut—and it is actually a radio cut— he is talking about a girl who saw his necklace and "started relaxing and that is what the fuck I call a chain reaction." Wow, that's tight, you know what I'm saying? So like, that was good wording, like as long as you are . . . being like creative about your art form, not how . . . somebody could be like "I'm a gun, 'cause I'm gonna blow up, BLAM!" You know what I'm sayin'? There is no talent in that. But, those people get Grammys. Those are the people that they want to get out there. They don't want our minds to actually think.

Conrad actually turns the discussion back to adults, record companies, and popular audiences who feed the negative aspects of the genre, but then blame youth for participating in it. David had a similar critique of rappers and other artists, particularly the overconsumption of commodities, which often meant a lack of "culture" or connection to "their" community:

I listen to a lot of soul music, like Jill Scott, Soul Child. I used to listen to Indie.Arie until I saw her in a Gap commercial and then it got me mad…I just like songs that does not promote disrespect or does not talk about "Yeah, I got a Benz, but I'm living in the projects," you know. I listen to like, hip-hop, but then it is like *real* hip-hop, I am not talking about, "I got pinkie rings" and, "I can't pay my rent 'cause all of my money is spent," or people who advocate for "I got gold grills in my mouth," but you don't understand why you got gold grills in your mouth and you don't know where it came from, or "I got dreads," [pauses and looks at my dreadlocks] not saying anything about you, but "I got dreads because I want to look cool," that's weak! [Instead] Like, "I got dreads because I want to fall back into my heritage, I want to fall back into my history, I want to fall back into my culture," you know what I'm saying?

Finally, Te summed up the critique of American culture's attack on hip-hop, by linking it to racism:

T: I listen to other music and everything they say is not beautiful, deep, and in-depth. So I'm like why do hip-hop music get scrutinized so much. And that's weird I was like do you like ever really think about why hip-hop get scrutinized, like, focus on what they sayin' and they not sayin' nothing different than other, than a lot of other music genres. They're really not saying too much different.

A: Why do you think it gets so scrutinized?

T: 'Cause of the people that's doin' it. Like . . . Black males are getting rich off it over night, you know, so it's getting scrutinized. Now, like, I listen to, like, [Bob] Marley and I listen to like Marilyn [Manson] and everybody else and all these other bands. And I'm like "Oh my God what did he say?" I was like "oh my God I can't believe he said this."

Like others, Te situates his comments in the context of U.S. discourse, which has historically singled out hip-hop as *the* culprit in perpetuating violence and misogyny among youth. However, he also suggests that this scrutiny is precisely because of the artists performing hip-hop: young Black men. It is this kind of critique that youth activists drew upon in their justification for using hip-hop as a social organizing tool: most notably because it is *the* way to get youth of color to an event. At the same time, listening to hip-hop creates a setting where youth are able to critique not only the genre itself but the racism, sexism, and violence that permeates American culture and their own lives.[30]

All I Need Is One Mic: Organizing Youth for Change

Using hip-hop to organize other youth around social and political issues is a growing trend in youth organizations. Reflecting a larger trend in hip-hop culture, youth organizations are using poetry as a political outlet for youth.[31] For example, Youth Speaks, a San Francisco nonprofit, trains youth as "slam" poets who use spoken word to articulate their experiences.[32] Committed to the philosophy that "the next generation can speak for itself," Youth Speaks focuses on developing leadership and critical thinking skills among youth. According to their mission statement,

> Youth Speaks is building the next generation of leaders through written and spoken word. Our innovative programs nurture and develop the youth voice and promote positive social dialogue across boundaries of age, race, class, gender, culture and sexual orientation. . . . By coupling public performance with educational opportunities, mentoring, and cooperative learning, Youth Speaks is committed to creating spaces that celebrate the youth voice and its essential role in the literary continuum.[33]

Here, the understanding is that for teenagers, the written and spoken word is intimately connected to youth leadership, positive social dialogue, and community organizing. Members of Teen Justice and

Multicultural Alliance told me that poetry slams were also how they "kicked it" with their friends. As a researcher, I attended several poetry slams sponsored by Youth Speaks with members from both of the youth organizations I studied. This form of cultural exchange and gathering allows youth to communicate their experience to a larger audience. Other youth empowerment organizations, such as the School of Unity and Liberation (SOUL), also embrace hip-hop and the written word in their social change efforts. As part of their training of youth organizers, SOUL rearranges the lyrics to popular rap songs as a form of anti-oppression education. By changing the words, they demonstrate how using an everyday cultural form is useful in organizing around political issues. In the view of Genevieve Negron-Gonzales, a former SOUL Bay Area director, "Using hip-hop and spoken word helps to bring those people—working-class youth and youth of color—into the organization in a way that wouldn't happen otherwise"[34]

Youth at Teen Justice also regularly used hip-hop in organizing for the Youth Center at Bayview High. One of the first events I attended was a hip-hop poetry slam. When I began attending leadership meetings, the youth were in the middle of choosing an event to advertise the center, eventually deciding on the poetry slam. Over the next several weeks, they discussed potential sites for the slam, which performers would be invited, and where to publicize. They also organized committees to contact other students on and off campus to rap, break dance, read poetry, and sing at the event. Youth were also responsible for hiring a deejay and security. More importantly, at one of the meetings, the youth decided they would only invite "positive" performers—meaning they didn't want people who cursed or talked about "bitches and hoes," because that would conflict with the organization's purpose of combating social injustice in their communities.

On the day of the poetry slam, Trisha, Jose, and David were standing at the bus stop in front of the Taco Bell at the corner of Thirty-fifth and MacArthur. This was the place where we usually picked them up since they lived in different parts of the city. The three of them piled into the backseat of Griselda's Honda and began to chat about the events leading up to the slam. This was one of their first major events for the Youth Center, and they chatted anxiously in the backseat, nervous about the reliability of the performers and whether or not the slam would attract a large crowd. The previous weekend I had gone with members to hand out fliers at different events in Oakland and Berkeley advertising the slam. Naseem's mother's boyfriend had offered his downtown bar and grill, which housed about two hundred people, as the event site. When we arrived, a group of youth was already gathered outside the front door. As we made our way through the line, I greeted Carlos, who was setting up to collect tickets at the door. He, like the others, had a mixture of excitement and anxiety about the event.

Griselda and I made our way into the room where the others were setting up the event. Typical of bars, the room was dark, with a small, wood-paneled dance floor situated in front of a slightly bigger stage. There was a deejay booth in the corner where the hired deejay, a Latino in his early twenties, was flipping through his record collection. Other Teen Justice members were milling about, decorating the walls with political posters of Yuri Kochiyama and Angela Davis, and lighting tea light candles on the tables. Conrad, one of the evening's emcees, was standing near the stage, going through the list of performers. "Have you guys seen the breakdancers?" he asked as we approached him and exchanged hugs. We only had about thirty minutes before the event started, and he, Naseem, and others were trying to track folks down.

In addition to the breakdancers, there were several singing groups, three or four poets, and a handful of rappers rehearsing in different corners of the room. Monica came up and told us that the group of four Vietnamese boys in the corner were 'Nvision , whom she had recruited for the event. The four of them were dressed in white dress pants and jackets, with long-sleeved black shirts. When Monica went to check on the food, Conrad nodded in the direction of the group and expressed his concern to me that this "wasn't really a poetry slam." When I asked him to clarify, he said, "A real slam wouldn't have any performers other than slam poets." And he should know; an established poet himself, Conrad was a member of the

Youth Speaks slam team and had participated in three national teen poetry slams.

As the place started to fill up, I took a seat in the audience and waited for the program to begin. I noticed that in addition to the parents and friends, there were several teachers standing in the corner talking to one another and to some of the youth. Mr. Thomas was talking to Ms. Shepard, who was there with her partner, a staff member at Bayview. To the left of the stage, there were rows of chairs, and the place was beginning to fill up. A large banner that read "Unity is Power" in red and black letters was taped to the front of the stage. The room became more and more packed with youth, and some parents, as the event began. The majority of the audience members were Black, with a significant number of Cambodian and Vietnamese, and smaller numbers of Latino youth. Some of the youth had donuts and sodas in their hands, which Monica had donated from her workplace. As I was cueing up the camera—Naseem asked me to videotape the proceedings—someone handed me the youth center petition, which was already being passed around. As I flipped through them the crinkled pages, I saw the names, addresses, and emails of youth along with their schools and grades—all with signatures in support of the center. I passed it along because Griselda had informed me that as an outsider to the neighborhood, school, and organization, I didn't have a vote.

At around 6 p.m., Conrad, who was emceeing the event, grabbed the microphone and introduced himself casually. "Hey y'all, my name is Conrad and this is the Teen Justice Presents Urban Thought Poetry slam—long title, huh?" he asked, winking at the crowd. I swear I saw one or two of the girls swoon. Rumor had it that most of the girls at Bayview had a crush on him. He, Eduardo, and David were among the most popular youth in Teen Justice, which spoke to their political enthusiasm and training but also, clearly, because of their looks. Griselda had a framed picture of the three of them standing on campus, striking what looked like their most serious, "activist" pose—lined up one behind the other, not smiling, and looking directly into the camera. It was poses like these, she told me that "got the girls." This seemed to be the case tonight as Conrad moved back and forth along the stage.

Conrad appeared both comfortable and skilled at energizing a large audience and seemed very aware of his ability to get a crowd "pumped up." He once told me after a meeting that he was going down to a local coffeehouse for an open mic poetry reading, where, he heard, they hadn't had anything exciting in a while. He smiled, saying in all seriousness, that he wanted to go there "to give them a little something." I was intrigued by his confidence and went to the reading. True to his word, after he read two poems—one about his love of poetry, likening the art form to a woman's body, the other about police violence in his neighborhood—the mostly adult audience was on its feet.

On the night of the slam, Conrad informed the crowd that he would be introducing the acts for the evening, ranging from rappers and spoken-word poets to R&B groups, Mexican dancers, and the Oaktown B-boys. The last act made the crowd cheer loudly. The B-boys were a local breakdancing group that performed at several events in the city and at Bayview. Conrad continued by reading a poem that he had written called "You wrong and you know you wrong," in which he called out members of the Black community for acting on their internalized racism, similar to his discussion with me about Black people and the use of the word "Nigga." He cited everything from dancing to misogynist rap lyrics to girls wearing fake contact lenses and hairpieces to Black police officers busting Black youth in the same neighborhoods where they had grown up. After every few sentences he would say, in a loud voice, "You wrong! And you KNOW you wrong!" to which the crowd would scream and clap their hands.

When Conrad finished, to loud applause, he introduced Janice, a former Teen Justice member, who had dropped out for other commitments. She was a short, light-skinned Black girl, dressed in tight jeans and a pink T-shirt. Her hair was straightened, and she was wearing lip-gloss that looked like icing on her lips. She looked similar to some of the other girls in the audience. Despite her dress, her delivery was serious. She talked about growing up in Oakland and the violence that she saw on the street around her home. She wasn't as skilled or well versed as Conrad, but the crowd applauded loudly for her. It seemed like she had a group of supporters near me, as they called out her name as she exited the stage. Next, a self-described half-Vietnamese, half-Chinese girl stepped up to the microphone. She was dressed differently than Janice; she wasn't wearing makeup and wore more loose-fitting clothes. Her hair was straight and shoulder-length, and she looked like she was both bookish and hippie. She had a laid-back tone as she read about what it was like to be someone who felt connected to her heritages only through her use of chopsticks, while at the same time she was alienated because she didn't speak "the language of her people."

As the night wore on, one of the more memorable performances was by a young girl who, visibly pregnant, sang "Other Side of the Game," a popular song by Erykah Badu. In this song, Badu talks about the difficulties she faces as a young mother with both a baby and a boyfriend. The opening lyrics are:

> Do I really
> Want my baby?
> Now, me and baby got this situation
> See brotha got this complex occupation
> And it ain't that he don't have education
> 'Cause I was right there at his graduation
> Now, I ain't sayin' that this life don't work
> But it's me and baby that he hurts
> Cause I tell him right
> He thinks I'm wrong
> But I love him strong

As the girl sang the lyrics of the song, she held on to her stomach, calling attention to her pregnancy. Through this performance, the girl brought her experience of teen pregnancy and motherhood, young womanhood, and race to the forefront. The girl drew upon the authenticity of hip-hop to connect with other youth. Several of the people sitting next to me knew the song, making her performance more significant because the girls sang along and applauded her when she finished. This call-and-response seemed to contribute not only to her performance but to the collective identity of the group as a whole: by participating in singing the song, audience members aligned themselves with the struggles of the young mother.

Throughout the night, Teen Justice members talked about the importance of building a youth center on their campus to address unmet needs—career counseling, mental health needs, and providing a safe place for youth to hang out. The night ended with a long "battle" between members of the B-boys breakdancing crew, in which different members formed a circle. While the youth were dancing, the deejay put on a popular song by Ludacris, whose lyrics indicated that he wanted to "lick his girlfriend from her head to her toe." I had heard this song sometimes in the car with some of the youth on our ride home from school and felt a little uncomfortable when I heard Eduardo sing along (even though this was a song I danced to often), suggesting the different places he wanted to lick his girlfriend—in the back of his Escalade, in the library, the candy store—as it seemed contradictory to my imagination of him as a youth activist who was only interested in political, underground hip-hop. Later, Naseem and Trisha expressed disappointment that the deejay included it in his musical rotation because it was contradictory to the purpose of the event. As people began to trickle out of the bar, we counted up the signatures for the slam—120 so far. There was more work to be done, but we left feeling like the night was a huge success.

The poetry slam was a significant event because it allowed youth to use hip-hop cultural forms in order to talk about their experiences as urban youth of color. Different performers took to the stage and expressed their feelings about important issues in their lives, like being pulled over by the police, growing up mixed race, having sex, and experiencing gang violence in their communities. In all of these instances, the youth interacted with the audience in a call-and-response manner. Each time a young person would take the stage, people in the audience would applaud and clap in support of the act. Teen Justice also drew upon the collective identity and community created at the poetry slam to distribute information and circulate petitions in support of the youth center. For example, between performances, members talked about issues relevant to the young people in the audience, like the "cycle" of violence, school suspensions, and intraracial conflict.

At both the individual and collective levels—the poetry slam, listening to hip-hop before a political event, or using it to connect with other youth individually—youths' use of hip-hop performance not only brings into being a collective identity or community, as Lipstiz suggests, but also unmasks the ways that power works in society and the varied ways that youth resist in their everyday lives. Specifically, youth transform the meaning and commercialization of hip-hop by using it in a political context.[35] This is similar to the strategies that previous activists used by incorporating folk music in the 1960s antiwar movement and repressed identities in the Chicano movement.[36]

Being linked to a community and taking on a hip-hop identity becomes part of an individual's consciousness. Further, deploying or utilizing a particular identity—in these instances, a hip-hop identity—is significant because it provides a space to articulate grievances that might not otherwise be talked about among youth. In this way, as Eduardo suggests, hip-hop culture is indeed a (big fat) tool. Youth use it to organize. More importantly, the performance of hip-hop serves as a forum to mobilize others into action, which is a goal of the youth at Teen Justice. As David said, "going to poetry night or something like that, and reading about [social change], and asking the audience, 'What are you doing about it? I know you guys are all conscious up here, going, ooh-ah, yeah, I know, yeah, I clap for that, but what are *you* doing about it?'" More importantly, their use of hip-hop to connect with other youth and talk about racism, violence, and other realities of the youths' lives helps to reveal where social movement organizing and activism has failed in recent years. By examining the importance of identity formation, scholars often overlook how the racism and violence of "wars" on drugs or welfare shape the everyday lives and life chances of youth of color. By using hip-hop to highlight such issues, the youth in this study have capitalized on an important cultural medium to raise consciousness, connect with others and strengthen their understandings about oppression and their everyday lives.

Conclusion

In this chapter, I have explored how youth use hip-hop as an organizing strategy in the twenty-first century. Specifically, we have seen how hip-hop culture becomes a tool that allows youth of color to transform their individual and organizational politics in their everyday lives. It is in these moments that hip-hop becomes the mechanism that youth utilize to make sense of their social location and social justice organizing. For the youth involved with Teen Justice, hip-hop culture was central in gaining support for the political issues that they were involved in. Organizers like Naseem, Conrad, David, and Eduardo explicitly view hip-hop as an important mobilizing tool with other teenagers. And, as Conrad indicates in his discussion of the political potential of hip-hop, poetry slams and other events got folks interested because "everyone is listening." Or, as David keenly observes, every generation has its moment and for post–civil rights youth, the moment is informed by hip-hop.

While youth use hip-hop to organize around structural change in their communities, hip-hop also influence their individual political (race, class, and gender) identities. As Courtney and David explained, hip-hop was important for them because they were able to write and express the things that happened in their communities in a form that reflected those communities. Te and Donelle also cited Tupac and other rappers as a central to their individual understandings of their raced and gendered location as young Black males. In spite of the more commercialized aspects of hip-hop, which the youth themselves critique, the important position it has in the lives and experience of youth of color, make it an important organizing tool.

By reconceptualizing the importance of popular culture in the everyday practices and organizational strategies of marginalized groups, scholars can "privilege the specific lived experience of distinct communities [and] also . . . search for those interconnected sites of resistance from which we can wage broader politics."[37] For post–civil rights youth, this is imperative in understanding their dual experience as both the subjects of history post–civil rights as well as objects of civil rights history. This approach must be understood as central to analyzing the importance of popular culture, social movement processes, and social change in the post–civil rights era.

5

QUEER YOUTH ACT UP
Tackling Homophobia Post-Stonewall

The world is not a safe place to live in. We shiver in separate cells in enclosed cities, shoulders hunched, barely keeping the panic below the surface of the skin, daily drinking shock along with our morning coffee, fearing the torches being set to our buildings, the attacks on the streets.

—Gloria Anzaldúa[1]

Gay brothers and sisters, you must come out. Come out to your parents. I know that it is hard and will hurt them but think about how they will hurt you in the voting booth! Come out to your relatives, come out to your friends, if indeed they are your friends. Come out to your neighbors, to your fellow workers, to the people who work where you eat and shop, come out only to the people you know, and who know you. Not to anyone else. But, once and for all, break down the myths. Destroy the lies and distortions. For your sake, for their sake, for the sake of the youngsters.

—Harvey Milk[2]

I use Gloria Anzaldúa and Harvey Milk's words to frame the queer experience for youth of color, post–civil rights. Not only do these youth navigate racism, ageism, homophobia, and abandonment as other youth in this study have, but they must also carve out a Lesbian, Gay, Bisexual, or Queer (LGBTQ) identity in the San Francisco Bay Area, a.k.a. the Gay Mecca. One-third of the youth in this study identified as queer (or gay, lesbian, bisexual, or questioning).[3] Throughout my research, I became more and more interested in how the youth incorporated this identity into their activism. For instance, homophobia was one of the key organizing frames that youth at Multicultural Alliance focused on in their anti-oppression workshops. More importantly, I was also interested in how current, popular discourses around same-sex marriage and the increasing visibility of LGBTQ people in mainstream media shaped their individual queer identities and overall sense of LGBTQ community.

For youth in particular, organizations like the Gay, Lesbian, and Straight Education Network (GLSEN), which has established thousands of Gay/Straight Alliances (GSA) in high schools across the country as well as other, local gay and lesbian youth organizations like the Lavender Youth Recreation Center (LYRIC) in San Francisco, and the Sexual Minority Alliance of Alameda County (SMAAC) in Oakland, suggest that resources exist for the ever younger experience of coming out as Gay in the post–civil rights era. In this chapter, I examine how the youth navigate and reference this contemporary landscape, some of which they participate in and celebrate, but also, because of their age and race status, were very absent from. I first noticed the complexities of this experience during a workshop sponsored by MA.

On a Friday afternoon in May, I went with Achilles to a Black gay panel sponsored by "the girls club," an after-school program for African American girls that MA had worked with before. Jen, one of the supervisors, told me she asked the organization to conduct it for several reasons: first, because of the rapport Jasmine, Shabee, and Frida had with the girls, and, second, because whenever she and Tanya, the other adult staff member, asked the girls to talk about gender, or sometimes in their everyday conversations, the girls would often say something homophobic. Recently, when they tried to interrupt their homophobia, one of the girls told them "there were no gay Black people anyway," to which the other girls agreed. Finally, as their supervisor and as a lesbian, Jen felt that she couldn't come out to them because they saw her on a regular basis, which made her fearful of their parents' reaction. As it was, she had to get permission slips for them to participate in the day's conversation. I wondered if, on some level, the girls were "acting out" with their homophobic remarks because of Jen's gender presentation. Even though she wasn't "out" to the girls, her presentation was strikingly different from Tanya's. First, she was white and Jewish, as opposed to Tanya, who was Black, wore long dreads, and casual, yet tight(er) clothes. The latter difference seemed to be the most striking, as Jen personally identified as "butch." Her daily gender presentation, consisted of a short, boyish haircut and casual, baggy men's jeans and button-down shirts. The girls may not have been told that she was a lesbian, but it seemed clear that she had a different gender (race and class) presentation than they did.

On our way over to the panel, Achilles asked me to participate, if I felt comfortable. I agreed, feeling a little protective of them as young, queer youth. It was an established practice at MA that the adults participated in whatever the youth agreed to do, as an act of solidarity, but also as a model for the participants. In addition, Achilles was the only MA intern on the panel that day, as the only Black gay youth in the organization. He also asked his boyfriend, DeShaun, and Chris's girlfriend, Shanae, to participate. They met us outside the elementary school where the girls club was held, near the MacArthur BART station. I had met DeShaun before when I took him and Achilles shopping for their prom in the Castro. I introduced myself to Shanae, whom I had heard about from Chris and Achilles—the four of them were friends—but had yet to meet. When we arrived, I noticed that, in addition to Jen and Tanya, an older African American woman was also present. As we sat down in chairs at the front of the room, Jen pointed out that the older woman was the mother of one of the participants, a girl who asked the interns how to spell "faggot" a couple of weeks earlier during an MA-led workshop in which they asked the girls to name some of the derogatory words they may have been called. Several of the interns—Jasmine, Shabee, and Frida in particular—thought the girl may be gay: she was very quiet, engaged in conversation only around queer/gay topics, and didn't seem as connected to the other girls in the club. On that day, her demeanor was the same, heightened by her mother's presence; she sat quietly with her shoulders sunk inward onto herself, her chin pushing into her chest.

The youth had their usual hour with the girls that day and, after they introduced us, Jen and Tanya spent the first five minutes collecting permission slips. Jen then gathered the girls into a circle and, standing at the chalkboard, reminded the girls why we were there: to talk about homophobia. She then asked them to brainstorm a few things they heard about or knew about gay people, which she wrote down on the board. A thin girl with braids raised her hand, "I know there's something about rainbows or pride or something."

"Yes, that's the rainbow flag, a symbol of gay pride," Jen said and wrote down rainbow flag on the chalkboard.

"Well, I know some people call people fags if they're gay," another girl said.

"Yes, derogatory statements like fags or dykes might be another thing people have heard," Jen said. I could feel the tension in the room: Tanya sitting back, moving from sheepish to tense, her eyes moving back and forth between Jen and the girls, unsure of where this was going. DeShaun, Achilles, and Shanae, on the other hand, eagerly listened to what the girls came up with, as the mother sitting behind her daughter, shifted in her seat with her arms folded. She reminded me of some of the women my grandmother went to church with, she dressed formally in a skirt and jacket, her hair was curled and styled; she was well put together. She also looked considerably older than I suspected most of the girls' parents were: late twenties/early thirties. We were near the end of the list, when one of the girls commented that she "doesn't know how this fits, but I have heard people say, 'I'll tear that blank [ass] up," she giggled and swept her hands together in a spanking manner. The four of us on the panel looked at each other quizzically as Jen asked for clarification, "What does that mean?"

"I don't know, I've just heard it before about gay people." Some of the other girls nodded.

"Okay," Jen said as she finished the list, saying that she wanted to get some of those terms and definitions out before we started the panel, so that the girls could think about those in relationship to the people who agreed to come in today, (or "real, live queers," I later scribbled in my notes).

The girls shifted their attention to us as Jen introduced us again. She then asked them to tear out a small sheet of paper and write down a question they wanted asked, which we would then choose anonymously, and would then read aloud. Once she collected them from each girl, she asked each of us to choose one from the bowl she placed them in.

We each chose a slip of paper and waited for our turn to speak. Before we started, however, the girl's mother set the tone by saying, "You know, I was once that way. You know, somebody was feeling on me once, but God saved me." She looked at us and then said, "Your souls are on your way."

The adults in the room became even tenser, if that was at all possible, Tanya put her face in her hands, looking resolved that this was, indeed a bad idea. And, it was an odd interaction, not just because of the mother's words, her interruption, or her disregard for the practice of letting the youth speak first, but also because of the way she said it: it seemed almost confessional. We sat in silence, frozen, for what seemed like a much longer time than it actually was. As Jen started to step in with an answer, Achilles, leaned back and, in his usual dry tone, said, "I'm already there, I know who I am" and, rolling his eyes, turned away from her. I could tell he was caught off guard and a little upset. DeShaun must have sensed it too and quickly responded, looking like a bridge as he tried to reach them both, with his hands out in front of him as he spoke, "Well, I'm a Christian and I actually sat down with my pastor and talked about it—because I was really going though it at the time—and we came to an agreement." He didn't elaborate on what the agreement was, but then went on to say, "You know how the Bible talks about spilling seeds, and that's not *really* a bad thing," which seemed to mitigate things for a moment: the mother smiled and seemed somewhat comforted by DeShaun's being a Christian and his ability to quote the Bible.[4]

Jen then moved the discussion back to the panelists, asking us to read aloud our questions, which varied. Shanae read hers first, "How did you know you were gay?" "How did I know I was gay?, she started, "I had always been around it and knew I was gay since I was younger, you know." Shanae was bubbly and smiling, and dressed in a similar style to the other Black girls at MA, Patti and Shabee. Today her long braid extensions were pulled back, and she had on a tight black shirt with sparkles on it, jeans, and black boots. She looked, in many ways, like she could have been one of the girls in the room, in spite of her age. This may have prompted one of the girls to tell her, "You don't look gay," and another, "Did you get sick of your boy-friend or something?" She took the comments in stride answering, "I get that a lot," and "No, I didn't have a boyfriend, I always liked girls."

Achilles read his question next, which was, "Are you bisexual?" to which one of the girls raised her hand, giggled, and said "I asked that question." He laughed as well, and said, "No, I never liked girls," he paused, "I mean, I had girlfriends and stuff, but, no." I was surprised by his candor in discussing his life with the girls—in a way that I hadn't seen him be before. At other workshops, he was often sullen, hanging back while others led, particularly with folks his own age. But, it was interesting to see him here, being his usual, dry self, but also very much engaged and clear about who he was, what our pur-pose was on the panel, and what he was doing there.

I was next, and read the question I drew: "Did you know you were gay in the fourth grade?" I couldn't help but think the question came from the girl whose mother was there, but couldn't read her actions or actually look at her for that long to read her reaction. I answered honestly, saying no, I didn't know I was gay but "knew I was differ-ent." That didn't seem to satisfy the girls, maybe because I was an adult, as one of the girls turned to Shanae, asking, "But you always knew." She nodded.

We wrapped up with Jen looking at the clock, as we had come to the end of the hour. She asked the girls to give a round of applause and thank us for coming, to which they gave us a collective "Thank you." The mother nodded to us, smiling while Tanya also smiled and thanked us for "enduring their questions," still looking a little embar-rassed. As we made our way out of the classroom and down the hall, the youth were silent until we got to my car, where they burst into excited laughter and conversation, pleased with the day's events. Achilles said, "That was really cool, I thought all the questions were going to be about sex, you know, 'does it hurt' and stuff like that." DeShaun and Shanae laughed and agreed that it went well and then laughed harder when Shanae said, "Yeah, I think that that mother was gay, the way she was talking!" I started the car and drove the couple of blocks to the BART station as they continued to debrief, excitedly, about their work.

As a researcher, my own queer identity was always central to some aspect of the research. For instance, I identified with and was perplexed by how "out" the queer youth were in their lives: to their peers, to their families, and in their activism. I came out in my twenties, like many of my peers, in college—and in the "safety" of Women's Studies—identifying and finally feeling at home with writers like Cherríe Moraga, Gloria Anzaldúa, and Audre Lorde. Women who, in similar and different ways, were telling my story: the story of coming out, being biracial in some instances, and the fear of losing our "home" communities as we carved out new ones, new families, and openly expressed our same-sex desires. It felt much easier for me to come out, because I was in the comforts of adulthood: I lived on my own and away from my family, I was educated, something my family was not, creating a safe distance that I enjoyed and was able to fully embrace as I created a different sense of home and family.

Those experiences profoundly shaped my interactions with queer youth in this study. Of the twenty-one youth who were central to the leadership of the two different organizations, seven of them identified as gay, lesbian, bisexual, queer, or questioning.[5] The two primary staff members, Griselda at Teen Justice and Margaret at Multicultural Alliance, also identified as queer and were out to the youth that they worked with. Given the contemporary context of queer visibility and identity, this experience was unique, as much of how we continue to understand queer identity is based on whiteness and white queers, whether in the visibility of shows like *Will and Grace*, the *L Word*, and public figures like Ellen DeGeneres. Or, in the establishment of gay neighborhoods like the Castro in San Francisco, Chelsea and Greenwich Village in New York City, and West Hollywood in Los Angeles. In all of these settings, the experiences of queer people of color are largely overlooked, invisible, or are lumped into the umbrella of "queer." As the girls club panel suggests, there is an understanding that people are gay, that there is such a thing as gay culture, but not gay people of color. If you look at mainstream media representations, this remains true. If one were to peruse these images or stroll these neighborhoods, it would appear that queer people of color do not exist, perhaps singularly in a sea of white friends, but not as a community.[6] Coupled with popular discourse of Black men and other men of color being on the "down low," made famous in books, songs, and television talk shows, the existence of queer people of color is sometimes linked to confusion, deviancy, and even death.[7]

Others have argued that the focus on visible queerness as whiteness is *strategic*, particularly in the development of a gay sensibility or aesthetic, one that is, ultimately, apolitical and based upon processes of inclusion and exclusion. As Charles Nero (2005) asserts in his discussion of queer integration and controlling images of Blackness in the gay community:

> In her famous essay "Notes on Camp," Susan Sontag prophesized that "homosexuals have pinned their integration into society on promoting the aesthetic sense." Successful television shows in the new millennium like Queer Eye for the Straight Guy, Will and Grace, and Queer as Folk, with their overbearing images of gayness as whiteness and as correct taste, certainly proves Sontag correct. But her prophecy was already evident in the 1970s with the formation of gay neighborhoods. . . . the fairly widespread controlling image of black gay men as impostors suggest that our exclusion from gay neighborhoods may be crucial for the formation of white inner-city outposts. In a sense, the malevolent black gay impostor legitimates the sense of fear that leads whites to prefer to live in racially homogeneous neighborhoods. Ultimately, this fear undermines the social justice rhetoric of the queer movement.[8]

The process of exclusion of Black men, as Nero suggests, and of youth of color, as I argue, works to undermine the social justice opportunities and the larger idea of a unified, LGBTQ community. Further, as Mary L. Gray suggests in her research on queer youth in rural Kentucky, "The logic of visibility—'being out and proud'—that organizes contemporary LGBT identities and social movements and saturates media representations of them (genericizing how LGBT people look or politically act) has made it harder, arguably impossible, for queer differences to go unnamed or unspoken in rural places."[9] The genericization that Gray discusses in her work continues to reflect a white model of gay identity and visibility, pointing to the racism present in the LGBTQ community. While Gray's example of the disconnect between "rural" and "queer," the inclusion of rural youth, many of whom are white, as a way to broaden definitions of queer identity does not address how racism informs the LGBTQ community. Queer youth of color, like the ones in this study must continue to search for images and movements that reflect their experience.[10]

Queer Alliances

In the post–civil rights era, schools have emerged as an important site for queer youth. Since the late 1990s, Gay/Straight Alliances (GSAs) have grown in size to four thousand active chapters nationwide and which are well represented in the San Francisco Bay Area.[11] At the time of this study, Xochitl was the president of her GSA, as was Frida's girlfriend, Tara. Evident of the important strides and benefits of the gay and lesbian movements, GSAs "strive to assure that each member of every school community is valued and respected regardless of sexual orientation or gender identity/expression."[12] However, by their own account and from the discussions with youth in this study, the establishment and presence of these organizations has not made homophobia or heterosexism easier for youth in the classroom, or on campus.

Recent studies point to GSAs as a primary source of empowerment for gay and straight youth alike.[13] As Fetner and Kush suggest, in the current sociohistorical context, "Youth are often shielded from information about LGBTQ lives; in many instances, college is the earliest opportunity for young people to take a course in lesbian and gay history or in the sociology of sexualities."[14] Thus, GSAs provide an important site for youth to congregate, see other queer people, and feel safe. In addition, GSAs represent a significant source of visibility and support for youth who are questioning and/or have come out as LGBTQ. In "Youth Empowerment and High School Gay-Straight Alliances," Russell et. al. suggests that "In schools that have GSAs, students and school personnel report more supportive climates for LGBT students. Further, sexual minority students in schools that have GSAs report lower rates of victimization and suicide attempts."[15] Indeed, GSAs have been central in young queer people's lives by providing a safe space, validation, coalition building, and visibility.

While GSAs have been firmly established in secondary schools throughout the country, an equally significant school presence is "fag discourse," what C. J. Pascoe describes as the constant, casual use of the word "fag."[16] In her study of masculinity at "River High School," she observed how "fag discourse functioned as a constant reiteration of the fag's existence, affirming that the fag was out there."[17] Fag discourse works to monitor straight and gay youth, primarily men, establishing the boundaries of masculinity and sexuality. It was clear that fag discourse structured the lives, and sometimes organizing, as the examples in chapter 2 demonstrate, of the young people in this study: it was part of their school climate, as well as the workshops that the youth led at MA. For instance, Chris, an eighteen-year-old Latina, and Achilles' best friend, discussed the role of fag discourse at her high school:

> It's like, there was a holocaust for the Jews and that was racism and everyone's like we can't let this happen again you know, and I'm sure the word nigger and cracker is still around, but [used] lightly—you only use that with your friends. And if you don't, you better be careful 'cause somebody is gonna come after you. Like if you say nigger in a classroom someone is gonna say something to you, more than likely. If you say faggot in the classroom it's more than likely that they're not.

The relationship between and usage of the derogatory words "nigger" and "faggot," as Chris points out, has been the topic of post–civil rights debate and has contributed to the debates comparing the civil rights movement (for African Americans) to the movement for civil rights among gays and lesbians. As screenwriter Barry Sandler states in Vito Russo's documentary film, *The Celluloid Closet*, "I never heard the word *nigger* used unless it's either by two Black people as a form of affection or by a totally bigoted Southern sheriff, a blubbering stereotype, to point out his ignorance. He would use that term, you see? Faggot is not used in that way. Faggot is used by just anyone talking to anyone else."[18] The film then shows a montage of seventeen film scenes where the word is used negatively and/or violently to denote a male character's sexuality. In effect, as Chris states, "faggot" is a word that youth are not surprised to hear in everyday conversation and popular representations, primarily because it doesn't hold the same social consequences as words like "nigger." She continued,

> Like even your teacher uses the word faggot and says, "Oh he looks like a faggot," or "Oh he's dressing like a fairy." Something like that, some little homophobic remark. And students are taught this and it's like, oh it's okay. Like if there was ever a holocaust again I don't think it would have to do with race, people of color, or something with gender, it'd probably be on people who are gay.

The use of "faggot" by authority figures, peers, entertainers, and even family members makes the word more acceptable, at the same time that it is condemned. In the post–civil rights, "post-Stonewall" period,[19] some have even argued that the word does not, in fact denote sexual orientation or a queer identity. As a recent op-ed piece in the *New York Times* suggests, "being called a 'fag,' you see, actually has almost nothing to do with being gay . . . it's really about showing any perceived weakness or femininity—by being emotional, seeming incompetent, caring too much about clothing, liking to dance, or even having an interest in literature."[20] While this may be true, the word may not be used solely to label someone as gay in the current historical moment, the description that the author and oth-

ers typically use is often synonymous with stereotypical character-
istics used to describe gay men, as demonstrated by Chris' teacher's
use of "fairy" to further describe the "faggot" he has identified in
his classroom. These instances mark the particular person as queer,
but also structure and determine the actions of others in the classroom, something that youth, including queer youth, internalize. For
instance, although Achilles was out and had a boyfriend , he struggled with being gay on an ongoing basis. He would often act this out
by targeting other, closeted, queer students at school:

> [Homophobia] was not important to me, 'cause I was like, well they
> don't know I'm gay, so, they can say all they want. I used to be like
> "hey faggot." I was not homophobic, sometimes I said it to be funny.
> Like this one boy who was walking fast and like trying to avoid me,
> and I'm like "You old faggot." I knew he was gay. I mean, you know
> you can smell it, [like] cheap cologne. I knew he was gay, and I don't
> know why I did that, but we almost got in a fight over it. He was like
> "What'd you call me?" and I was like "fag, duh, you're a fag." Now
> he's out and now I guess, I don't know, maybe we like grin at each
> other now."

The harassment that the youth themselves or their friends experienced was a regular occurrence among participants in this study.
For instance, I watched Frida, who had just come out the year I met
her, balance the struggle to accept her relationship with another girl
with the social exclusion from her peers at school. One afternoon I
picked her up directly from school and took her to a workshop. As
soon as she got in the car, she began telling me about her day, which
included two run-ins with other students who attacked her because
of her sexual identity. In the first incident, several girls were sitting
behind her in class, talking about how they didn't think it was right
for two women to be together. When Frida turned around to interrupt their conversation, explaining to them that she had a girlfriend,
they told her she was "nasty." Later, a boy called her a dyke when
she didn't speak to him in the hall. This same boy had been taunting
Frida on and off since he found out she had a girlfriend. She told me:

One day I was waiting for the bus with this guy that used to go to school with me and was my friend or whatever. And, he was talking to me and he was like "Oh, how you doing?" And, somehow my girlfriend came up and there was this other middle school kid there who was like, "Oh, you have a girlfriend?" And then said this whole homophobic stuff and they called me names.

I asked her what they called her and she replied, "Like, 'do you do this with a girl in bed?' And then, 'Oh, that's nasty!' And, 'Don't you believe in God?' and, 'Have you read the Bible?"

The presence of GSAs in Oakland high schools, including Frida's (where her girlfriend Tara was the president) didn't seem to meet the needs of the queer youth of color (and their allies) in this study. If youth talked about GSAs, they were often critical of the organization's lack of focus. For instance, Naseem was one of the straight allies in her GSA, where Xochitl was also president. When I sat down with Naseem and asked her about her activities with GSA, she answered:

> N: I'm not sure exactly what they're doing 'cause a lot of the people, who built the club up are seniors and then they left, so a lot of the people are—this is their first year even being in a club who are, who hold office like the President, Xochi's [*sic*] a freshman and Josh, he's the vice-president, well not for long.
>
> AC: How come?
>
> N: The only reason he's doing [it], like he's joined so many clubs, this year so he can put it on his college application and so he's been talking a lot like shit about Xochi to the sponsors so like they, he might lose his position.

Xochitl was also critical of the GSA—its role at her school, the people involved—often comparing it to her experience with Teen Justice:

> It's totally different, which is why we have the problems. We only really meet because we have to and it doesn't really work out. . . .

When the group is united it works better. We don't have much in
common and we don't talk much. . . .The thing is, that the people
who already go to the clubs, are already educated and all this.
They've had classes with this one teacher up there, Ms. Shepard,
and, if you've had her class, you're pretty much educated on that
subject [LGBTQ] very well because she makes it very known. And
practically it's those same people who go. And if they're already
educated on that, we're not really making any difference. And it's
hard to get other people to come to the club because they think
that's it's only gay people and they don't want to go in because they
don't want to be portrayed as gay. And even those students who are
gay, most of the people at Bayview don't want other people to know.
So they're like, if I go to a club meeting, people are going to know
I'm gay and they don't want that so most people don't go. And the
ones that do go are already educated, so we're not making a difference.

One of the problems with increased visibility for the LGBTQ
community in the twenty-first century is, as Xochitl suggests, that
visibility feigns as education. But, as Gray reminds us, "the increase
in visibility has not translated into pro-gay stances at the voting
booth or in the halls of Congress."[21] Seeing more and more queer
people in mainstream media, particularly those with celebrity statuses, makes larger audiences think they are familiar with gay lifestyle and experience. One striking example of this is in former President Bill Clinton's remarks about Pedro Zamora, an openly gay, HIV
positive activist who died shortly after he appeared on MTV's *The
Real World*: "Over the past few years Pedro became a member of all
of our families, now no one in America can say they've never known
someone living AIDS."[22] Clinton's conclusion that television serves
a site where the audience can claim relationships with "celebrities"
speaks to the current cultural landscape for queer youth of color. His
statements not only help to mask the experience of, not only people
living with HIV and AIDS, but also the violence that queer youth of
color routinely experience. A reality that the youth and their parents

are keenly aware of. As Xochitl told me in her discussion of her own visibility as president of her GSA:

> I'm out to my parents, but they believe that if I'm the GSA president and telling everybody that, "Hey, I'm gay" they don't want me to get gay bashed or anything. My mom feels that it's a shame to the family so she doesn't want nobody to know that I'm gay. From my dad, he just doesn't want me to get hurt from people knowing. He just thinks that if a lot of people know that I'll get hurt.

Xochitl points out here that despite increased visibility for gays and lesbians, queer youth of color continue to experience homophobia in their homes, at school, and at work. Discourses of mainstream visibility and representation continue to mask the everyday experiences of youth, unless those experiences are connected to violence and, sometimes, death.

Come Out, Come Out Wherever You Are?

A common story about queer youth and more often transgender youth of color, which persists in popular culture, reveals the violence that queer youth of color are subjected to because of their LGBTQ identity. If, as Chris suggests, a contemporary holocaust were enacted upon gay people, it seems to be targeted at queer and transgender youth of color in the post–civil rights era. As the murders of Steen Fenrich, Sakia Gunn, Gwen Araujo, Lawrence King, and Angie Zapata reveal, those living an LGBTQ lifestyle or even displaying "soft" traits, as in the case of little Ronnie Paris,[23] is still a dangerous road for youth of color. These were roads that the youth in the study were quite familiar with: organizing their lives, like many of us, around when, where, and who to come out to, and what consequences existed in their social circles. For instance, Monica, a nineteen-year-old Latina from Teen Justice, aligned her coming out process with safety:

> M: At my school I'm totally out, but at my job I don't feel safe coming out. But I was walking around with some of my co-workers and we were talking about gay people and I was like, "Can we not talk about that? That's an issue that I don't want to talk about."
>
> AC: What kinds of things were they saying?
>
> M: They were just like, I don't want her hanging out with my friends because she's gay and she might hit on them. Or, I don't know, things like that. And they were all like basically about guys and it was like, I don't know. They were talking about whether or not he was out I guess and they were like, yeah he's a fag. And that's why he can't handle stuff. I told them not to be talking about him because he was gay. But I talked to her on a more personal level because it was gonna be hard to talk with like five people there. And the person that said it was the most important person to me. I did tell them not to talk about that issue, at least not that issue around me and that's a really strong issue for me. And I walked away and I heard some whispering in the back but I didn't pay attention to it.

As Monica states, she routinely structures her day around settings where she feels safe to "come out" to people, given the amount of homophobia in her workplace. Despite recent hyper-visibility of queer identity and lifestyle, Achilles also noted the instances of violence that he witnessed among other queer youth at his school:

> I know Nina used to come to school who used to be a transgender, but now she is a boy or something. I don't know. She went to school and she was walking and she was, you know, trying to be cute that day, and an egg caught her! An egg caught her in the back of her wig and she took off her wig and you know, like combed the egg out or something, and it was like you know, "Who threw that?" I don't even know, and she said like "Well, why don't all of y'all line up?"

And they would just do things to mess with her, or like gay people, they would do things to mess with them.

In addition to the harassment they experienced at school, Chris and others talked about the constant fear of violence in their everyday lives. For instance, when I asked Chris more about her thoughts on the "gay holocaust," she told me about her own, steady occurrences of violence. She told me:

As a child, I experienced a lot of teasing and it gets to you at a certain point. . .And I kind of came to this place where I was like "Anyone says anything, fuck you" and people start[ed] to respect me. The only thing that I've gotten is when I'm with girlfriend because she's Black. And a lot of the Black people that we see they have a problem because I look like a punk white boy with a Black woman and she shouldn't be with me, she should be with them and some Black men get threatened. They usually think I'm a male so they act like they want to fight with me and I don't want to tell them that I'm a female because what are they going to do to me when they find out? Maybe they'll back off, maybe they won't. And [I] take precautions.

As these two stories suggest, much of queer teenagers of color's experiences are centered on safety and the everyday practice of being prepared to fight. Even if the youth are not "out," in different situations, they must still be prepared for potential violence. As Chris told me, when I asked her why she had to "take precautions" and if she had ever been in a fight before,

I haven't gotten into a fight, but once we were walking to my car and there was five Black guys and at first they were like, "Whatever," and they were trying to flirt with her [Shanae] and I was like whatever and we're walking to the car and they're following us and [I] quickly unlock the door and she got in and I got in and the next thing I know they started to kick my car and punching. And there was this guy standing in front of my car, like I'm really gonna stop it, and so I'm just driving it, I'm like, "That's his fault, if he's dumb enough to stand in my way." So I started driving and he moved and he punched my window—he didn't break it or anything—but this one guy put a huge dent in it. I don't know why they did it to this day. And why did they wait until I was in the car? Were they trying to scare me, put some fear in me? Job well done. I'm scared of Black men now. My best friend is a Black man. I'm not scared of him, but you know, when I see a group of Black males, I'm thinking "Oh shit, what are they gonna do, what are they gonna want?"

Chris' words highlight an experience of queerness that is marked, not by invisibility, but rather one that is marked by a heightened sense of distrust and fear. And, this was an experience that the youth had difficulty incorporating into their organizing in an effective way.

Shortly after she told me this story, Chris and Achilles led an interactive performance piece at an MA event organized to recruit new members. On this day, we were gathered at a local Unitarian church in Oakland, a regular spot for the organization's activities. Achilles and Chris were two of the youth who regularly participated in interactive theater, an exercise aimed at getting large groups to talk about stereotypes. On that day, the two of them and a former participant, LaRhonda, were sitting at a table in the front of the room as Margaret discussed the events planned for the rest of the day. As Margaret spoke, Chris draped her arm around LaRhonda and started whispering in her ear when Achilles yelled—purposely interrupting Margaret's talk—at Chris, "What are you doing, why don't you leave her alone?" Chris told him to mind his own business, and LaRhonda shrugged him off, telling him, "It's okay, we're just talking." But Achilles continued, somewhat viciously, as everyone else in the room stopped what we were doing and turned our attention to the three of them. Achilles confronted Chris in an accusatory way, saying, "Why do you always gotta hit on girls that ain't even gay?" Chris momentarily took her attention away from LaRhonda to respond to Achilles, who continued, "I can't stand how y'all always thinking you gotta be out and flaunting it even when she clearly doesn't want you. That's why everybody calls you a fuckin' dyke!"

These last words seemed to provoke the intended shock that Achilles sought. Margaret was pinned to her seat, her teeth clenched. Other adults in the room gasped and held pained expressions on their faces, looking around at the other adults in the room. One woman turned to me and raised her eyebrows with an expression that asked, "Did he really just say that?" It even seemed to stun Chris, who, after a few moments muttered a "shut up!" and they continued to go back and forth for a few more minutes until Margaret, looking uncomfortable, finally told them to "freeze." She then stood up and addressed the group, saying "Now, what just happened here?"

Audience members shifted in their seats a bit, as they realized this was an exercise, until a young African American male finally spoke up, "Well, he was just accusing her of hitting on this girl and called her a dyke, but, you know, that's not true about everyone." Another young person chimed in, "Who cares how people live their lives? We don't have to call each other names" with another young woman adding, "Yeah, you're supposed to treat people with respect; it doesn't matter if they are gay or not."

As members of the audience talked, the three performers stayed in character. When provoked, Achilles stood by his words, saying that "Well, I'm offended though, she shouldn't be hitting on girls all the time." These interactions seemed to be a test on both parts: the MA interns were showing their skills as performers and anti-oppression facilitators, and the potential recruits were showing their ability to take on similar roles in the future by analyzing oppression. Both Achilles and Chris joined Margaret in surveying the group: listening to their responses and waiting to see what others would say. Finally, Achilles and Chris confessed that they were "pretending," with Achilles proclaiming, as he put his arms around Chris, "This is my girl and I'm gay as hell!" Chris smiled, but didn't seem to share Achilles' enthusiasm.

Even though most youth who performed interactive theater would draw upon their own or other's experience to talk about stereotypes, Margaret later told me that in mixed crowds—like the one at this recruitment session—interns should choose their words more carefully, particularly when they discuss topics like homophobia. Staff and interns often checked in with the staff members at participating organizations to confirm that homosexuality and homophobia were appropriate topics to address. In the past, parents of youth involved in the workshops had protested their children discussing gay and lesbian issues. More importantly, Margaret felt that Chris and Achilles' performance, even though it created dialogue, was "interactive theater gone wrong" because the intention was to portray stereotypes about identities that the actors did not hold: youth who weren't parents would pretend to be pregnant, others who were not Arab American would pretend to be to get the group to talk about xenophobia, and so forth. Because both Achilles and Chris identify as gay, she felt that they were inflicting more "hurts" on their individual consciousnesses while trying to raise awareness.

Still, their performances moved beyond just an after-school activity to a dramatic approach to making homophobia more visible. As Goffman asserts, "when an individual plays a part he implicitly requests his observers to take seriously the impression that is fostered before them."[24] In this instance, Chris and Achilles' experiences with violence and ridicule in their personal lives spoke directly to a contemporary media landscape that celebrates same sex marriage, queer lifestyles, and visibility—suggesting again that homophobia was an important frame for organizing.

Performance has long been an organizing tool for queer communities, particularly in AIDS activism (see Cohen 1999; Epstein 1998; Gamson 1989, 1995; Rodriguez 2005; Román 1998; Shepard and Hayduk 2002). For example, in his study of gay male responses to AIDS, David Román (1998) found that performance was an "act of intervention" into U.S. cultural understandings of the AIDS epidemic. Specifically, AIDS theater performances—including drag shows, Broadway theater, and street theater—contributed to the overall understanding of people living with AIDS:

[M]any of these social performances are attempts to intervene in our understanding of AIDS as it takes its form and is sustained by the governing institutions of the dominating center of powers, and that these performances—acts of intervention, really—contribute, immeasurably and in ways impossible to register effectively, to the continual cultural negotiations of AIDS, sexuality, and citizenship in the local, regional, and national sphere.[25]

As Román suggests, the role of the gay male community's response to the AIDS epidemic has played a significant role in how AIDS, sexuality, and identity is understood in U.S. cultural discourse. Performance as social and political protest, in this instance, created a deeper understanding of the effect the disease had on the gay community in an era where little knowledge about AIDS existed. Queer youth of color utilize a similar strategy in their organizing efforts, not only against the media, which has failed to provide adequate representation or role models, but, in many cases, against their families as well.

Coming Home

Achilles and I had formed a fairly quick bond at Multicultural Alliance. He came back to the organization to work in January, months before he was to leave for college. I had different interactions with Achilles: in the office of MA, riding in the car on our way to and from workshops, taking him and DeShaun shopping for their prom outfits, and giving him rides home after work. Many of our conversations focused on race and the Black community, so much so that for a while when I asked him how he was or how his day was, he'd answer "Oh, you know, it was Black," or "I'm cool, you know, Black." This could mean a number of things but usually referenced that every experience he was in was shaped by his racial status. So, I found it surprising when I asked Achilles what the most important issue to him at the moment was, and he stated:

> A: I think homophobia is more of an issue for me than being Black, because being Black is almost some kind of reverence you get, or something like that. It's not reverence, it's . . . of course people are suspicious of you; of course people, whenever I open my mouth, people expect ignorant things to come out, and then they make it

a clear point that they are surprised that ignorant things did not come out. It's like "Oh you are so good, unlike the others of your race, we should put you on parade," you know, patronizing things like that. That's—whatever, I have learned to deal with that. I am like, "Okay, I know everybody else deals with that, you know, people are just, ugh, but like being gay is like, I know a lot of people who deal with it, but they don't deal with it in like, well, they don't deal with being Black in a good way, [but] they don't deal with being gay in a good way. They go out and they prostitute and stuff like that. I'm like, "Okay, that's cool, and that's not me." And like just little things like, just the fact that I have so much internalized trouble with homophobia and stuff like that, and I try to work through that and I'm like, "Oh my God, do I put my arm around my boyfriend in this movie theater? I'm like, "Am I going to have to fight because of this?" You know, do we hold hands? How close do we get? And sometimes I want to withdraw, but then I'm like no I don't want to withdraw, it's THEM, and then it's like, "Oh my God, I don't want to bust him out"—even though he says he's coming out—I am like, you know, it's almost like it's a secret or something like that, like I don't want to tell his business but I will tell mine, you know, I'm a fag, I'm gay, not queer, never been queer, you know? [Laughs] You're a lesbian.

A C: I am a lesbian.

I include the last sentence of this quote to point out the lack of role models that young queer people of color have despite the current landscape. Although we bonded fairly quickly over our shared Blackness, Achilles was quiet about his gay identity at first. I knew he was gay, having been told by Margaret and Ze shortly after I met him; however, he never "came out" to me personally. It wasn't until one day that we were returning from a workshop near Lake Merritt and, unintentionally, I mentioned that we were passing the house that my recent ex-girlfriend lived in. Without missing a beat, he asked, "Oh, do you want me to throw rocks at it or something?" I paused, contemplating it as a possibility, but said no. We laughed and then fell silent. After a minute or two, he asked, "So, you're a lesbian?" I replied, "Yes, I'm a lesbian." And he said, "Me, too, I have a boyfriend." It appeared I had gained his trust from that moment on. He intimated to me later that he had never actually met an *older* Black lesbian, which, it seemed, prompted him to point out this fact from then on.

Unlike mainstream images, the images of queer people of color, role models for queer youth of color in this study, were few and far between. When I asked who he looked up to, Achilles mentioned Caushun, the gay rapper as a possible role model because of his "homo-thug" status:

> I have never heard any of his lyrics. I look up to him. Because he looks straight and he challenges Black male masculinity, and he is like a public figure. He does not have to be out. He does not even have to take on like gay issues 'cause he looks like a straight person so, it's like, the fact that he is doing that he is an activist, 'cause it's like, he is calling into question a lot of sistahs and things like that. He is like forcing people to look at him like, "Look at me, I am gay, I don't fit any of your stereotypes, AND I can flow" . . . so, I think he is tight, because he is very controversial.

Controversial indeed, Caushun, the only out, Black, gay male rapper to receive any mainstream press and a subsequent record deal with Baby Phat records, turned out to be a fraud—a prank initiated by rapper, Ivan Matias, and actor/hairstylist Jason Herndon.[26] One night, Matias, a Brooklyn-based rapper, decided to play a prank on his DJ friend by calling a local hip-hop station pretending to be a "flamboyantly gay rapper," imitating his childhood friend Herndon.[27] Once buzz grew, Matias enlisted Herndon to act as Caushun, the gay rapper, who was interviewed in the *New York Times*, *Newsweek*, *ABC News*, the *Advocate*, and *Metroweekly*. However, the scheme failed when Matias exposed Herndon, as the face, not the voice, of Caushun. Still, Achilles didn't even have to listen to his music (which was never published) to cite him as a role model.

Because of the largely absent representations queer people of color in popular culture, the youth often looked to their immediate mentors as role models in learning about, understanding and being proud of their LGBTQ identity. For instance, Xochitl, a freshman at MA, compared her own struggles of accepting her attraction to other girls to Griselda being gay:

> My friend, she was gay and I don't know, like my dad always told us that it was normal and I thought you know, that's not right a girl is supposed to be with a guy and all that. And like, I stopped hanging out with her and my sister asked me why and she started telling the stuff that she had learned like it's completely normal and you know love is love and everyone is normal and I didn't have to think about it that way and it's normal you know and then Griselda, I saw her all proud and stuff and I just was starting to figure out that I liked girls and stuff and when I saw Griselda all proud of it and stuff I was like "I don't why I should be ashamed of it if other people are acting all proud and stuff." I think she helped me out a lot, just me seeing her.

Monica's relationship with Griselda was similar in that it shaped how she felt about incorporating queer issues into her social justice strategies.

> M: And I guess making a difference with one person, like Griselda made a difference with me and I can go and make a difference with someone else.
>
> AC: How did Griselda make a difference?
>
> M: She got me more involved, I was never in that state of mind and then I was like, yeah maybe I can make a difference too, you know. I was always that kind of person that would say as long as I can get by and my neighbor won't care and why should I care? I guess now in fact I do and I do want to make a difference.

In each of these instances, the youth took cues from their role models on how to accept and understand their sexuality and queer identity, at the same time that it influenced their commitment to addressing homophobia as a social justice/social change issue. Their struggles for acceptance, both internally and externally, became a central component of their activism, particularly with their families, friends, and at school. Monica, Xochitl, and Achilles also articulated a strong need for visible role models to accompany their coming out process, a process they struggled with at home. This was most clear in Frida's experience during the year that I spent at MA. For instance, when I asked her what issues were important to her, she relayed her experience of coming out and the implications it had on her home life.

> AC: So, what's the most important issue to you right now?
> F: Right now? There's a lot of issues, but right now I'd say homophobia.
> AC: How come?
> F: Just because I got in trouble and my life isn't the way I want it to be. It's not peaceful right now because of that.
> AC: So, you got in trouble for?
> F: Being gay.

I met Frida during my first week at MA. Less than a month later, Margaret, the program director, called me to let me know that Frida had been kicked out of her house and needed a place to stay. When I asked why, Margaret said she'd let Frida tell me when she arrived. I didn't know much about Frida or her home life at that point, so I was a little anxious about the meeting. Margaret had a previous engagement that night so she wasn't able to take her in. I was a little nervous about the slippery boundaries of this situation: she was being kicked out her of her house, I hadn't met her parents, and I barely knew her.

Margaret and Frida arrived at my house at around 6 p.m.. Margaret brought her inside, further trying to establish trust with me, I assume, letting Frida know it was okay. Or, rather, that I was okay. She stood in the doorway, looking fairly sullen and in her usual uniform of black: long-sleeved black shirt, black pants, boots, and dyed hair. Her eyes were puffy, as if she'd been crying. After Margaret left we sat down on the couch, and I asked her what was going on.

"Well, basically," she began, "I was at home with my girlfriend and my mom came home and caught us." I didn't ask her to elaborate at that point, as I was pretty surprised. In the weeks since I met her, Frida began dating a girl, Tara, who went to her school. This was her first girlfriend and, over the next few months, they had an on-again/off-again relationship. No one at MA knew she was dating a girl—Margaret had some idea, as she had mentioned Tara before, but nothing was confirmed until this incident.

While Frida was slowly coming out to some of her friends, her mother apparently didn't know she had started seeing Tara. As Frida and I talked some more over dinner, the scenario became more clear: Frida's mother came home after work to find Frida and Tara naked and in her bed. Not an uncommon story—especially if you watch current teen movies—many teenagers experiment with sex, typically in their own homes. Most parents would be upset to find their seventeen year old, naked, in their bed with anyone. However, finding Frida, who had never dated girls previously, with Tara seemed to be more than her mother could handle. Upon finding the two of them in her room, Frida's mother began yelling at her in Spanish, asking her if she thought she was a man and calling her a derogatory name for "lesbian"—which Frida wouldn't repeat to me—and then told them to get out of the house.

"I wouldn't even say that about someone I didn't like, you know?" Frida told me, looking like she was reliving the experience as she sat in my living room. Instances like this one, happened several times throughout the year that I worked with MA and affected Frida's work. On another occasion, Ze, the executive director, called the office to see if anyone there—myself, Margaret, Lana, and Achilles—had seen or heard from Frida, who had been missing for the last twenty-four hours. A week or so later, she surfaced, having boarded a bus to New York City, staying on it, and riding back to Oakland because she didn't have a place to stay.

Achilles experienced a similar reaction from his mother after he came out, which was shortly after he started working at MA. This story emerged when I asked about his family's response to his organizing work and he said, "I think my mother thought it [Multicultural Alliance] was the devil for a long time. Maybe she thought it made me gay or something." This seemed to be an ongoing struggle between Achilles and his mother, who also had a similar reaction to the work he did with SMAAC, a specifically queer organization that he worked at prior to Multicultural Alliance:

> A: SMAAC, however, she was very adamant about, like, "No, you are not gonna work there."
>
> AC: How come?
>
> A: Because of the Gay Youth Center. She was, like, it can only make him gayer. So, I guess she had this dream of me like suddenly being like "You know what, Mom? I was wrong for being gay, I am sorry." But I guess she saw SMAAC interfering with that. But, I worked there anyway, and I guess she kind of accepted it.

Even before he came out and began organizing with MA, Achilles experienced homophobia in his family, who thought he was gay at an early age. One of the more poignant and personal moments I saw him talk about his family was when Frida, Clark, Margaret, Jasmine, Achilles, and I were practicing a popular education exercise at MA. Before the youth tried out any of the exercises in their workshops, they first did a "run through" with one another to verify the usefulness of each exercise. On this day, we were tweaking "Derogatory Words," an activity that we were going to use with the younger, elementary school students.

We were all sitting around the office, and Margaret asked us to gather around the couches, in a circle. She went into what felt like teacher mode, saying, "Okay you guys, we're gonna do the derogatory words exercise so folks can think of different ways to do it with people. Now what I want you to do is write down a list of words that you never want to be called again. Do that in silence—just make a list—and then we'll come back together as a group and discuss at least one of them, okay?"

We all dutifully wrote down all of the words that we didn't want to hear again; Margaret, who reiterated that as adults, we were not exempt from any of the exercises that the youth had to participate in. Each person sat in silence, some longer than others, and, as it became clear that we were finished with our lists, she asked for a volunteer to read something off their list. Some of us looked at each other nervously, others looked at the floor. We had been through several of these exercises with one another and sometimes talked about our experiences informally. However, each time we had to "get personal," we all stumbled over our words, even though this was their training and was what they expected of the youth in their workshops. Achilles looked out the window, sighed and then started the conversation,

> "Well, one of the things I wrote down was 'sick.' I never want to be called sick again."
>
> "What do you mean by sick?" Margaret asked, looking a little surprised by the harshness of his words.
>
> "Well, it's like my grandmother, you know?" The rest of us knew and nodded our heads, he had told us about his grandmother many times, who had a particular way of expressing what she thought of people. "Well," he continued "she hasn't ever said it to me, but whenever she talks about gay people—I mean she don't even say gay people, she says 'faggots' or 'bull daggers.' She always says how they sick and stuff like that." The rest of us were still and silent as he spoke, even though he laughed nervously and even smiled as he talked. He paused briefly, which gave Margaret room to ask, on cue, "And how did you feel when you heard this?" "It didn't make me feel anything really," he said a bit defensively, " 'cause I know that's not me." He paused for a minute, and then, shrugging, said, "But, you know I guess if you hear it enough times, you start to think it's true."

For many queer people of color, the notion of home, family, and chosen family that we have come to understand as members of the LGBTQ community is a complicated one. Feminist and Queer Theorists have long described this, specifically the complicated nature of coming out in our biological families or communities, under the call of the LGBTQ community, as Harvey Milk's speech suggests, to come out to our families, our friends, to everyone (see Holland 2005; Johnson 2005; Reddy 1998). Milk's words, intimately tied to political action and social change, are also deeply connected to and portrayed as a symbol of personal, individual liberation, an emergence from the ever-isolating, dark closet (see Butler 1991; Sedgwick 1991). On the other hand, Achilles' words highlight how racism and heterosexism shape the coming out experience for queer youth of color—hinged on the complex positionality of communities of color. His discussion of his grandmother echoes E. Patrick Johnson's discussion of his own grandmother's words about queers, or "quares" as excessive:

> My grandmother uses "quare" to denote something or someone who is odd, irregular, or slightly off-kilter—definitions in keeping with traditional understandings and uses of "queer." On the other hand, she also deploys "quare" to denote something excessive— something that might philosophically translate into an excess of discursive and epistemological meaning ground in African American cultural rituals and lived experience. Her knowing or not knowing vis-à-vis "quare" is predicated on her own "multiple and complex social, historical, and cultural positionality."[28]

And, the continued absence of this culture-specific positionality has allowed the gay and lesbian movement to solidify itself closer to the mainstream. This happens, often, without regard for the experiences of people of color, for whom coming out continues to be a risky endeavor—ultimately read as choosing one identity over the other. As Anzaldúa reflects about her own "choice to be queer":

> For the lesbian of color, the ultimate rebellion she can make against her native culture is through her sexual behavior . . . It is a path of knowledge—one of knowing (and of learning) the history of oppression of our Raza. It is a way of balancing, of mitigating duality. . . .Though "home" permeates every sinew and cartilage in my body, I too am afraid of going home.

Although written more than twenty years ago, Anzaldúa's words continue to resonate in the lives of queer youth of color.

Monica was one of the more shy TJ participants, and her participation was kind of off in the background: she wasn't on the leadership team until later in the year but played a key role in the practical side of building the Youth Center, rather than giving speeches, talking with adults, or organizing poetry slams. When I met her, she had a boyfriend, Jay, who some of the other youth suspected was gay. Monica's coming out was a bit of a surprise, primarily because of how quiet she was—no one knew much about her. Before I interviewed her, we had had one or two in-depth conversations about the center, but mostly our interactions did not go past greeting one another. She was a senior the year that I began conducting research at TJ and, immediately upon graduation, she moved out of her parent's house. That summer I ran into her with Griselda at the San Francisco Dyke March, where she agreed to be interviewed for this project. Our interview lasted two hours, was conducted at her house, and focused primarily on her coming-out process, something she was currently in the midst of. Most of this process centered on her relationship with her family:

> M: I think I've never talked about my [sexuality] with my parents. I mean, I actually never saw myself in a serious relationship like that. It just isn't me. But, I came out and it was totally hell. Until recently, I was meant to—I guess I was homophobic in a lot of ways and I was scared of what I knew in a lot of ways. About myself, that I would put myself in positions and now I'm like "Why did I do things that I didn't, that I wasn't comfortable with and that I did to put up a front?" And it's like, why did I do that? And then I was the one who had a boyfriend but it was like every six months or I would call them once in a blue moon. And it's like I didn't hang out with him, I was with my friends. But whenever anybody would ask, do you have a boyfriend, I would be like "Oh yeah!". And I was like "Oh, I love him! [laughs]"And you know, my mom has always pushed—my mom bought a guy home the other day for me to meet: an older guy at that and I was like, "Why?"

And I guess it's because this is the longest time I've been without a boyfriend.

AC: So you can't talk to your parents about being gay?

M: No, not unless I want to go into deep therapy. And I know that's not going to change anything but I think it would send my mom to the crazy house because she went through a lot with my sister. Both of my sisters, at the same time, my one sister coming out and then the other one being sexually active. And it's like, those are both things that are never talked about in the house and it was like one's a whore and the other one was like "You're still a kid, how could you know that you're gay." She took them to therapy and I think it helped her a lot. But, it will be different with me and she hoped that I was the only virgin and straight person or daughter that would give her kids and that she will be proud of. And she's totally completely wrong, but you know. I don't think that way until I actually want to let them know. I'm ready to let them know, but I guess they're not ready to hear that. I can't go through the whole emotional [experience] of my mom not talking to me. . . . I hope she won't push me away or I hope that—that one of the things, I've been the person that's always brought people home and it's very important for my family to meet everybody. Like, my friends, I don't have a very large circle of friends, but they know them and all my boyfriends—all three of them—they've eaten at the house before and interacted with them. And I guess it's always been important for me to do that. So it's going to be hard for me to say "Hey mom, can I bring her home?" 'cause she says, "I don't want her at my house" to my sister. So I don't see what would be the difference for me.

For Monica, the concept of home was about her biological family: her mother, her sisters, her father, but also about bringing her people home—the three boyfriends she'd had in her life, her friends, and now, at nineteen, her girlfriend. Like many gay people, the youth in this study sought refuge from their families of origin outside of the household. However, as Monica's experience with her parents suggests, coming out as queer, particularly for women of color, continues to be seen as an act of rebellion.[29] In addition to the harassment that they experienced at their schools and among their peers, their immediate families were equally as exclusionary. In fact, at times, this was where they experienced the most "punishment," leaving them to navigate their queer identity, outside of the two organizations, on their own.

Conclusion

The experiences that queer youth of color have in the post–civil rights era suggest a culture in which homophobia is present and is, in many ways, as oppressive as it was prior to the gay liberation movement—particularly in relationship to the mainstream media exclusion of the lives of queer people of color. American cultural discourse constructs and reinforces a dialogue that reassures us that homophobia is on the decline, evidenced by the current organization around same-sex marriage rights and several states' recognition of same sex marriage (albeit not in California).[30] Popular understandings of equality are evident in civil rights discourse that contends that no "special rights" or preferences are necessary for gays and lesbians. At the same time that this discourse defines the contemporary LGBTQ experience, the violence (often constructed as bullying) directed at LGBTQ teenagers, including LGBTQ suicides, has shaped the LGBTQ youth experience. Ultimately, popular discourses surrounding gays and lesbians, and sometimes the LGBTQ movement itself, fails to incorporate the everyday experiences of youth, like the ones in this study, into larger discussion of sexuality (and race) in the United States. In response, queer youth activists incorporate their experiences with homophobia into their social justice activism in an effort to challenge dominant ideology and practice in their workplaces, at school, and at home, while at the same time constructing and understanding where their identity fits within larger understandings of gay identity, lifestyle, and community.

6

BIG SHOES TO FILL
Activism Past and Present

The youth at Teen Justice and Multicultural Alliance participated in social change in a number of ways: through the Youth Center collaborative, anti-oppression workshops, hip-hop culture, and interactive theater. In this chapter, I explore these activities in relationship to popular and academic definitions of activism. Specifically, I ask if these activities, values, tools, and identities that the youth have created indeed constitute activism as it is defined in popular and academic discourse. Additionally, I examine the idealized cultural image of activism, and ask how this image informs youths' definitions of activism.

There are indeed repertoires of activism that have emerged from the civil rights movements and charismatic leadership. These repertoires shape the overall understanding of activism, which is often linked to large social movements. Participants at TJ and MA are uniquely influenced by the idealized cultural image of activism because they have grown up in Oakland, California. The rich, political history of Oakland has shaped youths of color's political opportunities as well as their understanding of their roles in social change. As other scholars have suggested, community ties and a shared sense of identity are crucial to participation in social movement activism.[1]

In this chapter, I explore how youth build upon the idealized cultural image in their definitions of organizing work at TJ and MA and their understandings of activism. Some youth differentiate themselves from these idealized images while still defining themselves as activists. For instance, when I asked Achilles if he thought of himself as an activist, he said, "I am more of your activist like 'well what do you think about it, do you think it's right?' I am not like your ACT

UP activist, or anything." Here, he suggests he is indeed an activist, but he disidentifies with the strategies and tactics of such organizations as ACT UP. Other youth, particularly at TJ, incorporated the idealized image of activism into their identities as activists. I also discuss how both approaches to activism can co-exist in the practices and consciousness of the youth in these organizations. Based on the youths' definitions, I offer a critique of dominant popular and academic understandings of activism and social change, carving out a clearer definition of youth activism post–civil rights.

Where is the New Youth Movement?

Although California has a number of youth empowerment organizations in the Bay Area and throughout the state, there was no direct mention by the staff of the organizations I examined of any larger youth movement. Moreover, during my research neither organization worked in collaboration with any other youth empowerment organizations in Oakland.[2] Under these circumstances, I began to question how the youth in the study perceived themselves in relationship to a larger youth movement. Previous social movements, such as the civil rights movement, involved coalitions of various social movement organizations. For instance, the Student Non-violent Coordinating Committee (SNCC), the Southern Christian Leadership Conference (SCLC), and the Congress of Racial Equality (CORE) worked on similar civil-rights issues, predominantly on ending racist voting laws toward Blacks. In this study, TJ advocated community organizing against social injustice at the institutional level, and MA concentrated on "healing the hurts" of a community by examining how internalized racism, sexism, and homophobia shaped young people's lives. The goals of the organizations provided youth with the tools to change their communities. Still, there was no mention of *activism* in the missions, vision, or handouts for the organizations.

I was confronted directly with the question of how youth activists understand their activities in relationship to previous social movements on a field trip with TJ. Throughout the eighteen months

I worked with the group, TJ included tactics of older activists and used long-standing organizing tactics in their organizational events. The youth made field trips to see various civil-rights leaders speak in the area, including Yuri Kochiyama, a Japanese-American civil rights activist. On this particular day, I was asked to chaperone the youth on a Black Panther Tour of Oakland with David Hilliard, former chief of staff of the Black Panther Party. I readily accepted the offer. Like the youth, I was excited to meet a living, "famous" member of the Black Panther Party. At around 3:15 p.m. a chartered bus pulled up in front of the office of TJ. Mr. Hilliard stepped off the bus, dressed in a black sweatshirt, a jacket with "Black Panther Tour" insignia on the front, black jeans, and black sneakers. He was neither friendly nor unfriendly, just nonchalant. I introduced myself and the youth—Eduardo, David, Trisha, Charles, and Naseem—standing near the entrance of the building that housed TJ. We climbed on the tour bus and were introduced to the driver, an older African American man.

We took our seats; there were about twenty of us—one of the other leadership teams and an adult chaperone joined us that day. Mr. Hilliard prefaced the tour by telling us that we would be visiting nine different sites and getting off the bus at several of them. He suggested that we leave our questions for the end of the afternoon. We started off to the first site, driving down Martin Luther King, Jr. Blvd. to the house that Huey P. Newton, co-founder of the Black Panther Party, grew up in. There was nothing extraordinary about the house; it was a single story, white clapboard house with dark green shutters and green steps on the front porch. It was currently up for sale, which made some of the youth question how much the sale price was and whether people knew who once lived there. Mr. Hilliard took out a notepad and wrote down the realtor's information, saying that he might try and raise some money to buy it for the party. We stopped in front of the house for a few minutes while Mr. Hilliard told us a little bit about Huey Newton's history: he was born in Louisiana, raised in Oakland, and went to school around the corner at Merritt College, which later became Children's Hospital. He met Bobby Seale, who lived a few streets over, in elementary school, but it wasn't until college that they started the Panthers.

We turned the corner and passed Bobby Seale's childhood home, and the bus made its way up to Fifty-fifth and Market. As the bus was stopped at the corner, Mr. Hilliard pointed out the stoplight that was one of the first Panther Party victories. The Panthers organized community members to demand the installation of the light because motorists at the intersection were killing young people. Some of the youth around me whispered they had seen this reenacted in the movie *Panther*. The rest of the tour unfolded in this way: We went to several different former Party locations, including the first Black Panther office, which is now "It's All Good Bakery." This was one of the places where we stepped off the bus to view black-and-white pictures of Black Panther members on the walls. I stood behind several of the youth as they peered into the eyes of Panther members, some whom appeared close to their age.

The group grew somber as we moved into West Oakland and pulled up in front of the house where Bobby Hutton (or "Lil' Bobby") was shot. There they were silent, as Hilliard described the scene that day: police ambushing the house where Eldridge Cleaver and Bobby Hutton were, and police shooting Hutton upon their surrender. Youth had the same reaction when we made our final stop on the tour, the site where Huey Newton was shot, at the corner of Ninth and Center. They stood quietly on the sidewalk as Hilliard told us about the final years of Newton's life.

As we climbed back on the bus and made our way back downtown to the TJ office, Mr. Hilliard took a couple of questions from the group. David had been curled up in one of the seats with his girlfriend, Natasha, from one of the other TJ groups. He piped up, "Yeah, what kind of work did you do with other organizations?" To which Hilliard replied that in addition to Asian groups and women's groups at the time, the Panthers also worked with gay rights organizations, "Something a lot of people didn't know." He then quoted one of the writings by Huey P. Newton in which he claimed that just as Black people need rights, the homosexual man needs rights that members of the party should respect. Eduardo, who was sitting in front of David and his girl, raised his hand next. Mr. Hilliard called on him, and Eduardo asked him "What do you think of the youth movement? Do you think there is one for our generation?" Hilliard replied, "Actually, I see the most things happening in hip-hop. In fact," he said, "we're doing some collaborative work with a hip-hop group here in the Bay Area. That's where I see the youth movement the most, is in hip-hop." Eduardo and David smiled and nodded their heads at one another in response. The bus pulled up in front of the downtown building that housed TJ, and we trailed off the bus and gathered in front of the building. A male passerby asked us what we were doing, and the youth responded in different voices, "We just went on a Black Panther Tour." I asked the man to take a picture of us together, and Charles, who had been silent for most of the trip, encouraged us to put our fists in the air, a symbol of solidarity associated with Black power.

The trip with David Hilliard and the questions Eduardo and David asked made me think about what, if anything, each organization said about activism. How did the organizations talk about activism and activists, and incorporate these discussions into their activities at TJ and MA? After the Black Panther Party tour, Eduardo told me he wrote a paper on the Black Panthers and presented it to his leadership class at Bayview High. Other youth reflected on how the Black Panthers' previous struggles directly impacted their lives. For instance, Naseem took pride in knowing the Black Panthers did their political work in the East and West Oakland neighborhoods where she grew up:

> I like that it was—even though like it's the guns that people see first—but there is this other part that people don't even know about. Like, not everyone else has went on the Black Panther tour and all this stuff happened like right there or next door to you or down the street. And I like that it happened here in Oakland and [that] we have some kind of connection here.

Here, Naseem uses an idealized cultural image of the Black Panther Party in relationship to her growing up in Oakland. As she states, it is often "guns first" that people see in popular images, invoking the ways that Black Panther Party members are often portrayed as gun-toting activists. Two of the more popular images of the Black Panthers include Bobby Seale and Huey P. Newton standing in front of a Black Panther Party for Self-Defense office, with Newton holding a shotgun. Another, of Newton alone, shows him sitting in a wicker chair, eyes fixated directly on the camera, with shotgun in his right hand. These images have come to symbolize the party by removing them, entirely, from the social and political context that they emerged in, which, as Naseem states, a lot of people don't know about.

There were other ways the youth incorporated the idealized cultural image of activism into their repertoires of the organization. For instance, in addition to organizing support for the Youth Center, TJ collaborated with other school organizations at Bayview to sponsor an event during a second Youth Solidarity week. This year, the week culminated in an on-campus assembly highlighting social justice issues relevant to youth. Teen Justice members invited participants from several breakdancing groups on campus, traditional dance and folklore groups, local singing groups, and hip-hop poets.

As I sat down in the audience, I noticed that the walls were lined with flags of various countries—Yemen, Palestine, Cuba, Puerto Rico, and South Africa. There were also posters of famous leaders, writers, and activists like Yuri Kochiyama, James Baldwin, and Malcolm X. When emcees from TJ introduced each act, they gave a brief introduction about one of the featured leaders. Naseem, who helped organize the event, told me the purpose of showcasing these particular leaders was to show how they fought for more than just a single issue against multiple oppressions. This seemed to connect previous activists to the struggles of the youth today. As she explained, "the speakers were supposed to show how these people fought for more than their race's rights or their ethnicity's rights." Most of the speakers did acknowledge the ways in which the various leaders struggled for different rights. For instance, when Xochitl stepped up to the podium to talk about James Baldwin, she noted that he was a gay writer and activist who also worked in the civil rights movement. Naseem explained to me that the goal was to show how he wasn't just Black or gay but that the oppressions he experienced and fought against were interconnected, which she felt was similar to the struggles of youth today. In these instances, the youth incorporated the individual leader image of activism into their organizing work.

Invoking the Idealized Cultural Image

Most of the youth I interviewed were aware of the idealized cultural image of activism, often describing images of activists in their discussions of role models for their own activism. For instance, Courtney told me Angela Davis is someone to whom she looks as a role model:

> Angela Davis, she—I've seen her speak twice—she's just really cool. She's just a cool lady; she knows what's going on. And I was reading her [book] *Blues Legacies and Black Feminism* and she just put it out there and she really knows what's going on. And I really like her style. So she's definitely been an influence in terms of activism.

Making social change accessible and connecting with other people are important tools in contemporary youth activism. As individuals increasingly rely on technology for social interactions (i.e., the Internet), "reaching people" seems to be an important goal for youth activists. Davis's and other activists' establishment of such connections influenced the youths' own activist strategies. For instance, David talked about the influence Malcolm X has had on his activism because of his ability to connect with and lead people:

> I look up to, you know, Malcolm X—and I am not just saying that, because like he is one of the people who is most remembered—but I look up to him and I look up to people who are really into majority organizing and have contributed a lot to organizing, and I look at them as leaders. The reason I look up to Malcolm X is because he knew what was going on back then and he took initiative and he was preaching and used his words to influence people.

Here, David acknowledges the overexposure of activists like Malcolm X, someone who is the most remembered, but also explains a deeper exploration of X's strategies as an activist focused on "majority organizing." Like his critique of hip-hop, David moves beyond commercialized images of activism to define his own tools for organizing, based on a larger model of social movements.

Instead of focusing on one person, Naseem talked about the civil rights movement as a whole in relation to her definition of activism, particularly because a shared sense of struggle that she, and others in the youth movement, are currently involved in. For instance, when I asked her what she thought activism was, she said, "When I hear that word I think of like the civil rights movement. And not just like Malcolm X, but when you said that, that's the first thing that popped in my head. And even though you would know that [the movement today is] not that big of a movement, it's still somewhat like it." Although she takes the emphasis off of an individual leader like X, Naseem still invokes the idealized cultural image of activism by pointing to the civil rights movement itself as a model of activism. However, she also uses it in contrast to a movement she feels exists today.

Although youth like Naseem, David, and Courtney looked to (and occasionally criticized) an idealized cultural image of activism in relationship to their own activism, for other youth the idealized cultural image was so overwhelming that they could not identify themselves as activists. For example, Trisha had difficulty thinking of herself as an activist because the expectations seemed too high:

> Like to call yourself an activist, you have to fill really, really big shoes, 'cause all these people who did all this stuff and worked so hard. It's hard to call yourself—it's hard when there are all these people. Like it's hard, especially in Oakland, 'cause the activists we have like the Black Panthers who did these mass things like help feed the children . . . and that's so cool and it's so big. I think it's hard to call yourself an activist because it covers so much and you have to do so much. I think you have big shoes to fill.

For Trisha, the expectations embodied in the idealized cultural image were compounded by growing up in Oakland, a city where the Black Panthers organized. While this was something that she thought was cool, it also made it difficult to think of herself as an activist. Her statement implies that because the Panthers were from Oakland, contemporary youth activists might feel pressured to take on similar activist roles. This is a potential effect of the idealized cultural image in popular culture: it overshadows competing definitions of activism and impedes an individual's self-definition as an activist.

Xochitl also had difficulty thinking of herself as an activist because she felt she "wasn't doing enough." She was the president of her high school GSA, a key organizer in mobilizing support for the Youth Center at Bayview, and a leader of a recent high school walk-out to protest the U.S. invasion of Iraq. She thought an ideal activist is one who has enough resources to participate *fully* in social justice struggles:

AC: So, do you think of yourself as an activist?

X: [pauses] No.

AC: How come?

X: I see more of an activist as someone who is out there protesting and I don't know, I don't feel that I do enough to become an activist.

AC: So, you feel like you have to be protesting in order to—

X: No, not just protesting but I don't know, but just doing more things. Like with Teen Justice at Bayview we're focusing on getting the Youth Center together and we haven't been doing nothing else—except for some people went to Sacramento, the capital, to protest the budget cuts. But, I don't know, I feel like an activist is someone who does a lot and spends all his or her time trying to change stuff. I don't think I spend enough time doing stuff to call myself an activist.

Xochitl, like others, articulates cultural expectations of what it means to be an activist—someone who is out protesting "all the time." These expectations, which have become her own, made it difficult for her to call herself an activist. This difficulty was a common theme among some of the participants in this study. Most of the youth were in high school, which limits their time to organize. Still, there was a tendency to define activism in relationship to an idealized cultural image of activism where activists are at every meeting and every protest.

Another participant, Jane, an intern at MA, also grappled with calling herself an activist because she wasn't contributing as much as she thought appropriate, based on an idealized cultural image of activism:

> I don't know, [an activist is] just someone who is always out there, always doing something that they believe in, and pushing for it and, I guess, I don't know, I don't really think of myself as an activist at all, because I am not always out in the community. I am not doing it with 100 percent of my efforts. I am just, I just don't feel like an activist. I don't feel like all of the people that I have seen who were activists, I don't feel at all like I am contributing to anything like they are.

Jane and Xochitl, like Frida's comments in the Introduction, suggest that an activist is a person who devotes 100 percent of her time to the "cause." Even though both Jane and Xochitl were involved in organizations in addition to the ones studied here, and engaged in more social change activities than the average person, they still considered an activist as someone outside of their reach. Here, the social construction of the idealized cultural image actually impedes the ways in which some youth define their activism. Further, it helps to establish an understanding that a person is never doing enough to change the system and that activism is something that happened in the past. These same explanations of activism resonate in academic understandings of resistance. Ultimately, the message is that being an activist is a full-time career, not accessible to anyone unless they are giving 100 percent of their time to the cause. These definitions played a central role in the ways the youth identified themselves as activists, as well as the political identities and community they created with others.

Building Youth Activism at Work: Staff Expectations

To get a larger understanding of youth activism and youths' understanding of their own activism, I talked with the staff at Teen Justice and Multicultural Alliance. At TJ, Griselda had clear expectations of activism for both the youth and herself, which she communicated in different ways. For instance, her office, where many of the youth made phone calls to city council members and wrote letters to funding organizations, was filled with photos of the youth as well as a poster of Malcolm X's anthem "By Any Means Necessary" in which Malcolm X sits with his head tilted and his chin resting on his thumb and forefinger. The poster didn't stick out as the most important image on the wall; rather it was tucked in and behind photos of the youth on the Bayview leadership team, some standing in front of a group of youth at a summer training, and between TJ press clippings. There was a connection between the photos on the wall and the work the youth and Griselda did at the organization. This was also evident in Griselda's own definition of activism:

> There is so much economic and social injustice and I don't think we're at a point—and I don't think it's safe or even realistic to say that we could accomplish a revolution. Ideally, I think this society should practically be turned on its head, but I really would like to devote my life to something that is realistic and tangible in my life. What motivates me is that there is so much injustice that is visible on the streets and so much injustice that my family and my friends—people I care about—have experienced in their lives. . .I can't just sit and watch things that are wrong and not do anything about it. I mean, obviously I can't solve all the problems—none of us can solve all the problems—but I think we have to do what is in our power.

Griselda's definition of activism, ultimately, is to turn society on its head. However, she also focuses on the everyday realities that shape her friends and family's lives, much like the youth in this study. She was also clear that this was a key strategy, the use of individual power, to challenge oppression. When I asked her if she thought of herself as an activist, she quickly answered yes.

In contrast to TJ, youth at MA were not inundated with historic images of activists. The office at MA wasn't covered with photos of social activists or quotes from them. Rather, there were pictures of different communities of color in "third-world" countries (the executive director, Ze, was also a photographer). Staff rarely talked about or incorporated information about past leaders or activists into their training agendas.[3] But, as staff members told me, the focus of the organizations was less on painting one picture of activism and more on allowing the youth to carve out their own understandings of social change, organizing, and activism. This decision was based upon their own struggles with the idealized cultural image of activism and organizing, as well as on their own individual agendas.

In accordance with the mission statement of the organization, both Ze and Margaret were clear about centering the organization's goals on youth and community development by advocating an understanding of interpersonal and internalized oppression. But they were less clear about the youths' roles as activists. They also connected their definitions of activism to their own personal goals and identities as activists. Long excerpts of their interviews demonstrate their philosophies of activism and social change. First, Ze discusses both the goals of the organization as well as his own identity as an activist:

> z: I think the goals as I see them are young people developing community with a group of other young people. And I think that means creating new communities and that's fine. Young people thinking about things that they may not think about all the time, but thinking about them in a different context. Providing them with tools too, that the traditional educational system doesn't provide. Making them be critical thinkers, that's really, really important. Yeah, critical thinkers about themselves and society on many levels. Having some skills to act in whatever way they want to act and having a support network to make that happen. And [by]acting, I think that young people—not only young people—but that

we can create an environment that people can talk about things that we normally don't talk about and make changes—small or large.

Q: So, do you think of yourself as an activist?

ZE: I go back and forth about that. I think that I am an activist in small groups and like I guess that I consider myself in the way that in the broad sense that Multicultural Alliance is an activist [organization]. Meaning that when I am in a small group of folks, I'm trying to do a lot of work to change people's perceptions and language and in terms of people's actions and my own. And then the work that I do professionally is to move an agenda forward. And I feel like I am part of that, but I don't fashion myself as an activist. And I guess it's because I compare myself to people that are pretty hard-core. I meet people and I feel like I'm not doing enough and I'm not doing this or I'm not doing that and they are pretty hard core.

Q: What are they doing?

ZE: They're just like making it out to every public function and educating themselves about the issues and speak really clearly about everything. You know they really have a clear message that they're putting out there. . . . And I sometimes feel like okay, do these other people see me as an activist? Or, am I a good enough activist? You know, some of those questions. So, that feels like a little more complex question than [one that can be answered] yes or no.

Ze's discussion of activism reflects the idealized cultural image of activism, like "hard core" activists—people who are clear about their cause and educating themselves about different issues. His evaluation of his activism in relationship to others influences his goals for the organization (which he claims is activist) and the young people. For instance, he never suggests that the youth are activists, but rather that they should be trained as critical thinkers and given "the tools" to act in whatever way they desire.

On the other hand, Margaret was more clear about her relationship to activism and her goals for the organization. When I asked her about what her agenda was for MA, she explained that while she wished to focus on social change and ending oppression, she first wanted youth to understand the ways in which the belief in or internalization of stereotypes were as much a tool of the oppressive system as racism, sexism, and homophobia:

> I knew pretty early on that I really wanted to address internalized oppression with young people, because I felt like that to me and my value system, that . . . was what I really most wanted to accomplish. You know, I know that the larger picture thing, you know "how to dismantle oppression" was too big of a picture for me to think about, but if I knew how to really get young people to think about how they've been affected by their own internalized racism or their own internalized sexism or what-have-you, then there would be a major change in their lives and a major change in their community . . . but it's not overwhelming in the same way that creating a whole new government or getting rid of capitalism or, you know like some of the larger mobilization or organizing movements are too overwhelming.

In this statement Margaret critiques the "larger picture" of social change, which includes social movements, because they are too overwhelming. Rather, she felt her personal and political goals rested on understanding internalized oppression and how it affects youths' lives before they could change the larger community, something she demonstrated to the youth at MA.

Identity, Resistance, and Social Change

One of the central aspects of previous youth-led social movements such as the civil rights movement was the creation of individual and group identity among movement participants. Research on social movements suggests that identity formation is a key component of social-movement participation.[4] New social movement scholars have examined the importance of identity—at both the collective and individual level—in relationship to the civil rights movement, the women's movement, and the gay and lesbian movement. Overwhelmingly, researchers conclude that central to the formation of social movement identities are a series of individual relationships.[5] These relationships not only sustain individuals' involvement within the movement, but also influence their motivation for participation, their recruitment strategies, and the various roles they take on within the movement.

Scholars have identified community ties as an important motivation for individual and collective movement participation. For instance, in their work on social networks and social activism, Doug McAdam and Ronelle Paulsen found that a strong sense of social ties was necessary for individual movement participation. Studying the recruitment process for participants in the Freedom Summer campaign, the authors conclude many of the participants were already linked to the movement through friends, family members, or involvement in other organizations that were "ideally suited" for activism in the civil rights movement.[6] Ultimately, they argue that individual activism is shaped by a person's participation in other, similar organizations or through linkages to other social movement participants. Identity and personal experience shape not only social networks and ties but also potential leadership roles among participants. Specifically, how participants capitalize on their race, class, or gender statuses to mobilize other movement participants is central to their leadership role within the movement.

Personal connections also facilitate individual commitments to social movements. For example, in her book *How Long? How Long? African-American Women in the Struggle for Civil Rights*, Belinda Robnett examines how Black women's leadership was crucial to the overall success of the civil rights movement. Black women's secondary status as females often excluded them from formal leadership roles in upper echelons of the movement, but they often took on leadership at the grassroots level. Because they weren't always in the public eye, participation at this level often allowed women to rely on "emotions and spontaneity." The use of emotions allowed them to connect with potential participants on a more personal level and mobilize them into the larger movement. They thus acted as "bridge leaders" by using tactics to link the larger movement organizations and goals to individuals in the community. As Robnett states, "activities of bridge leaders in the civil rights movement were the stepping stones necessary for potential constituents and adherents to cross formidable barriers between their personal lives and the political life of civil rights organizations."[7] The efforts of women to connect on a more personal level during the civil rights movement were key to the success of the movement.

Other scholars suggest individuals are predisposed to activism because of the structure of the communities with which they identify. For example, Aldon Morris argues that particular individuals are already predisposed to social movement participation because of the structure and culture of the communities into which they were born. For instance, Blacks were ready to participate in the civil rights movement because of their experiences with racism in the United States. Further, internal structures in the Black community helped facilitate participation in the movement. Specifically, "local movement centers" like the Black church were sites for coordinating movement activities, distributing information to potential participants, and providing financial resources to the movement.[8] Because these sites were already established as part of the community, they were central to the participation and nourishment of movement participants, making participation almost an organic aspect of being a member of the Black community. The role and support of the Black church was crucial to the spread of collective action in the Black community because it provided a space to articulate shared grievances and mobilize for social change.

In chapter 4, we saw how the youth capitalized on their identity as part of the hip-hop generation to mobilize other youth and sustain their own activism. Similarly, youth drew upon their personal experiences as queer, Black, Latino, or Asian to lead anti-oppression workshops with other youth. In addition to these aspects of their identity, they also used the structure of their communities as youth to inform their individual activist identities, which motivated their participation in the organizations as well. The youth in this study became involved in TJ and MA because of their links to other members or organizations. For instance, Achilles became involved in MA through Chris, who was already an intern. As Achilles states:

> my friend Chris was in Multicultural Alliance and she was like "You should come" and I'm like "Um, I don't know, I don't want to come." And then Ze made the classes kind of fun and he was kind of eccentric, so I said, "You know this could be fun, so why not give it shot? So I gave it a shot and I found out it really was fun.

Courtney also became involved because of her involvement with other youth organizations. However, it was also clearly linked to her role as an outsider as well. Asked how she got involved in social change work, she replied:

> In high school . . . because I was a homebody and I wasn't part of the popular crowd, I was just known as a smart kid. I was in all honor classes so my drive was "I'm going to go college and I'm going to do something cool with the community," so that's just when I started to get involved. I started volunteering at Kaiser Hospital and then I got involved with the Volunteer Center and I was on the youth board for that. And then from there, I discovered diversity stuff, like diversity issues, which has become my issue. And I did that junior year— we developed a diversity team at my school. My school was, I was [in] the second graduating class so everything there was new. I was the founding president of that of that club and everything. From there, that branched off into all of the counties and Multicultural Alliance and from there I got connections to the Bay Area, a bunch of organizations like Multicultural Alliance. It all just branched off from high school involvement.

Other youth, like Clark, from MA, and Conrad, from TJ, became involved because of previous experiences in which they questioned their environment. When I asked Clark how he became involved in MA, he suggested that the organizational framework fit with his own thinking. Specifically, when asked why he got involved in the organization, he answered:

c: I think it is because I had a lot of questions growing up, and I spent most of my time thinking about why do we have religion, why do we have all of this stuff? I had questions and I felt that Multicultural Alliance or an organization could help me or something. That's why I did it.

AC: Why Multicultural Alliance?

c: I don't know, it was the only organization I saw that dealt with the issues. [Like] "Why is there religion, why is there racism, homophobia?" all of that stuff. That's why I chose Multicultural Alliance.

Like Clark, Conrad was also committed to social change and critical thinking prior to his involvement with the organizations. More importantly, he became involved with Teen Justice because of the "carelessness" he observed in his community. As he explains:

So one form of being careless is to not care about [your] community, so you destroy your community. Or, you don't care about yourself, so you use drugs. Or you murder people because you don't care about your community, or you commit suicide because you don't care about yourself. Things like that are going on in my community all of the time. You join a gang because you don't feel like your self worth is enough, like you walking down the street by yourself is enough to protect you—you know what I am saying?—so you join a gang.

Conrad uses these personal experiences of growing up in Oakland as a base for his activism. Moreover, his activism transcends OFCY expectations of youth empowerment in that he does more than avoid the realities in his community; he organizes to change them. In all of these instances, the youth build on their prior experiences and race, class, and gender identities to construct their identities as activists.

The importance of identity formation is perhaps most evident in studies of gay activism. Since the Stonewall rebellion of 1969, the gay and lesbian movement has been a visible source of change as

well as a safe haven for gays and lesbians. The gay and lesbian movement has influenced the coming-out processes among people who
identify as gay or lesbian. Mary Bernstein's work on gay and lesbian
activism details the effects that the coming-out process has on individual and collective identity. Based on her analysis of gay activism
in four different U. S. cities, she suggests it is imperative to explain
"the structural relationship between identity and mobilization, when
identity is a goal of collective action."[9] Coming out as gay or lesbian
(or bisexual, queer, or transgender) not only challenges the dominant culture's perception of the gay and lesbian community but con-
tributes to the transformation of the participants involved, particularly because it links individuals to a larger community.

The importance of identity is also clear in Steven Epstein's study
of AIDS activism. Epstein argues that the gay and lesbian movement
is important because participants "are conscious of their own active
involvement in a public and contested process of identity construction."[10] By examining the production of knowledge and identity in
struggles between AIDS activists and the state, Epstein argues that
movement participants took on "expert" positions. The AIDS activists in his study established a unique relationship to the state and
pharmaceutical companies in that they were able to draw from the
already existing knowledge base of the gay and lesbian movement
to make demands upon the state. More importantly, they used their
personal experience as gay individuals who had witnessed the dec-
imation of the gay community due to the AIDS crisis or who had
suffered from the disease themselves. Drawing upon their personal
experiences provided AIDS activists with more knowledge than did
the doctors and pharmaceutical companies trying to find a cure for
AIDS. Because of their ability to label themselves and construct
their own experience, AIDS activists transformed their identities
from clients or "victims" to experts in the AIDS struggle.[11] A strong
knowledge base along with a well-defined identity is central to social
movement organizing and social change.

Like the AIDS activists in Epstein's study, youth of color in the
post–civil rights era are better equipped to understand what is
"best" for the community because of their personal experiences with

violence, racism, and homophobia. They become experts because of the tools and strategies they use in light of their particular socio-historical context, where the oppression they experience is masked by discourses around the victories of civil rights. Moreover, popular understandings of an idealized cultural image of activism often omit other ways of participating in social change. For the youth activists in this study, the assertion of an activist identity is almost impossible within the idealized cultural framework. Teenagers of color do not fit in with the dominant representations of activism. The power of these repertoires is reflected in the youth's definitions of activism. In some cases, these definitions impinge on an individual's sense of herself as an activist. In others, it challenges them to construct their own definitions of activism.

"I Am Active, Therefore I Am an Activist": Youth, Resistance, and Activism

Most of the youth I interviewed who identified their organizing work as activism were also very clear about the types of activism in which they participated, still conscious of the ideal activist. Several of the participants played with the word activism to describe the activities in which they were involved and how they conceded to the overall definition. For instance, Frida who didn't like the word activist because of the stereotypes associated with it, said that for her, making a change means "being active." To her, being active may simply mean "speak[ing] to people [about] anything that comes up basically. Like if they're talking about something and you hear them you just get them thinking and relate it to them."

Conrad used the same definition of being active, but he employed it to explain activism and attributed his involvement to the way he was raised:

> If activism is being active, then I am an activist. I think that word is so big, activist. You know, my mother advocated for youth, when I was growing up, you know what I am saying, and she was active in my growth. My mother led marches up to the school to find out

what was going on, you know what I am saying? And she revolution-
ized the theory that was put in my mind about being less because
of my color or just being less in general because of the way I was
brought up, you know what I am saying? She rallied me and my sisters together to clean up the house on Sundays and it was not really
about us cleaning up the house, really, but it was about us coming together to do something. So, when I think about being active,
I think about rallying these people together against some kind of
cause. . . I mean active in the sense of having an active awareness of
what is going on and caring.

Here, Conrad argues that he is an activist because he brings
people together for a cause. He also speaks to the different levels
of activism in that it can mean rallying people together or actively
advocating on behalf of others, as his mother did. Similarly, David,
who also considers himself an activist, interpreted the meaning of
the word activism as being "active" for a cause. As he states:

I do consider myself to be an activist. . . . Activism means you are
doing something to contribute to the struggle. If you are not doing
anything to contribute to the struggle, like, then you are not an
activist, believe me, because the first part of the word activism, is
active, so you have to be active, and if you are not active, then you
are not an activist. And being an activist, you have to sacrifice a lot
of things you have to like give up your time for it, and you have
to participate and you have to support and you have to create, and
you have to make change, and when you change something like you
change your goals . . . that is change.

David, like Frida and Conrad, thinks that activism at its base
involves being active for change. Because he is changing something,
he locates himself within an activist model. At the same time, he
acknowledges others' understanding of an activist as someone who
makes sacrifices and gives up his time for a cause. While these youth
break down the word activism to include being active, talking to
family members, or rallying people for a cause, they are also clear

that activism includes sacrifices, such as giving up your time. Others, like Clark, define activism as part of one's everyday interactions in the community. Clark recounted:

> I mean, just having to deal with people, I guess. I mean, being a tutor is like a whole new activism also. You are out there, working, like teaching them, and having a regimen to follow. There is something else more, like going to college. You are educating people and then it's giving them the chance to make them realize what you can do.

Clark's definition of activism is linked to education, indicating the struggles that remain around obtaining and education for urban youth of color. He also articulates this as "a new kind of activism," in contrast to previous struggles. This distinction is significant in that it highlights the organizing sites that are available to teenagers—education, as a primary site. There is a strong relationship between his philosophy of activism and his work as an intern at MA.

Most of the interns at MA adopted the strategy of consciousness-raising and self-reflection as part of the activism. Further, they took the skills they learned in both organizations and used them to organize other youth. For example, Shabee, a sixteen-year-old intern at MA, explained her definition of activism by evoking Margaret's philosophy almost exactly:

> I do think that I'm like a small activist in my community and just doing things to better myself and my community. In that type of way I am, but I don't think that I do stuff to receive mass recognition or my own holiday but I think I am. Basically, because like I'm doing something to make a change in my community. Also, not just in my community, but hopefully in the entire world—you know if that person passes on it to that person and then the next person and on and on, you know what I mean? Like you can't always change a person, but you can inform them. In that type of way I'm an activist.

Shabee suggests activism happens at different levels. Some levels warrant your "own holiday," like Martin Luther King Jr. perhaps, while a different approach such as starting with one person can eventually change a community and then possibly the whole world. Monica articulated a similar approach of starting with the people around her, such as members of her family. When I asked her if she thought she was an activist, she replied:

> s: In some ways. I mean I don't know, maybe in small ways just like teaching my little niece or nephew things that they might not have known otherwise. And like in Teen Justice and at home, by fighting for what I believe in.
>
> a c: What kinds of things do you fight for at home?
>
> m: Well, my parents are of the belief that this is a great country and that there's nothing wrong with it and I mean I love this place, I wouldn't want to be anywhere else. But, there is a lot of things you can change and there are many ways you can go about it and we're always having arguments about it. . . . And if we have something so far and it's good, why can't we make it very good or perfect? I mean, nothing is perfect, but we can always try. And I guess homophobia has always been an issue and I always try and fight for that.

Clark, Shabee, and Monica's strategies of interrupting homophobia and educating others in their everyday interactions are part of their activist identity. These strategies challenge popular understandings of activism that center on individual leaders or large-scale social movements. Even though contemporary social movement activity is often absent from popular discourse, the youth create distinct activist identities that reflect their surroundings: school, family, and friendships. Perhaps Lana, at MA, best summed up this element of youth activism. When I asked her if she thought what she did was activism or if she was an activist, she said:

> Yeah, 'cause I never shut up. I'm always like, "Well I think that you should," or "I think that people should think about it like this," and

you just have to see a different side. . . . I think you can be an activist if you're spreading the word. If you spreading a positive message or whatever, 'cause if you're an activist, you're supposed to be doing something for a cause. And, you know, so as long as people are doing something and it's for a cause, it doesn't really have to be like, let me go to a protest or that kind of thing. I can be an activist just by having a conversation with you and telling you what I think. . . . It doesn't have to be in a big auditorium with a lot of people or anything like that. If you're out there spreading the word, you're considered an activist in my opinion.

In Lana's view, the key to contemporary activism and social change is to "never shut up." She, like other youth in this study, consistently emphasized the importance of speaking up and challenging friends, family, and others in everyday conversation. These definitions challenge the idealized cultural image of activism by reframing the definition of what it means to be an activist. For instance, while they agree an activist is someone who makes sacrifices and commits much of her time to social change, they also very ardently believe they are activists, albeit sometimes on a much smaller scale. And, their primary goal is to start by educating the folks around them. Using this approach, youth commit to spreading their message and building community, one person at a time.

Activism as Everyday Practice: Norms, Values, and Resistance

Other works in sociology and cultural studies have looked at various forms of resistance, which include but are not limited to large-scale social movements.[12] For instance, in her study of female community workers and poverty, Nancy Naples developed the term "activist mothering" to describe the type of activism in which the women were involved. Emerging from their role as biological mothers and "other mothers" in the community, Black and Latina women in her study combined their activism with what they considered everyday caretaking. As Naples states, "activist mothering not only involves nurturing work for those outside one's kinship group but . . .

comprise[s] all actions, including social activism, that addressed the needs of their children and community.[13] Verta Taylor takes this analysis one step farther in her study of postpartum depression support groups. She argues the success of the movement exists in the face-to-face interactions, rather than the larger postpartum movement. She states, "The emotion culture of the postpartum self-help movement is not simply an extension of women's traditional nurturing roles but grows out of a conscious awareness of the significance of emotional control for upholding gender differences"[14] In each of these works, the authors contend that social movement organizing and activism is rooted in the everyday interactions and activities of the women involved, at the same time that they may not fit into dominant discourses of social movement activism.

Inside and outside of Sociology, scholars have focused on how individuals participate in cultural movements, create liberatory ideologies, and establish norms in their everyday lives. For instance, feminists of color have long used culture as a tool of resistance against dominant ideology and oppression, specifically by incorporating new ways of being and understanding into their repertoires for social change. The Combahee River Collective, a group of Black lesbian feminists, issued a statement during the second-wave feminist movement in which they acknowledged the importance of using language in an effort to dismantle the structures of oppression. They stated that "even our Black women's style of talking/testifying in Black language about what we have experienced has a resonance that is both cultural and political. We have spent a great deal of energy delving into the cultural and experiential nature of our oppression out of necessity because none of these matters have ever been looked at before."[15] For these women, the use of language is a political act in that it challenges dominant ideologies and is a liberatory strategy for the (marginalized) women involved. Similarly, the youth in this study build on their experiences, language, and culture to educate others and create a movement.

Central to the feminist goal of challenging ideology was building a movement through education—and building upon culture to frame their activism and define it. While it was important for feminists of color to formulate a new ideology based on anti-racist, sexist, and homophobic understanding, it was also crucial to share this understanding and ideological commitment with others. Black feminist scholar bell hooks outlined this plan of action in her discussion of feminist revolution and social change. She argued that a shift in ideology is essential for building a mass movement and impending social change:

> To build a mass-based feminist movement, we need to have a liberatory ideology that can be shared by *everyone*. That revolutionary ideology can be created only if the experiences of people on the margin who suffer sexist oppression and other forms of group oppression are understood, addressed, and incorporated. They must participate in feminist movement as practice, we have been satisfied with relying on self-appointed individuals, some of whom are more concerned about exercising authority and power than with communicating with people from various backgrounds and political perspectives.[16]

She not only calls for a new platform for revolutionary change, based on one-on-one education but also critiques traditional movement models of revolution and change. The definitions and strategies that youth use to define their activism provide a critique of large-scale social movements. Youth activists describe their activism as rooted in their everyday activities and practices, rather simply than large-scale strategies.

Conclusion

Youth activism takes place through participation in nonprofit youth empowerment organizations where they are trained as organizers, facilitators, and leaders around various national, international, and local issues. Drawing upon activist models of the past, contemporary youth are involved in traditional modes of protest and organizing, such as attending social protests and organizing social events to educate the public. For instance, students in the Bay Area and Los

Angeles participated in several walkouts protesting the U.S. invasion of Iraq. In addition, youth take organizing tools into their everyday interactions at school, at work, with their families, and among their friends. My in-depth interviews with youth at Teen Justice and Multicultural Alliance revealed this strategy to be the one youth employed most frequently and which they felt was most effective. For them, interrupting homophobia or racism in the places with which they were most familiar—at school, home, and in their neighborhoods—was the most meaningful practice and was linked to how they thought about social change, their role in it, and their overall identity as activists. By performing these acts of resistance and identifying as activists, the youth challenge the dominant understanding of activism by taking action to change their communities, however they define them. Their actions also suggest it is imperative that social movement scholars acknowledge these strategies in their overall understanding of contemporary activism and social change in order to get a richer understanding of activism and social change.

Social movement theory has influenced contemporary understandings of activism, resistance, and social change by using models of collective behavior, resource mobilization, political opportunity, and new social movements. While some of these theories, which focus primarily on large-scale movements, often fall short of explaining contemporary youth activism, recent scholarship has challenged this approach. Youth are involved in an activism that merges a popular understanding of traditional social movement strategies that rely on structural change (and sometimes utilizing these methods) with changing ideological frameworks and a contemporary landscape influenced by changing attitudes toward race, age, class, and sexual orientation. Like recent scholars, Naples and Taylor among them, I use the voices of the youth to further interrogate social movement theory by examining the everyday acts of resistance in which the youth are currently involved.

7

CONCLUSION
Sampling Activism

Although ya try to discredit

Ya still never read it

The needle, I'll thread it

Radically poetic

Standin' with the fury that they had in '66 . . .

Still knee-deep in the system's shit . . .

Fist in the air, in the land of hypocrisy

—Rage Against the Machine

There are no new ideas, just new ways of giving

those ideas we cherish breath and power in our own living

—Audre Lorde

On November 4, 2008, Barack Hussein Obama was elected president of the United States. Personally, I was overcome with emotion: he was the first Black president. I immediately called my eighty-two-year-old grandmother, who is Black, and my mother and father, and we cried about this historic moment. As a researcher, I was also interested in the discussions of youth activism that accompanied his campaign and election. Newspaper headlines, television anchors, and everyday conversationalists concluded that President Obama had "galvanized the youth vote" and that youth activism was at new heights during his campaign. Youth were motivated more so than ever before, demonstrating a strong commitment to civic engagement and political activism.

Quickly, it seemed, discourse turned to the decline of youth activism in headlines that read, "How to keep youth motivated," and "What was the key to continued youth involvement in politics?" The momentum behind the election of Barack Obama, and the numbers of young people under the age of thirty who voted for him—66 percent —was a visible component of his campaign. One Penn student said, "It's like, one of my rights. . . . For me, it's the first one that came to mind when I turned eighteen."[1] For African American youth in particular, voting is a key component of the history of being Black in this country: the passage of the Voting Rights Act of 1965 was, in large part, passed because of the organizing work of African American (youth) organizations like SNCC, CORE, and SCLC. The platform that Obama ran on—community organizing—seemed to speak to a generation of youth, like the ones in this study, who disidentified with the model of leadership that currently exists. He also spoke directly to ongoing, intergenerational discourse, declaring, "this is your victory" to young people who "rejected the myth of their generation's apathy."[2] While important in challenging the dominant discourse of youth and apathy, these discussions fail to recognize other forms of political engagement that youth engage in, especially younger teenagers who are not allowed to vote in the United States. More importantly, none of the youth in this study mentioned voting as something they looked forward to, nor did they mention it as part of their civic duties. Rather, their civic engagement included resisting racism, sexism, and homophobia in their communities.

An equally important development that emerged during Obama's campaign was the discussion of race and a so called "postracial" era, as evidenced by the election of the first African American president.[3] This era is also characterized by a growing divide between two generations of African Americans: members of the civil rights and post–civil rights generations—the latter of whom didn't always see themselves as leaders of the Black community. For instance, Cory Booker, the current mayor of Newark, New Jersey, where African Americans make up more than 50 percent of the population, states:

> I don't want to be pigeonholed . . . I don't want people to expect me to speak about *those* issues . . . I want people to ask me about nonproliferation. I want them to run to me to speak about the situation

in the Middle East. . . . I don't want to be the person that's turned to when CNN talks about black leaders.[4]

At the same time that the postracial conversation focused on a movement that "transcends" race, it was peppered with stories of voters who distributed racist fliers of President Obama with watermelon and fried chicken in the background.[5] While it appears that many celebrate the color-blind era, when a Black man can be elected president, racism continues to shape how we view people of color.

Both conversations—the rise in youth activism during the election and the postracial moment—highlight some of the arguments I have made in this book. The coverage of youth activism before, during, and after President Obama's election is indicative of how we as a culture define social movements and, subsequently, youth activism by relying on "surges" of activity: voting, massive demonstrations, and marches, which are based on idealized repertoires of activism. At the same time, this dialogue simultaneously blames and celebrates youth involvement and apathy, while overlooking the important, ongoing work on the part of youth activists. Many of the young adults that mobilized for Obama's presidential campaign may have been longtime organizers trained in organizations, similar to the ones studied here, since their teens. However, these moments are routinely read as a singular event that politicizes already apathetic youth, rather than the building of an ongoing youth movement. In this book, I have offered a critique of popular and academic discussions of activism and social change that rely on this model by examining how teenagers in organizations like Teen Justice and Multicultural Alliance are trained to organize and participate in social change, developing skills far beyond, as OFCY's vision states, "meaningful participation."[6]

Youth activists in the contemporary context experience racism, sexism, and homophobia in an era quite different than previous generations. In chapters 2 and 3, I demonstrate the impact of the dual reality that youth experience of benefiting from the social reforms and policies since the 1960s, as well as suffering the loss of many social services, including the elimination of affirmative action in California. More importantly, I argue that youth activism and the youth activists themselves are influenced by a current politics of abandonment of urban youth of color. This impacts youth activism in several ways: First, they are directly targeted as urban youth of color through formal and informal policies of surveillance. These policing techniques happen in different sites: their schools, their neighborhoods, at work, and in their families. Second, this landscape also impacts the social policies and opportunities available to youth who are encouraged to navigate the field of the current backlash, laden with increased violence in their communities, the rise in the prison industrial complex, and a deteriorating education system. These factors are ones that organizations like OFCY encourage youth to simply "avoid." Voting becomes one of the rewards for avoidance and survival. This discourse, one of civil rights gains, civil rights backlash, and surveillance has directly shaped contemporary youth activism. As Kitwana states, "in part due to previous generation's victories, today's 'enemy' is not simply white supremacy or capitalism" (Kitwana 2002, 149). The youth in this study all discussed how these enemies emerged in their schools, at work, and at home.

Discussions of race and racism, and how it intersects with class, gender, and sexuality, were topics of youth activists' everyday discussions, which drew upon their own experiences. As Te and Conrad described in chapter 3, being an African American teenager meant that race and racism was something that they strategized around and talked about daily, as it was central to their mobilization efforts as well as their daily experience. Similarly, Lana told me she participated in MA and social change because

> I think I'm involved in all these things because I wasn't happy and I'm still not happy with how society views, I don't want to say minorities, but what society *considers* minorities, you know people of color? So, it's like how can we change society's view on us? You know as a Mexican-American female, it affects me all the time. . . . Well, maybe by focusing on changing the younger generation and by educating the younger generation grows, then some of those things will stop, or racism will stop or at least decrease.

For Lana, like the other youth in this study, their organizing vision is long term, moving from generation to generation. Each of the youth that I have maintained contact with, continue to organize, several for Multicultural Alliance and Teen Justice, an indication that their vision focuses on building *a movement*.[7]

Youth activism is as much about the activities they engage in as it is about the context that they organize in. While anti-oppression workshops, collaborative meetings, poetry slams, and interactive theater are important for providing the movement with certain boundaries, they are only part of the definition of activism for teenagers in the post–civil rights era, equally important is the social-cultural context in which contemporary youth activism has emerged. A moment where, as Foucault suggests, power is decentralized, with multiple "enemies" for youth to address, both at the institutional and interpersonal levels. Traversing this landscape, while not easy, is at the core of youth activism and is what makes it unique: they combine organizing against particular laws in some instances, with engaging in everyday social change processes in their social networks. In chapter 6, for example, the youth articulated the kinds of activism that they are involved in, perhaps a more "micro" approach based on talking to those closest to them: friends, family, and peers. Youth activists construct their definitions of activism by juxtaposing what they learn at each organization, the idealized cultural image of activism, and their status as youth who experience both the benefits of civil rights and the backlash against those same rights. In an effort to mobilize others, youth turn to popular culture, which has taken on a significant role in defining the contours of youth activism—how they mobilize, the tools they use, and the role models they identify with. Like Stuart Hall's (1993) discussion of popular culture, youth activism provides a site for youth to engage with and utilize images of urban youth, previous social movements, and discourses of activism to understand and construct their experiences.

In order to fully understand the scope of contemporary youth activism in the twenty-first century, researchers must continue to confront two realities: (1) there is a dominant representation of activism in U.S. public discourse that informs our understanding of previous civil rights victories; (2) this discourse in turn influences how people think of themselves as activists. An idealized cultural image of an activist is based upon (but not limited to) the civil rights leaders, struggles, and participants in previous social movements. Like others, youth find it difficult not to include these activists and their strategies in their work. Some, like Trisha, feel the definition of activism requires too much to actually claim, while Frida critiques the expectations. At the same time, youth activists look up to these leaders and incorporate their teachings into their resistance strategies, organizing tools, and political identities as activists. For instance, David looked up to Malcolm X because, "he is someone who is most remembered," and for Naseem, activism made her think of the "civil rights movement." This idealized definition of activism and the iconic status of previous activists dominate the social, political, and geographical landscape that the youth organize in. As Trisha, Conrad, and Naseem suggest, living in Oakland makes it particularly difficult to escape the idealized image of activism, because the legacies of the Black Panther Party and other movements are ever present.

These Are the Breaks: Toward A Theory of Youth Activism

We often look to youth, as a culture, to spearhead social change. At the same time, teenagers are overwhelmingly categorized as apathetic. Typically, these "youth" are college students, many well beyond their teenage years. Yet, if popular discourse continues to single out youth for the future of social change, we must re-examine the definitions, strategies, and tactics of social movement activism, not to mention youth. The tactics and definitions that teenagers employ in this study are an indication that popular and academic discourses of activism need to continue to explore social change activities that happen outside of large-scale social movements, and with a critical understanding of the role of popular culture in the post–civil rights era. This is particularly crucial for understanding activism among those teenagers who occupy a disenfranchised social status and rely heavily on popular culture to organize their peers. Throughout the preceding chapters, I have turned to hip-hop to understand these changes.

Youth activism is a lot like a hip-hop sample, which, as it sounds, is the process of taking samples or loops of previous records and incorporating them into new sounds or contexts. Deejays (or producers) search for the "break," or the richest part of a song—what a crowd may respond to the most—and loop it back into a new sound that audiences will recognize and resonate with.[8] In *Making Beats: The Art of Sample-Based Hip-Hop*, Joseph G. Schloss argues that this process of looping "changes the entire sensibility within which this sound is interpreted."[9] Youth activism is similar to this process in that activists draw upon previous social movement tools, images and texts, geographic landscapes (i.e., the San Francisco Bay Area), popular constructions of urban youth of color, hip-hop culture, and their own personal experiences, utilizing a bricolage approach to mobilizing other youth. Eduardo listens to the same music the "homies and homegirls" listen to construct his movement frame, while Patti and Lana juxtapose the use of the words "Nigga" and "faggot" to encourage other youth to talk about homophobia. Courtney participates in a "blackout" or sit-in to protest the treatment of African American students at UC Berkeley. And while many have critiqued sampling for its "unoriginal" form, the process is a staple of this generation. The activist tool kit is a loop. And in the current context, it may be all they have.

Like hip-hop, which Schloss argues is "based on a cyclical form . . . derived from the approach of early hip-hop deejays, who used turntables to repeat drum breaks from funk and soul records,"[10] it is impossible to explain contemporary youth activism, without acknowledging how previous social movements and social movement actors inform the landscape, tools, and ideologies of contemporary youth activists. Organizations like Teen Justice and Multicultural Alliance sample the ideology and practice of the civil rights, feminist, and gay and lesbian movements to train youth organizers and/or facilitators in each organization. Margaret, for example, emphasized the important connection between structural and individual forms of oppression in everyday conversations with youth and the organizational structure of MA. She prioritized internalized oppression so that the youth would feel like they had some control and an understanding of the larger aspects of racism, homophobia, and sexism. Griselda had a slightly different approach at TJ, where she encouraged youth to make connections between civil rights activists like Yuri Kochiyama and Black Panther Party member David Hilliard in their formation of their own activist identities and approaches. Youth combine this training with the "funk" and "soul" of the Bay Area, including local histories of hip-hop, into their mobilizing efforts.

In the context of this landscape, youth activism takes on a distinct nature. Some of this is reflected in the vision and mission statements of the organizations that train youth activists. The primary missions of Teen Justice and Multicultural Alliance are quite different: one focused on instilling youth with long-term organizing skills to combat structural oppression in their communities; the other committed to healing the internal and external "hurts" caused by the "demons" of racism, sexism, and homophobia, but each aims to address the dual realities that youth activists face in the post–civil rights era. Similar to the consciousness-raising tactics of feminist movements, youth engage in the practice of understanding their social location and its relationship to their social justice organizing. In other words, there was nothing that they asked others to do that they weren't willing to examine or understand about themselves: the "stereotypes" and "derogatory words" exercises that each organization used to have youth examine their own internalized racism, for instance, often translated into the work that they did with other youth.

The post–civil rights landscape challenges youth activists to employ new tactics and incorporate old ones in ways that may never have been intended, reflecting a hip-hop sample. The incorporation of commodified ideas and images of social movement leaders and activists in contemporary youth activism are used in ways that could never have been imagined during previous social movements or among the social movement actors themselves. And while youth activism is not entirely new, similar to Audre Lorde's quote at the beginning of this chapter, the question isn't about social movement "newness." Cultural workers have long used culture and cultural images—the Pachuco, the pink triangle, and Negro spirituals—to mobilize others. However, what is important about youth activism is the use of highly commodified images to organize others and inform their own social and political location. Youth spin hip-hop lyrics, the images and words of political leaders like Angela Davis, Malcolm X, and the Black Panthers as frames for the movement as well as their own activist identities. In some cases, youth reject the idealized cultural image because they feel they cannot live up to it. In others, the youth explore other definitions that more aptly reflect their situation as urban youth of color. Similar to the genre of hip-hop, admittedly political in its beginnings, but, some argue, minstrelized in its current form, youth simultaneously rely upon and reject the commodified, popular understandings of activism in their social justice organizing. And, this in turn, creates new frameworks. Imani Perry suggests in her analysis of hip-hop:

> If any art form is to sustain a compositional framework, it should be hip-hop because its very roots lie in the use of the commodity to dislocate the commodity. The philosophical democracy at the participatory heart of the art form will continue in the underground, in live venues, people rhyming on the street, in parties, clubs, and dances, in the newer forms of music that constitute variations of hip hop and even in folks leaning to the side while driving bopping their heads.[11]

Like hip-hop, the approaches that youth activists employ in their activism provide a solid base from which to address the dislocation, or decentralization of power that operates in the post–civil rights era.

As Foucault's work suggests, the decentralization of power indicates that the goals and strategies of social change must also shift. For instance, while it is important to challenge the state on discriminatory laws that target youth of color, it may not always be a primary goal of youth activism. Rather, because the urban communities that youth live in are still shaped by racial and economic segregation and increased surveillance, being an activist means not only transforming that community but also transforming the paths that have been laid out for them as youth of color. As the youth suggest, activism may simply mean being *active* under these circumstances. Getting an education may be a form of activism in that it challenges anti-affirmative action laws that have significantly hindered youth of color's ability to do so in California. Then, by challenging the oppression around them—sometimes among staff, parents, and peers—youth challenge dominant discourse, which is rooted in civil rights progress. Because youth often describe their activities *as* activism, scholars need to continue to examine how others define not only activism but also their everyday life experiences post–civil rights.

While Foucault's analysis of power is useful to explain the landscape and contours of youth activism, others have rightly critiqued his theory because it allows him to envision a world, as Nancy Hartsock suggests, "in which things move, rather than people, a world in which subjects become obliterated or, rather, recreated as passive objects, a world in which passivity or refusal represent the only choices."[12] Instead, she calls for individuals to "recognize that we can be the makers of history as well as the objects of those who have made history."[13] Rather than being relegated to the status of passive subjects, the youth in this study act as both the objects of previous civil rights struggles as well as the subjects of a burgeoning youth movement—which Lana, Conrad, Eduardo, David, and Naseem talk about as a social movement. And these youth were not confused about their participation in the construction of history. They were building a movement, providing others with the tools to navigate the landscape they have been handed. What that movement looks like, how it is framed and how it operates may or may not look like the dominant construction of a social movement, itself both real and imagined. But the question of "newness" is no longer the question. The question now is whether the rest of us are going to join the fight. In the words of the rock band Rage Against the Machine, "You are the witness of change, and to counteract, we gotta take the power back."

APPENDIX
Notes on Navigating "the Field":
Insider Status, Authority, and Audience

Recently, I received a text from one of the participants in this book, with whom I have maintained contact since I conducted this research. The text read, "I'm having an identity crisis. How did you know you were into girls?" Since we met, when she was a teenager, and now as a young adult, she has entered into her first relationship with a woman. She has asked me much about my own experience over the last couple of years, as she has come to understand her "queer" identity. I answered back quickly and personally, suddenly reminded of the distance between the time I met her and the closeness between her experience as a young woman of color exploring her sexuality and my own. Her question also brings up three significant issues related to the methodological implications of this research. First, it relates directly to ethnographic discussions of "the field"; particularly the dilemmas associated with entry, being there, and ultimately leaving the field (see Burawoy 1991). Second, it evokes a discussion of temporality in ethnographic research, specifically a split between "activist time" and "academic time" (Geertz 1973; Clifford 1994).Finally, it also references important discussions of authority and adult status that are associated with ethnographic studies of youth (Best 2007; Taft 2007; Pascoe 2007; Fields 2008; Gray 2009). I consider all three of these discussions in this examination of the ethnographic implications of working with youth of color as a Black, queer, feminist.

Navigating the Field

Throughout this book, I have tried to highlight my particular race, class, gender, and sexuality status as it relates to key moments in the research. I came to this project out of an interest in combining my own personal, political, and academic interests in youth of color. I met Griselda through a mutual friend. The following week I was being introduced to the youth as someone who studied youth, activism, and hip-hop. I have written elsewhere about being raised on hip-hop as a Black teenager and the complications of remaining true to hip-hop culture as a young feminist (Clay 2007).Those years rushed back as I got to know the youth in this study. Outside of observing moments like the poetry slam or riding around in cars with the youth as we listened nonstop to hip-hop, I identified with much of the music the youth listened to, as well as the political discussions that ensued about hip-hop's relevance. My relationship to hip-hop was also questioned throughout my research. For instance, on the first day that I arrived at the Teen Justice meeting, Conrad approached me afterwards to see "what I knew about hip-hop," after having been introduced as someone who studied it. It was a genuine question, but also a moment of sizing up, seeing what kind of knowledge I would bring to the scene, maybe how "down" I was. I fumbled for some kind of answer, which didn't suffice at the time, and he, as well as many of the other youth at TJ, didn't interact much with me until months later.

In that first interaction, my authority and the trust I was able to establish with the youth was questioned and ultimately defined my relationship to those participants early on. For the first eight months at Teen Justice, I had a very traditional researcher role. I recorded weekly field notes on collaborative meetings and leadership meetings, which I later transcribed in more detail. In addition, I ran errands, volunteered for various events, and accompanied youth to different activities throughout the Bay Area. They viewed me as another adult in the scene, one, it seemed, they didn't trust very much. While I was routinely greeted with smiles and sometimes hugs, it wasn't until I had been observing there for a full year that I began conducting interviews with the participants. I was surprised that the majority of the tape-recorded interviews lasted close to two hours and were often quite personal, ranging from their political work to their coming out processes. With Conrad, Naseem, and Trisha, we laughed and joked throughout the time we were together, like old friends. In those instances, the interviews felt like conversations as I covered questions related to how they became involved in the organizations they worked with, whether they identified as activists, and their definitions of social change.

My relationship to the youth moved much more quickly at Multicultural Alliance, where I also worked as an employee. I stated in my interview that I was a conducting research at another organization and was interested in doing the same at MA. This role, at times, made it much easier for them to forget that I was a researcher. I took weekly field notes (sometimes more than once a week) at the workshops they facilitated and during their trainings. Although I established rapport with the youth fairly quickly, I didn't begin conducting interviews with them until I had worked with them for six months, as way to move beyond rapport to trust. However, I had almost the exact opposite experience at MA than I did at TJ; because the youth knew me so well, it was difficult for them to take the formal interviews seriously, reminding me of the various roles I took on in this research. For instance, Jasmine would laugh at some of my questions, telling me throughout most of the interview, "but you already know this stuff," while Lana spoke directly to the microphone during our interview saying, "do you all hear that out there?" and then turned to me and said, "be sure to put that in your book." In each setting, Teen Justice and Multicultural Alliance, I tried to navigate the various roles I inhabited at the same time that I sought to avoid the authority-establishing "having been there" moments that adult researchers studying youth inevitably encounter (see Taft 2007).

"Oh, so you're a _____"

Although I cannot (and would not) deny my role as an adult, authority figure, in the scene, that role was a bit more complicated as a queer woman of color. I was clearly an adult, and a supervisor in some cases, but I was also someone that they identified with, looked up to, and relied upon as a woman who came from a similar background as theirs. Perhaps because of these relationships, I have remained in touch with many of the youth from this study, through the organizations themselves; since this research formally ended in the summer of 2002. I have worked with Teen Justice in different capacities, as a community advisory member, a mentor, a volunteer, and a fund-raiser. Each of these roles, arguably, has muddied my objective authority since I "left" the field. But, it also points to an assumption that as researchers we actually ever leave the "field," or that it's even a possibility, especially when that field consists of our own activism, social statuses, and community. And, which fields are we talking about, specifically? Research? Activism? The social fields of race, gender, and sexuality? Those lines are not always clear and, in this instance, they often overlapped.

One of the key aspects of feminist ethnography is an examination of our role as researcher/outsider, even as we observe and participate (Collins 1989; Viswaseran 1994; Grindstaff 2002). Even as we have been encouraged to "start where we're at," many times we are also expected to maintain a somewhat outsider stance, knowing that we are not *really* part of the group that we study and that, eventually, we will leave the participants (Lofland and Lofland 1995). This is especially true in research studies of teenagers. Most of us maintain an adult status that is separate and distinct in that we have all both "been there," but are also in various stages of our distance from the category of youth (Best 2007; Taft 2007). As a researcher, my research goals were clear: two years observing specific events, and conducting formal and informal interviews. As an activist, my work with both organizations only ended recently. As a mentor and friend, my relationships have been ongoing—receiving texts, running into former "participants" at the university where I teach, on the street in my neighborhood, at conferences and, of course, on Facebook. I highlight these statues in an effort to demonstrate the difficulty in maintaining impenetrable boundaries around the field, authority, and knowledge.

I went into this research as an observer, a cultural worker, activist, and ally to youth, but also as a working-class, queer, Black woman. I found it difficult to separate myself out from the research and the youth that I studied. Not only did I live in Oakland, I traipsed around the same neighborhoods, the same coffee shops (later, the same bars), and went to the same protests as the youth. In some instances, I was also going through the same kinds of relationship woes as a queer woman in my twenties and early thirties. I fell in (and out) of love twice during the course of my research and made the decision to be open—sometimes it wasn't as much a decision as a negotiation—with the youth I was working with. I commiserated regularly with Achilles about dating other Black queer folks, talked to Jasmine and Frida about the importance of practicing safe sex as a woman having (or contemplating having) sex with other women, and was always challenged to answer honestly about whether or not I practiced what I preached. As someone who came out to my family much later in my late twenties, I was also grappling with some of the same struggles of coming out to my extended family that Xochitl, Monica, Achilles, and Frida described. As Juana María Rodríguez (2003), describes, the challenge of this writing and reflection then "becomes how to conceptualize subjectivity through both semiotic structures (discursive spaces) and agency (identity practices) by investigating the ways these fields work to constitute, inform, and transform one another" (Rodríguez 2003, 5). Writing this book has not only challenged my understanding of my relationship to the research, but also how (who) this text will be read. In conclusion, I consider the ethical implications involved with conducting research on a group I have been so intimately connected with on different levels and writing for a diverse, but still primarily white audience.

Who and When: Audience, Activism, and Temporality

Sociology, like other academic disciplines, has been informed by a heteropatriarchal approach to understanding race and racial identity, sexuality, gender, and an understanding of "the empirical subject." As Roderick Ferguson describes, "universalizing heteropatriarchy and understanding that universalization as whiteness and through American citizenship defined the core of sociological reflection about African American culture" (Ferguson 2004, 18). That lens continues to inform studies of people of color, queer bodies, and the scholars of color ourselves. How to conduct research, write about and reflect upon youth of color, queer youth, and my own queer body has been challenging in this context. I was first introduced to the discipline as a graduate student at the Center for Research on Women at the University of Memphis, where we were taught to critically examine how the intersections of race, class, gender, and sexuality informed our role as researchers and scholars. Central to every project and each class was a clear understanding of the ways that racism, capitalism and classism, sexism, and, to some degree heterosexism, contributed to the reading of people of color and white women in sociological theory and methodology. Therefore, it was our responsibility to participate in praxis, as an outsider within (Collins 1989). It was within this frame that I entered the field, collected and analyzed data and, eventually wrote this book.

As an outsider within the discipline and the field, I grappled with describing physical attributes of youth of color, and explaining details of their lives and backgrounds, which often mirrored media images of "urban youth" (an often default term for Black and Latino). Revealing conversations about Black people and the LGBTQ community that I had with Achilles, my own experiences straddled the line between "thick description" and insider status. And, while I write as an academic, I also write for the people that I studied (as much as they're interested) and other community activists. In this way, I aim to understand, as others have, how "the academy can contribute to social change efforts outside of university walls (Naples 1998, 6). Still, I have been confronted with established boundaries between academia and activism, time and space. For instance, participants have asked me, "when is the book coming out? We did that so long ago." Or, in response to things that have been central to my understanding of the work that the youth did, I have received an "Oh yeah, I forgot we did (or said) that." Both instances challenge and expose the "distinct temporal registers of past, present, and future" that exist between age, academia, and activism (Halberstam 2005, 78).

Questions of status, authority, temporality, and audience are ones that I hope scholar-activists/activist-scholars will continue to explore in their discussions of marginalized groups. I have examined my own struggles and successes with these questions in an effort to contribute to this discussion. And while our relationships to the participants, the field, and the work are not up for debate, *how* our identities and relationships to the methodological process construct our own and our readers' knowledge of our work, ultimately, should be.

NOTES

NOTES TO CHAPTER 1

1. See Mary Benson, *Nelson Mandela: The Man and the Movement* (New York: W. W. Norton, 1986).
2. See Sudhir Alladi Venkatesh, "Gender and Outlaw Capitalism: A Historical Account of the Black Sisters United 'Girl Gang,'" *Signs: Journal of Women in Culture and Society*. 23, no. 31 (1998): 683–709; and "The Social Organizations of Street Gang Activity in an Urban Ghetto," *American Journal of Sociology* 103, no. 1 (July 1997): 82–11; Andy Bennett, *Popular Music and Youth Culture: Music, Identity, and Place* (New York: Macmillan, 2000); Debra Gaines, *Teenage Wasteland: Suburbia's Dead End Kids* (New York: Pantheon Books 1991); Dick Hebdige, *Subculture: The Meaning of Style* (London: Routledge, 1979); George Lipsitz, "We Know What Time it is: Race, Class, and Youth Culture in the Nineties," in *Microphone Fiends*, ed. T. Rose and A. Ross. (New York: Routledge, 1994): 17–28; Angela McRobbie, *Feminism and Youth Culture: From Jackie to Just Seventeen* (London: Macmillan, 1991); Paul Willis, *Profane Culture* (London: Routledge and Kegan Paul, 1978).
3. See Jeff Chang *Can't Stop, Won't Stop* (New York: Macmillan, 2005); Nelson George *Hip Hop America* (New York: Penguin Books, 1999); Robin D. G. Kelley, *Freedom Dreams: The Black Radical Imagination* (New York: Free Press, 2003); Bakari Kitwana, *The Hip-Hop Generation: Young Blacks and the Crisis in African American Culture* (New York: Basic Civitas Books, 2002); Mary Pattillo-McCoy, *Black Picket Fences: Privilege and Peril Among the Black Middle Class* (Chicago: University of Chicago Press 1999).
4. Doug McAdam, *Freedom Summer* (Oxford: Oxford University Press, 1988); Aldon Morris, *The Origins of the Civil Rights Movement* (New York: Free Press, 1984); Sidney Tarrow, *Power in Movement: Social Movements and Contentious Politics* (Cambridge: Cambridge University Press, 1998); Benjamin Shepard and Richard Hayduk, *From ACT UP to the WTO: Urban Protest and Community Building in the Era of Globalization*, ed. B. Shepard and R. Hayduk (London: Verso, 2002).
5. A growing number of researchers have begun to study teenage political participation. For instance, see Hava Rachel Gordon, *We Fight to Win: Inequality and the Politics of Youth Activism* (New Brunswick: Rutgers University Press, 2009).
6. See Morris (1984)

7. Gamson, "Silence, Death and the Invisible Enemy: AIDS Activism and Social Movement 'Newness,'" *Social Problems* 36 (1989): 351–67.
8. Todd Gitlin, *Letters to A Young Activist* (New York: Basic Books, 2003): 20–21.
9. In *The Hip-Hop Generation*, Bakari Kitwana defines this generation as "Blacks born between 1965 and 1984" (Kitwana 2002, 27). Alternately, Jeff Chang's discussion of the generation questions these time and race brackets and includes a movement from "politics to culture" (Chang 2005, 2). Moreover, a narrow frame, ending in 1984 is insufficient, if one defines themselves as such. I fall in between these discussions and acknowledge the importance of being raised on hip-hop at the same time that the genre itself was growing up. I use this term to define the generation of people born after hip-hop became commercialized.
10. Pattillo-McCoy (1999), 93.
11. See Robert Charles Smith, *Racism in the Post–Civil Rights Era* (New York: SUNY Press, 1995); Eduardo Bonilla Silva, *White Supremacy and Racism in the Post–Civil Rights Era* (Boulder, CO: Lynne Rienner Publishers, 2001); Kitwana, *Hip-Hop Generation*; Ollie A. Johnson and Karin L. Sanford, *Black Political Organizations in the Post–Civil Rights Era* (New Brunswick: Rutgers University Press, 2002); Chang (2005).
12. As evidenced in the 2003 murder of fifteen-year-old Sakia Gunn, who was murdered while standing at a bus stop in New Jersey.
13. See Michel Foucault, *Discipline and Punish* (New York: Pantheon Books, 1977).
14. See Gamson (1989)
15. See William J. Wilson, *The Declining Significance on Race: Blacks and Changing American Institutions*, 2nd ed. (Chicago: University of Chicago Press, 1980); Douglas S. Massey and Nancy Denton, *American Apartheid: Segregation and the Making of the Underclass.* (Cambridge: Harvard University Press, 1993); Robin D. G. Kelley, *Race Rebels; Culture, Politics, and the Black Working Class* (New York: Free Press, 1994); Lipsitz 1994; Ann Arnett Ferguson, *Bad Boys: Public Schools in the Making of Black Masculinity* (Ann Arbor: University of Michigan Press, 2000); Mary Bucholz, "Youth and Cultural Practice," *Annual Review Anthropology* 31 (2002): 525–52.
16. See Robert O. Self, *American Babylon: Race and the Struggle for Postwar Oakland* (Princeton: Princeton University Press, 2003); Marie "Keta" Miranda, *Homegirls in the Public Sphere* (Austin: University of Texas Press, 2004).
17. Or, at any rate, this genre is supposed to reflect the lives of urban youth as myth and reality about the origins of hip-hop in urban areas of New York City attest. However, since its emergence, hip-hop has been commercialized, exploited, and redefined, effectively emptying the popular music, lyrics, and message of any political content.

18. See Bennett (2000); Todd Boyd, *Am I Still Black Enough for You?: Popular Culture From the 'Hood and Beyond* (Bloomington: Indiana University Press, 1990); George (1995); Lipsitz "We Know What Time It Is"; S. Craig Watkins, *Representing: Hip-Hop Culture and the Production of Black Cinema* (Chicago: University of Chicago Press, 1998).

19. Local hip-hop summits have been established in many cities the United States, including New York, Los Angeles, Atlanta, Seattle, Washington, DC, and Chicago. In 2003, Philadelphia's hip-hop summit effectively organized over 11,000 voters with an objective to register "two million more" in the 2004 election.

20. See Ryan Pintado-Bertner and Jeff Chang, "The War on Youth," *Alternet*, April 1 (2000); and Chang (2005); See also Victor Rios, "The Hyper-Criminalization of Black and Latino Male Youth in the Era of Mass Incarceration," *Souls: A Critical Journal of Black Politics, Culture, and Society* 8, no. 2 (2006): 40–54.

21. See Karl Marx, "Das Capital, vol. 1," in *The Marx-Engels Reader*, 2nd ed., Robert C. Tucker, ed. (New York: W. W. Norton, 1978).

22. See Dick Hebdige, *Subculture: The Meaning of Style* (London: Routledge, 1979) for an in-depth discussion of the conversion of subcultural signs into mass-produced objects, effectively rendering them as fashion.

23. Wimsatt (2002), 46.

24. Davis (1996), 90.

25. See Tarrow (1986).

26. Marita Sturken, *Tangled Memories: The Vietnam War, the AIDS Epidemic, and the Politics of Remembering*. See also Sturken, *Tourists of History: Memory, Kitsch, and Consumerism from Oklahoma City to Ground Zero* (Durham: Duke University Press, 2007).

27. Sturken (1997).

28. Ibid., 13–14.

29. George Lipsitz, *Time Passages: Collective Memory and American Popular Culture* (Minneapolis: University of Minnesota Press, 2001).

30. Robin D. G. Kelley, *Freedom Dreams: The Black Radical Imagination* (Boston: Beacon Press, 2002).

31. Michael Omi and Howard Winant, *Racial Formation in the United States: From the 1960s to the 1990s* (London: Routledge, 1996), 88.

32. Quoted in McAdam (1988), 12.

33. See DJ Kool Herc, "Introduction," to *Can't Stop, Won't Stop*, by Jeff Chang (2005), xi–xiii.

34. See Ann Swidler "Culture in Action: Symbols and Strategies," *American Sociological Review* 41, no. 2 (April 1986): 273–86.

35. See T. Denean Sharpley Whiting, *Pimps Up, Ho's Down: Hip Hop's Hold on Young Black Women* (New York: NYU Press, 2007) for a recent discussion on gender, misogyny, and hip-hop.

36. I use pseudonyms for the organizations, high schools and individuals in this study (with the exception of the city of Oakland and funding organizations) in an effort to protect the identities of the youth participants.
37. Burawoy (1991), 5.
38. The youth in this study range between thirteen and twenty-one years of age.
39. I conducted in-depth interviews with the adult site coordinator at Teen Justice and the executive director and program director at Multicultural Alliance. I also conducted informal interviews with adults not central to the scene, including teachers, community members, parents, other staff members, and board members.
40. See Anselm Strauss and Juliet Corbin. *Basics of Qualitative Research: Grounded Theory Procedures and Techniques* (Newbury Park, CA: Sage Publications, 1990).

NOTES TO CHAPTER 2

1. For an in-depth history of Oakland, see Elizabeth L. Bagwell, *Oakland: The Story of a City* (Oakland: Oakland Heritage Alliance, 1982). Also, see Robert O. Self, *American Babylon: Race and the Struggle for Postwar Oakland* (Oxford: Oxford University Press, 2005); and Christopher Rhomberg, *No There There: Race, Class, and Political Community in Oakland* (Berkeley: University of California Press, 2004).
2. See Bagwell (1982).
3. Ibid.
4. Blacks began moving into West Oakland because of its close proximity to the railroad and the shipping industry, which employed Blacks. Bagwell (1982).
5. Ibid., 206.
6. Since this study, Washington High School, like other schools in the area has undergone "small school reform," breaking up the traditional high school unit into smaller units.
7. Although I do not agree with the negative connotations associated with the words "ghetto" and "inner city," for the purposes of this project I use them to create a mental picture that we have internalized as people living in the United States.
8. In this study, I use the racial/ethnic identities that the participants used to describe themselves. *Xicano* (*Xi* is pronounced *Ch*) is an alternative spelling of *Chicano*, a political term for Mexican Americans.
9. Passed in 1994, Prop. 187 eliminated social benefits like medical care and public education to undocumented immigrants. This law also required public employees and law officials to report undocumented immigrants to the INS. In 1998 a U.S. district judge ruled Prop. 187 unconstitutional. In 1996 Prop. 209 was passed, which eliminated affirmative action in the state by outlawing "preferential treatment" for

individuals in public education or employment. California youth were actively involved in opposing both of these initiatives.

10. Legislative summary, Measure K, November 1996.
11. Mission Statement, Oakland Fund for Children and Youth (OFCY).
12. OFCY Evaluation Workshop Youth Development Assets Handout.
13. Ibid.
14. Ibid.
15. Ibid.
16. OFCY Youth Survey 2001–2002.
17. OFCY Evaluation Workshop Youth Development Assets Handout.
18. Program Overview, 4-H, http://4-h.org/
19. See Quentin Hoare and G. Nowell Smith, eds., *Selections from the Prison Notebooks of Antonio Gramsci* (New York: International Publishers and Lawrence and Wishart, 1971), 234.
20. McFarland and Reuben (2006).
21. See Amy Best, *Prom Night: Youth, Schools, and Popular Culture* (New York: Routledge, 2000).
22. Wheeler and Edelbeck (2006).
23. Ibid.
24. Mission Statement.
25. Handout, "Teen Justice Project Fact Sheet."
26. Bayview has its own city bus line that transports students twice a day from the flats to the hills.
27. Since the program wasn't fully developed at the time of their recruitment, staff members had individually recruited each of the youth. For instance, Deborah, one of the adult coordinators before Griselda, recruited Eduardo during a lunchtime informational meeting. In the beginning, Deborah and other adult coordinators recruited students by walking around the lunchroom, approaching students, and asking them if they were interested in joining an organization that addresses student needs and initiates change in the schools. Eduardo agreed and became one of the first members of the leadership team.
28. I was curious about and sat in on one of these interview processes, which consisted of the potential members answering such questions as "Why do you want to be a member of Teen Justice," "How do you define leadership," and "What will you get out of being a core member?" demonstrating a commitment to leadership and individual change. At times, the process was also fairly light, as potential members were also asked questions like, "What kind of music do you listen to," and "What is your favorite soda?"
29. Bayview's total student population was more than 2,000 at the time of this study. The racial/ethnic breakdown of students was 43 percent African American, 24 percent Asian, 19 percent Latino/Hispanic, and 11 percent white. Over 45 percent of the students were identified as "economically disadvantaged."

30. Handout, Youth Center Business Plan.
31. I worked as a part-time program coordinator, which helped facilitate my research process at Multicultural Alliance. Other staff included the program director, Margaret, and Ze, the executive director.
32. Vision Statement.
33. William Upski Wimsatt, "My Generation: A Young Visionary Sizes Up the Emerging Youth Movement." *Utne Reader* 113, September/October (2002): 46–47.

NOTES TO CHAPTER 3

1. Kevin Weston "Youth Work Together to Address Racism," in Jinn (1999). <http://www.pacificnews.org/jinn>.
2. Jason Ma, "East Bay Youths Fight Violence Together," *Asianweek* 21, no. 5, September 23, 1999.
3. Ness (2004); Venkatesh (1997; 1998).
4. I use Kimberle Crenshaw's definition of violence, described in "Mapping the Intersectionality, Identity, and Violence Against Women of Color," *Stanford Law Review* 3 no. 46 (July 1991): 1241–99. Here, she describes the domestic violence that women of color experience in their relationships as similar to the violence embedded in the intersection of institutionalized oppressions of racism, sexism, classism, and, often, citizenship status.
5. See Verta Taylor, "Social Movement Continuity: The Women's Movement in Abeyance," *American Sociological Review* (1989). Also, Traci M. Sawyers and David S. Meyer, "Missed Opportunities: Social Movement Abeyance and Public Policy," *Social Problems* (1999); and David S. Meyer and Nancy Whittier, "Social Movement Spillover," *Social Problems* 41 (1994): 277–98.
6. See Michael K. Brown, Martin Carnoy, Elliott Currie, Troy Duster, David B. Oppenheimer, Marjorie M. Shultz, and David Wellman, *Whitewashing Race: The Myth of a Color-Blind Society* (Berkeley: University of California Press, 2003).
7. Ibid.
8. See Verta Taylor, "Social Movement Continuity: The Women's Movement in Abeyance," *American Sociological Review* 54, no. 5 (1989): 761–75.
9. See, among others, Niko Koppel, "Are Your Pants Saggin'? Go Directly to Jail," *New York Times*, August 30, 2007. Several states, like Arkansas, have recently banned sagging pants in schools.
10. Bonilla-Silva (2002), 194.
11. See Patricia Hill Collins, *Black Sexual Politics: African Americans, Gender, and the New Racism* (New York: Routledge, 2005), 55.
12. See Patricia Hill Collins, *From Black Power to Hip-Hop: Racism, Nationalism, and Feminism* (Philadelphia: Temple University Press, 2006), 3–4.

13. This is especially true in hip-hop culture, where African American rappers are rewarded with celebrity status because of their participation in perpetuating images of African American men as "gangstas" or "pimps." For an in-depth discussion of this phenomenon, see also S. Craig Watkins, *Representing: Hip-Hop Culture and the Production of Black Cinema* (Chicago: University of Chicago Press, 1998).

14. His flip statement points to the reality of this generation of African Americans who have been significantly shaped by the evolution of crack cocaine in urban communities. Whether real or imagined connections, as Achilles suggests, there aren't many Black people who don't know about crack. Also, see Richard Iton, *In Search of the Black Fantastic: Politics and Popular Culture in the Post–Civil Rights Era* (Oxford: Oxford University Press, 2008).

15. See specifically, "Performing Disidentity: Disidentification as a Practice of Freedom," in Jose Esteban Muñoz, *Disidentifications: Queers of Color and the Performance of Politics* (Minneapolis: University of Minnesota Press, 1999), 161–79.

16. Ibid., 11–12.

17. http://www.acri.org/209_argument_for.html

18. Taken from the title of hip-hop group Dead Prez's "They Schools," which critiques white racism in education, from a personal and political standpoint. The chorus repeats "They schools don't teach us shit, my people need freedom, we tryin' to get all we can get. All my high school teachers can suck my dick, telling me white man lies straight bullshit. They schools ain't teachin' us what we need to know to survive. They schools don't educate, all they teach the people is lies."

19. Collins (2006), 48.

20. K. Gwynne Coburn and Pamela A. Riley, "Failing Grade: Crisis and Reform in the Oakland Unified School District" (Harvard Civil Rights Project, July 2000). These rates disproportionately affect students of color. While California dropout rates are around 24 percent, the rates for Black youth are 41 percent, Native Americans 31 percent, Latinos 30 percent, and Pacific Islanders at 28 percent.

21. Xochitl was a freshman at the time of this study.

22. See Michel Foucault, *Discipline and Punish* (New York: Random House, 1977), 202.

23. Ibid., 200–201.

24. Montclair is an Oakland neighborhood east of Piedmont. It is home to Montclair Village, an upscale shopping district.

25. Foucault (1977), 200–201.

26. See Robin D. G. Kelley's in-depth discussion of urban Black males in "Kickin' Reality, Kickin' Ballistics: Gangsta Rap and Post-Industrial Los Angeles," in *Race Rebels: Culture, Politics and the Black Working Class* (New York: Simon and Schuster, 1994), where he argues for an understanding of contemporary Black manhood that is distinct from previous

generations. Cornel West evokes a similar discussion of nihilism in the Black community in *Race Matters* (New York: Vintage Press, 1994). Also, see Ann Arnett Ferguson, *Bad Boys: Public Schools in the Making of Black Masculinity* (Ann Arbor: University of Michigan Press, 2000).

27. See Aldon Morris, "The Black Church in the Civil Rights Movement: The SCLC as the Decentralized, Radical Arm of the Black Church," and Bobby Seale, *Seize the Time: The Story of the Black Panther Party and Huey P. Newton* (Baltimore, MA: Black Classic Press, 1996).

28. Cornel West describes an increasing nihilism, particularly evident in Black communities, demonstrated by a "lived experience of coping with a life of horrifying meaningless, hopelessness, and most important, lovelessness . . . result[ing] i[n] a numbing detachment from others and a self-destructive disposition toward the world." See West, *Race Matters*.

29. See Robin D. G. Kelley, *Race Rebels: Culture, Politics, and the Black Working Class* (New York: Free Press): 210.

NOTES TO CHAPTER 4

1. Dead Prez, "They Schools," *Let's Get Free*. Audio CD.

2. Of course, not all of hip-hop does this; many explicitly political hip-hop groups like Dead Prez, The Coup, and Talib Kweli have not achieved the commercial success of artists like Jay Z, 50 Cent, and Lil Wayne.

3. See Angela Ards, "Organizing the Hip-Hop Generation," in *That's the Joint!: The Hip-Hop Studies Reader*, ed. M. Forman and M. A. Neal. (New York: Routledge, 2004): 25–26. Chang (2005); George H. Lewis, "Social Protest and Self-Awareness in Black Popular Music," *Popular Music and Society* 2, no. 4 (1973): 327–33.; Kitwana (2002); S. Craig Watkins, *Hip Hop Matters: Politics, Pop Culture, and the Struggle for Soul* (New York: Beacon Press, 2005).

4. See Ron Eyerman and Scott Baretta "From the '30s to the '60s: The Folk Music Revival in the United States," *Theory and Society* 25, no. 4 (August 1996): 501–43.

5. Although the body of work is vast, for an introduction to studies on the relationship between youth and hip-hop culture see, among others, Andreana Clay, "Keepin' It Real: Black Youth, Hip-Hop Culture and Black Identity, *American Behavioral Scientist* 46, no. 10 (June 2003): 1346–58; Jeff Chang *Can't Stop, Won't Stop: A History of the Hip-Hop Generation* (New York: Picador Press, 2005); George Lipsitz, "We Know What Time It Is: Race, Class, and Youth Culture in the Nineties," in *Microphone Fiends*, ed. T. Rose and A. Ross (New York: Routledge, 1994): 17–28; Tricia Rose, *Black Noise Rap Music and Black Culture in Contemporary America* (Middletown, CT: Wesleyan University Press, 1994); and S. Craig Watkins, "Black Youth and the Ironies of Capital-

ism," in *Representing: Hip-Hop Culture and the Production of Black Cinema* (Chicago: University of Chicago Press, 1998).

6. See Todd Boyd, *The New H.N.I.C (Head Niggas in Charge): The Death of Civil Rights and the Reign of Hip-Hop* (New York: NYU Press, 2002); Jeff Chang, *Can't Stop, Won't Stop*; Bakari Kitwana, *Why White Kids Love Hip-Hop: Wankstas, Wiggers, Wannabes, and the New Reality of Race in America.* (New York: Basic Civitas Books, 2006); Tricia Rose, *Hip-Hop Wars*; T. Denean Sharpley-Whiting, *Pimps Up, Ho's Down: Hip-Hop's Hold on Young Black Women* (New York: NYU Press, 2007); and S. Craig Watkins, *Hip-Hop Matters: Politics, Pop Culture, and the Struggle for Soul* (New York: Beacon Press, 2005).

7. See Rosalinda Fregoso, *The Bronze Screen* (Minneapolis: University of Minnesota Press, 1993).

8. See Gary Alan Fine (1995); Joshua Gamson (1989); Anne Kane "Theorizing Meaning Construction in Social Movements: Symbolic Structures and Interpretation during the Irish Land War, 1879–1882," *Sociological Theory* 15, no. 3 (November 1997): 249–76; David Román (1996); and Ann Swidler (1986).

9. Boyd, *The New H.N.I.C* (2002); see also Epstein, *Impure Science* (1997).

10. Stephen Duncombe, *The Cultural Studies Reader* (New York: Verso Press 2002), 5–6.

11. All of the youth in this study were born after MTV was launched in 1981.

12. See Stuart Hall, "What Is This 'Black' in Black Popular Culture?" *Social Justice* 20, no. 1–2 (Spring-Summer 1993): 104–15.

13. See Paul Gilroy "'After the Love Has Gone': Bio-Politics and Etho-Poetics in the Black Public Sphere," in *Back to Reality?: Social Experience and Cultural Studies*, ed. A. McRobbie (Manchester: Manchester University Press, 1997):,92.

14. Tupac Shakur 1998. "Changes." *Greatest Hits*. Audio CD.

15. Michael Eric Dyson, *Holler if You Hear Me: Searching for Tupac Shakur* (New York: Basic Civitas Books, 2001). Also, Sam Brown and Kris Ex, eds., *Tupac: A Thug Life* (New York: Plexus Press, 2005); Derek Iwamoto, "Tupac Shakur: Understanding the Identity Formation of Hyper-Masculinity of a Popular Hip-Hop Artist" *The Black Scholar* 33, no. 2: 44–49; Armound White, *Tupac: Rebel for the Hell of It* (New York: Thunder's Mouth Press).

16. Dyson (2001), 138.

17. See Bakari Kitwana, *The Hip-Hop Generation: Young Blacks and the Crisis in African-American Culture* (New York: Basic Civitas Books, 2000); Mark Anthony Neal, *Soul Babies: Black Popular Culture and the Post-Soul Aesthetic* (New York: Routledge, 2002); Imani Perry, *Prophets of the 'Hood: Politics and Poetics in Hip-Hop* (Durham: Duke University Press, 2004).

18. Rose (2008).
19. The lyrics go on to say "these teachers can 'suck my dick,'" which Trisha wouldn't finish.
20. Tupac spent his high school years in Marin City, California, but many, perhaps because of his involvement with Digital Underground, claim him as an Oakland native.
21. Rose (2008), 142.
22. Fregoso (1993), 665.
23. Lipsitz (1994), 36.
24. See Robin D. G. Kelley (1994); Rose (1994); and Chang (2005).
25. See Joan Morgan, *When Chickenheads Come Home to Roost: A Hip-Hop Feminist Breaks It Down* (New York: Simon and Schuster, 1999); Gwendolyn Pough, *Check It While I Wreck It: Black Women, Hip-Hop and the Public Sphere* (Middletown, CT: Wesleyan University Press, 2004); and T. Denean Sharpley-Whiting, *Pimps Up! Ho's Down: Hip-Hop's Hold on Young Black Women* (New York: NYU Press, 2007) for an introduction to this discussion.
26. Erving Goffman, *The Presentation of Self in Everyday Life* (New York: Penguin Books, 1959).
27. Cash Money is a record label that houses such artists as Lil' Wayne, Mack 10, Juvenile, and Bow Wow.
28. Many point to this time as the release of "Rapper's Delight" in 1979. See S. Craig Watkins for a detailed discussion of the nuances of this debate in *Hip Hop Matters* (New York: Henry Holt, 2005).
29. A Tribe Called Quest, "Check the Rhime," *The Low End Theory*. Jive Records, 1991.
30. See Robin D. G. Kelley (1994) for an in-depth discussion of the relationship between American values and hip-hop music.
31. A recent *New York Times* article showcased the Def Poetry Jam, the first hip-hop event on Broadway. Def Poetry Jam is a competitive poetry event produced by the Def Jam record label founder Russell Simmons. When asked why hip-hop was making its debut on Broadway, Simmons explained, that "If I'm in a high school in the ghetto right now and I ask, 'Who writes poetry?' or 'How many of you have a book of rhymes?' 80 percent of the class raises their hands."
32. According to Poetry Slam International (www.poetryslam.com), slam poetry is the "competitive art" of poetry performance. It puts a dual emphasis on writing and performance, encouraging performers to focus on what they're saying and how they say it.
33. www.youthspeaks.org.
34. Macmillan (2002).
35. Bling-bling often refers the flashy, expensive style of some hip-hop artists. This style includes expensive jewelry, cars, clothing, etc.
36. See Eyerman and Baretta (1996) and Fregoso (1993).

37. See Cathy J. Cohen, "Punks, Bulldaggers, and Welfare Queens: The Radical Potential of Queer Politics?" *GLQ: A Journal of Gay and Lesbian Studies* 3, no. 4 (1997): 437–65.

NOTES TO CHAPTER 5

1. Gloria Anzaldúa, *Borderlands/La Frontera: The New Mestiza* (San Francisco: Aunt Lute Books, 1987).
2. "That's What America Is," speech given on Gay Freedom Day in San Francisco, as quoted in Randy Shilts, *The Mayor of Castro Street: The Life and Times of Harvey Milk* (New York: St. Martin's Press, 1982).
3. I am not sure what attracted queer youth to each organization. I sat in on the interview process for the youth at Multicultural Alliance, and it wasn't a part of their recruitment strategies or youth that they targeted. Chris and Achilles were in their final year at the organization, and, as Achilles suggests, both came out in the context of Multicultural Alliance. Both Ze and Margaret were open about their sexual orientation as heterosexual and lesbian, which provided a safe space for the youth, but it wasn't clear that this was a motivating factor in the youth participating in the organization. This was similar at Teen Justice, where fewer of the youth identified as queer, but all of the youth were aware that Griselda had a girlfriend.
4. I had to look up his quote later to understand what he meant (see Gen. 38:9).
5. Others came out later on, after this study, including Lana. And, several years later, Chris began to identify as male, transgender, or female to male (FTM).
6. This is changing to some degree: with reality television shows and cable television with more and more queer characters of color. MTV, as always, has emerged as the frontrunner, with shows that feature characters like the bisexual Tila Tequila, "regular" queer folks on the *Real World* and *Road Rules,* as well as some representation on mainstream shows like the *L Word*'s Bette and later, Tasha, and the first kiss that Will had on *Will and Grace* with Taye Diggs's short-lived character. Still few, if any of these characters (including Tequila) are politically identified, and most notably for the hip-hop generation, there are no "out" hip-hoppers, although there is much speculation, leaving the representation of queer people of color that these youth identified with practically nil.
7. See Sharon P. Holland, *Raising the Dead: Readings of Death and (Black) Subjectivity* (Durham: Duke University Press, 2000).
8. See Charles I. Nero, "Why Are Gay Ghettoes White?" in *Black Queer Studies: A Critical Anthology,* ed. E. P. Johnson and M. G. Henderson (Durham: Duke University Press, 2005): 228–48.

9. Mary L. Gray, *Out in the Country: Youth, Media, and Queer Visibility in Rural America* (New York: NYU Press, 2009).

10. There have been significant, though limited, images of LGBTQ people of color in popular culture in the past decade. For instance, Tila Tequila, a presumed bisexual protagonist on her television show, *A Shot At Love with Tila Tequila* on MTV, in which sixteen lesbians and sixteen straight men vied for her love in a dating contest. Other visible celebrities include Wanda Sykes, an African American who recently came out as part of the protest of Prop. 8, the California proposition against same-sex marriage.

11. In California, the Gay-Straight Alliance Network allows GSAs to stay connected to one another via http://gsanetwork.org/.

12. Mission Statement, Gay Lesbian Straight Education Network (GLSEN), which created the Gay/Straight Alliance. For more information visit: www.glsen.org.

13. See Tina Fetner and Anna Kush, "Gay-Straight Alliances in High Schools: Social Predictors of Early Adoption," *Youth Society* 40 (2008):114–32; and Stephen Russell et al., "Youth Empowerment and High School Gay-Straight Alliances," *Journal of Youth Adolescence* 38 (January 2009): 891–903.

14. Fetner and Kush (2008), 118.

15. Russell et al. (2009), 893.

16. See C. J. Pascoe, *Dude! You're a Fag: Adolescent Masculinity and Fag Discourse* (Berkeley: University of California Press, 2007).

17. Pascoe (2007), 60.

18. See Vito Russo and Rob Epstein, *The Celluloid Closet* (Sony Pictures Classics, 1995).

19. Similar to the post–civil rights era, post-Stonewall may be referred to as the historical moment after the Stonewall riots at the Stonewall Bar on June 28, 1969, in New York City. These riots are credited, of course, with the spark of the contemporary Gay Rights/Gay Liberation Movement in the United States. Post-Stonewall, in this sense refers to the LGBTQ social movement since that time as well as recent developments that have significantly shaped the LGBTQ community, including the AIDS epidemic and movement, the establishment of "out" gay neighborhoods like the Castro, increased gay visibility, and the younger and younger process of coming out for LGBTQ teens. See John D'Emilio, *Making Trouble: Essays on Gay History, Politics, and the University* (New York: Routledge, 1992), among others, for further discussion of this moment.

20. See Judith Warner, "Dude, You've Got Problems," *New York Times*, April 16, 2009.

21. Gray (2009), 122.

22. "The Life of Pedro Zamora: From MTV to the Big Screen," *Living Out Loud with Darian* blog. February 23, 2009. Retrieved December 4, 2008.

23. Ronnie Antonio Paris was a three-year-old African American boy who died of severe brain trauma as a result of his father "teaching him how to box." During the father's trial, Ronnie's mother testified that his father suspected his three-year-old was gay and wanted to toughen him up.
24. Goffman (1959), 4.
25. Román (1998), 101.
26. See Tanisha Alston, "Ivan Matias: Hip-Hop's Secret Trapped in the Closet," *All Hip-Hop.com* (2007): May.
27. "Gay Rapper Exposed as Fraud," Entertainment News, *Advocate,* May 12, 2007.
28. See E. Patrick Johnson, "Quare Studies," in *Black Queer Studies: A Critical Anthology*, ed. E. P. Johnson and M. G. Henderson (Durham: Duke University Press, 2005), 125–57.
29. At the same time, the number of suicides and bullying on the part of LGBTQ youth is often reported and focused on by the media as it relates to boys.
30. These assumptions are exemplified in news headlines, for example, "Do We Still Need Affirmative Action?" a *Newsweek* cover in January 2003, as well as the current media frenzy over same-sex marriage and recognition of same sex marriage and/or civil unions in states like New York, Iowa, and Connecticut.

NOTES TO CHAPTER 6

1. See Doug McAdam and Ronelle Paulsen, "Specifying the Relationship between Social Ties and Activism," *American Journal of Sociology* 99 (1993): 640–67; Aldon Morris, *The Origins of the Civil Rights Movement* (New York: Free Press, 1984); and Belinda Robnett, *How Long? How Long? African American Women in the Struggle for Civil Rights* (Oxford: Oxford University Press, 1997).
2. During the first decade of the twenty-first century, Teen Justice, began working with other, local youth organizations around different social justice issues in the community.
3. Since this study, MA developed a summer program that focused on various leaders and their philosophies. For instance, one of the first "visionaries, that they focused on was Mahatma Gandhi.
4. New social movement theories analyze recent social movements as a departure from a traditional approach focused on revolution as the primary goal of collective action. See Epstein (1998); Anne Kane (1997); Alberto Melucci, "A Strange Kind of Newness: What's 'New' in New Social Movements?" in *New Social Movements: From Ideology to Identity*, ed. E. Larana, H. Johnston, and J. R. Gusfield, 249–76 (Philadelphia: Temple University Press, 1994); and Belinda Robnett (1997) for an outline of new social movements, identity, and culture.

5. Melucci (1994).
6. See McAdam and Paulsen (1993).
7. Robnett (1997), 19.
8. See Morris (1984).
9. See Mary Bernstein, "Celebration and Suppression: The Strategic Uses of Identity by the Gay and Lesbian Movement. *American Journal of Sociology* 103, no. 3 (November 1997): 561.
10. Epstein (1998), 21.
11. Ibid.
12. See Neil J. Smelser, *Theory of Collective Behavior* (New York: Free Press of Glencoe, 1963).
13. Nancy Naples, *Community Activism and Feminist Politics: Organizing Across Race, Class, and Gender* (London: Routledge), 1998.
14. Verta Taylor, *Rock-a-By Baby: Feminism, Self-Help, and Postpartum Depression* (New York: Routledge, 1996), 20.
15. Combahee River Collective, "A Black Feminist Statement," in *This Bridge Called My Back*, ed. G. Anzaldúa and C. Moraga (New York: Kitchen Table Press, 1981 [1977]), 213–14.
16. bell hooks, *Feminism: From Margin to Center* (Boston: South End Press, 1984), 161, emphasis added.

NOTES TO CHAPTER 7

1. Jennifer Steinhauer, "Road to November: The Youth Vote in Pennsylvania," *New York Times,* October 13, 2008.
2. See Obama's Victory Speech, transcript, *New York Times*, November 5, 2008.
3. See Mat Bai. "Post-Race: Is Obama the End of Black Politics?" *New York Times Magazine,* August 6, 2008.
4. Ibid.
5. See, "Issue of Race Grows With Obama in the Lead," *MSNBC* News, December 2008.
6. See also Hava Gordon, "Gendered Paths to Political Participation," *Gender and Society*, 22, no. 1 (2008): 31–55; Shawn Ginwright and Taj James, "From Assets to Agents of Change: Social Justice, Organizing, and Youth Development," *New Directions for Youth Development* 96 (Winter, 2002): 27–46.
7. Multicultural Alliance has since closed but still operates as an online discussion board. Teen Justice is still going strong, with assets of $1.5 million, youth centers on several Bay Area high school campuses, and leading community social justice campaigns.
8. See Jeff Chang (2005), for a vivid description of this process by deejays Kool Herc and others in the early days of hip-hop. See also Nelson George, "Sample This," in *That's the Joint!,* ed. M. Forman and M. A. Neal (New York: Routledge, 2004).

9. Joseph G. Schloss, *Making Beats: The Art of Sample-Based Hip-Hop* (Middletown, CT: Wesleyan University Press, 2004). 139.

10. Ibid., 138.

11. Imani Perry, *Prophets of the 'Hood: Politics and Poetics in Hip-Hop* (Durham: Duke University Press, 2004), 203.

12. See Nancy Hartsock, "Foucault on Power: A Theory for Women?" in *Feminism/Postmodernism*, ed. L. Nicholson (New York: Routledge, 1990), 157–75.

13. Ibid.

BIBLIOGRAPHY

A Tribe Called Quest. 1991. "Check the Rhime." *The Low End Theory*. Jive Records.

Alston, Tanisha. 2007. "Ivan Matias: Hip-Hop's Secret Trapped in the Closet." *All Hip Hop.Com*. May.

Andes, Linda. 1998 "Growing Up Punk: Meaning and Commitment Careers in a Contemporary Youth Subculture." *Youth Culture: Identity in A Postmodern World*, edited by J. Epstein. Walnut Creek, CA: Blackwell Publishing, 212–31.

Anderson, Benedict. *Imagined Communities: Reflections on the Origin and Spread of Nationalism*. London: Verso.

Anzaldúa, Gloria. 1987. *Borderlands: La Frontera*. San Francisco: Aunt Lute Books.

Ards, Angela. 2004. "Organizing the Hip-Hop Generation." In *That's the Joint: The Hip-Hop Studies Reader*, edited by M. Forman and M. A. Neal. New York: Routledge Press, 25–26.

Badu, Erykah. 1997. "The Other Side of the Game." *Baduizm*. Universal.

Bagwell, Elizabeth L. 1982. *Oakland: The Story of a City*. Oakland: Oakland Heritage Alliance.

Bai, Matt. 2008. "Post-Race: Is Obama the End of Black Politics?" *New York Times Magazine*, August 6.

Blackwell, Maylei. 2003. "*Cuauhtémoc*, Chicana Feminisms, and Print Culture in the Chicano Movement, 1968–1973." In *Chicana Feminisms: A Reader*, edited by G. F. Arredondo, A. Hurtado, N. Klahn, O. Nájera-Ramírez, and P. Zavella, 59–89. Durham: Duke University Press.

Bennett, Andy. 2000. *Popular Music and Youth Culture: Music, Identity, and Place*. New York: Macmillan.

Benson, Mary. 1986. *Nelson Mandela: The Man and the Movement*. New York: W. W. Norton.

Bernstein, Mary. 1997. "Celebration and Suppression: The Strategic Uses of Identity by the Gay and Lesbian Movement. *American Journal of Sociology* 103, no. 3 (November): 531–65.

Best, Amy L. 2000. *Prom Night: Schools: Youth, Schools, and Popular Culture*. New York: Routledge Press.

———. 2007. *Representing Youth: Methodological Issues in Critical Youth Studies*. New York: NYU Press.

Bonilla-Silva, Eduardo. 2006. *Racism Without Racists: Color-blind Racism and the Persistence of Racial Inequality in the United States*. 2nd ed. Lanham, MD: Rowman and Littlefield.

Boyd, Andrew. 2002. "Irony, Meme Warfare, and the Extreme Costume Ball." In *From ACT UP to the WTO: Urban Protest and Community Building in the Era of Globalization*, edited by B. Shepard and R. Hayduk, 245–53. London: Verso.

Boyd, Todd. 1994. *Am I Black Enough For You?* Bloomington: Indiana University Press.

———. 2002. *The New H.N.I.C (Head Niggas in Charge): The Death of Civil Rights and the Reign of Hip-Hop*. New York: NYU Press.

Brown, Elaine. 1992. *A Taste of Power: A Black Woman's Story*. New York: Pantheon Books.

Brown, Michael K., Martin Carnoy, Elliott Currie, Troy Duster, David Oppenheimer, B. Shultz, Marjorie M. Schultz, and David Wellman. 2003. *Whitewashing Race: The Myth of a Color-Blind Society*. Berkeley: University of California Press.

Bucholz, Mary. 2002. "Youth and Cultural Practice." *Annual Review Anthropology* 31: 525–52.

Burawoy, Michael. 1991. *Ethnography Unbound: Power and Resistance in the Modern Metropolis*. Berkeley: University of California Press.

Butler, Judith. 1991. *Gender Trouble: Feminism and the Subversion of Identity*. New York: Routledge.

Bynoe, Yvonne. 2004. *Stand and Deliver: Political Activism, Leadership, and Hip Hop Culture*. Brooklyn, NY: Soft Skull Press.

Carter, Shawn. 1999. "Public Service Announcement." *The Black Album*. Def Jam Recordings.

Chang, Jeff. 2005. *Can't Stop, Won't Stop: A History of the Hip-Hop Generation*. New York: Picador Press.

Clay, Andreana. 2003. "Keepin' It Real: Black Youth, Hip-Hop Culture, and Black Identity." *American Behavioral Scientist* 46, no. 10 (June): 1346–58.

———. 2007. "'I Used to be Scared of the Dick': Queer Women of Color: Hip-Hop, and Black Masculinity." In *Home Girls Make Some Noise!: Hip-Hop Feminism Anthology*, edited by G. D. Pough, E. Richardson, A. Dusham, and R. Raimist, 149–65. Monroe, CA.: Parker Publishing.

Cloward, Richard A., and Lloyd E. Ohlin. 1966. *Delinquency and Opportunity: A Theory of Delinquent Gangs*. New York: Free Press.

Coburn, K. Gwynne, and Pamela A. Riley. 2000. "Failing Grade: Crisis and Reform in the Oakland Unified School District." Harvard Civil Rights Project. July.

Cohen, Cathy J. 1997. "Punks, Bulldaggers, and Welfare Queens: The Radical Potential of Queer Politics?" *GLQ: A Journal of Gay and Lesbian Studies* 3, no. 4: 437–65.

———. 1999. *The Boundaries of Blackness: AIDS and the Breakdown of Black Politics*. Chicago: University of Chicago Press.

Collins, Patricia Hill. 1986. "A Comparison of Two Works on Black Family Life." *Signs* 14, no. 4 (Summer): 875–84.

———. 2005. *Black Sexual Politics: African Americans, Gender, and the New Racism*. New York: Routledge.

———. 2006. *From Black Power to Hip-Hop:* Philadelphia: Temple University Press.

Combahee River Collective. 1981 [1977]. "Combahee River Collective Statement." In *This Bridge Called My Back*, edited by C. Moraga and G. Anzaldúa. New York: Kitchen Table Press.

Davis, Angela. 1996. "Afro Images: Politics, Fashion and Nostalgia." In *Names We Call Home*, edited by B. Thompson and S. Tyagi. New York: Routledge: 87–91.

Dead Prez. 2000. "Behind Enemy Lines." *Let's Get Free*. Loud Records.

Duncombe, Stephen. 2002. *Cultural Resistance Reader*. London: Verso.

Dyson, Michael Eric. 2001. *Holler if You Hear Me: Searching for Tupac Shakur*. New York: Basic Civitas Books.

Epstein, Jonathan, ed. 1998. *Youth Culture: Identity in a Postmodern World*. Malden, MA: Blackwell Publishing.

Epstein, Steven. 1998. *Impure Science: AIDS, Activism, and the Politics of Knowledge*. Berkeley: University of California Press.

Eyerman, Ron, and Scott Baretta. 1996. "From the '30s to the '60s: The Folk Music Revival in the United States. *Theory and Society* 25, no. 4 (August): 501–43.

Ferguson, Ann Arnett. 2000. *Bad Boys: Public Schools in the Making of Black Masculinity*. Ann Arbor: University of Michigan Press.

Ferguson, Roderick. 2004. *Aberrations in Black: Toward a Queer of Color Critique*. Minneapolis: University of Minnesota Press.

Fetner, Tina, and Kristin Kush. 2008. "Gay-Straight Alliances in High Schools: Social Predictors of Early Adoption." *Youth Society* 40:114–32.

Fields, Jessica. 2008. *Risky Lessons: Sex Education and Social Inequality*. New Brunswick: Rutgers University Press.

Fine, Gary Alan. 1995. "Public Narration and Group Culture: Discerning Discourse in Social Movements." In *Social Movements and Culture*, edited by H. Johnston and B. Klandermans, 127–43. Minneapolis: University of Minnesota Press.

Foucault, Michel. 1977. *Discipline and Punish*. New York: Random House.

Fregoso, Rosalinda. 1993. *The Bronze Screen: Chicana and Chicano Film Culture*. Minneapolis: University of Minnesota Press.

Freire, Paulo. *Pedagogy of the Oppressed*. New York: Continuum Press.

Gaines, Donna. 1991. *Teenage Wasteland: Suburbia's Dead End Kids*. New York: Pantheon Books.

Gamson, Josh. 1995. "Must Identity Movements Self-Destruct?: A Queer Dilemma." *Social Problems* 42, no. 3: 390–407.

———.1989. "Silence, Death and the Invisible Enemy: AIDS Activism and Social Movement 'Newness.'" *Social Problems* 36:351–67.

George, Nelson. 1999. *Hip Hop America*. New York: Penguin Books.

———. 2004. "Sample This." In *That's the Joint!*, edited by M. Forman and M. A. Neal, 504–9. New York: Routledge.

Geertz, Clifford. 1973.*The Interpretation of Cultures*. New York: Basic Books,

Gilroy, Paul. 1997. "'After the Love Has Gone': Bio-Politics and Etho-Poetics in the Black Public Sphere." In *Back to Reality?: Social Experience and Cultural Studies*, edited by A. McRobbie, 83–115. Manchester: Manchester University Press.

Gitlin, Todd. 2003. *Letters to a Young Activist*. New York: Basic Books.

Goffman, Erving. 1959. *The Presentation of Self in Everyday Life*. Garden City, NY: Doubleday.

Gordon, Hava Rachel. 2009. *We Fight to Win: Inequality and the Politics of Youth Activism*. New Brunswick: Rutgers University Press.

Gray, Mary L. 2009. *Out in the Country: Youth, Media, and Queer Visibility in Rural America*. New York: NYU Press.

Grindstaff, Laura. 2002. *The Money Shot: Trash, Class, and the Making of TV Talk Shows*. Chicago: University of Chicago Press.

Halberstam, Judith. 2005. *In a Queer Time and Place: Transgender Bodies, Subcultural Lives*. New York: NYU Press.

Hall, Stuart. 1993. "What is this 'Black' in Black Popular Culture?" *Social Justice* 20, no. 1–2 (Spring-Summer): 104–15.

Hartsock, Nancy. 1990. "Foucault on Power: A Theory for Women?" In *Feminism/Postmodernism*, edited by L. Nicholson, 157–75. New York: Routledge.

Hebdige, Dick. 1979. *Subcultures: The Meaning of Style*. London: Routledge.

Hirshi, Travis. 1969. *Causes of Delinquency*. Berkeley: University of California Press.

Holland, Sharon P. 2000. *Raising the Dead: Readings of Death and (Black) Subjectivity*. Durham: Duke University Press.

———. 2005. "Foreword: 'Home' Is a Four-Letter Word. In *Black Queer Studies: A Critical Anthology*, edited by E. P. Johnson and M. G. Henderson, ix–xiii. Durham: Duke University Press.

Hooks, bell. 1984. *Feminism: From Margin to Center*. Boston: South End Press.

International Institute for Sustainable Development. 1995. *Youth Sourcebook on Sustainable Development*. Winnipeg, Manitoba: IISD.

Iton, Richard. 2008. *In Search of the Black Fantastic: Politics and Popular Culture in the Post–Civil Rights Era*. Oxford: Oxford University Press.

Johnson, E. Patrick. 2005. "Quare Studies." In *Black Queer Studies: A Critical Anthology*, ed. E. P. Johnson and M. G. Henderson, 125–57 . Durham: Duke University Press.

Kane, Anne E. 1997. "Theorizing Meaning Construction in Social Movements:Symbolic Structures and Interpretation during the Irish Land War, 1879–1882." *Sociological Theory* 15, no. 3 (November): 249–76.

Kaye, Jeffrey. 1999. "The Hip-Hop Phenomenon." *NewsHour with Jim Lehrer*. Official transcript. February 24.

Kelley, Robin D. G. 1994. *Race Rebels; Culture, Politics, and the Black Working Class*. New York: Free Press.

———. 2004. *Freedom Dreams: The Black Radical Imagination*. New York: Free Press.

Kitwana, Bakari. 2002. *The Hip-Hop Generation: Young Blacks and the Crisis in African-American Culture*. New York: Basic Civitas Books.

———. 2006. *Why White Kids Love Hip-Hop: Wankstas, Wiggers, Wannabes, and the New Reality of Race in America*. New York: Basic Civitas Books.

Koppel, Niko. 2007. "Are Your Pants Sagging?: Go Directly to Jail." *New York Times*. (August 30th).

Lee, C. 2002. "The Impact of Belonging to a High School Gay/Straight Alliance." *High School Journal* 85, no. 3. (February-March): 13–26.

Lewis, George H. 1973. "Social Protest and Self-Awareness in Black Popular Music." *Popular Music and Society* 2, no. 4: 327–33.

Lipsitz, George. 1994. *Dangerous Crossroads: Popular Music, Postmodernism, and the Poetics of Place.* London: Verso.

———. 1994. "Foreword," *Race Rebels: Culture, Politics, and the Black Working Class,* by Robin D. G. Kelley. New York: Free Press.

———. 1998. "Consumer Spending as State Project: Yesterday's Solutions and Today's Problems." In *Getting and Spending: European and American Consumer Societies in the Twentieth Century,* edited by S. Strasser, C. McGovern, and M. Judt. Cambridge: Cambridge University Press.

———. 2001. *Time Passages: Collective Memory and American Popular Culture.* Minneapolis: University of Minnesota Press.

Lofland, John, and Lyn Lofland. 1995. *Analyzing Social Settings: A Guide to Qualitative Observation and Analysis.* Belmont, CA: Wadsworth Press.

Lorde, Audre. 1984. "Learning from the '60s." In *Sister Outsider: Essays and Speeches.* Berkeley, CA: Free Crossing Press.

McAdam, Doug. 1988. *Freedom Summer.* Oxford: Oxford University Press.

McAdam, Doug, and Ronnelle Paulsen. 1993. "Specifying the Relationship between Social Ties and Activism." *American Journal of Sociology* 99: 640–67.

McFarland, Daniel A., and Reuben J. Thomas. 2006. "Bowling Young: How Youth Voluntary Associations Influence Adult Political Participation." *American Sociological Review* 71, no. 2: 401–26.

McRobbie, Angela. 1991. *Feminism and Youth Culture: From Jackie to Just Seventeen.* London: Macmillan.

Ma, Jason. 1999. "East Bay Schools Fight Violence Together." *Asianweek* 21, no. 5. September 23.

Mansbach, Adam. 2005. *Angry Black White Boy.* New York: Three Rivers Press.

Marx, Karl. 1867 [1978]. "Das Capital, vol. 1." In *The Marx-Engels Reader,* edited by R. C. Tucker, 2nd ed. New York: W. W. Norton.

Marx-Feree, Myra, and Beth B. Hess. 1995. *Controversy and Coalition: The New Feminist Movement Across Three Decades of Change.* Rev. ed. New York: Twayne Publishers.

Massey, Douglas S., and Nancy Denton. 1993. *American Apartheid: Segregation and the Making of the Underclass.* Cambridge: Harvard University Press.

Melucci, Alberto. 1994. "A Strange Kind of Newness: What's 'New' in New Social Movements?" In *New Social Movements: From Ideology to Identity,* edited by E. Larana, H. Johnston, and J. R. Gusfield, 249–76. Philadelphia: Temple University Press.

Meyer, David S., and Nancy Whittier. 1994. "Social Movement Spillover." *Social Problems* 41:277–98.

Miller, Jody D. *Getting Played: African American Girls, Urban Inequality, and Gendered Violence.* New York: NYU Press.

Miranda, Marie "Keta." 2004. *Homegirls in the Public Sphere.* Austin: University of Texas Press.

Morgan, Joan. 1999. *When Chickenheads Come Home to Roost: My Life as a Hip-Hop Feminist.* New York: Simon and Schuster.

Morris, Aldon D. 1984. *The Origins of the Civil Rights Movement: Black Communities Organizing for Change.* New York: Free Press.

Morris, Aldon D., and Carol McClurg Mueller. 1992. *Frontiers in Social Movement Theory.* New Haven: Yale University Press.

Muñoz, Jose. 1999. *Disidentification: Queers of Color and the Performance of Politics.* Minneapolis: University of Minnesota Press.

Naples, Nancy A. 1998. *Community Activism and Feminist Politics: Organizing Across Race, Class, and Gender.* London: Routledge.

———. 1998. *Grassroots Warriors: Activist Mothering, Community Work, and the War on Poverty.* New York: Routledge.

Nas. 2001. "All I Need Is One Mic." *Stillmatic.* Columbia Records.

Nero, Charles I. 2005. "Why Are Gay Ghettoes White?" In *Black Queer Studies: A Critical Anthology,* edited by E. P. Johnson and M. G. Henderson, 228–48. Durham: Duke University Press.

Noguiera, Ana. 2002. "The Birth and Promise of the Indymedia Revolution." In *From ACT UP to the WTO: Urban Protest and Community Building in the Era of Globalization,* edited by B. Shepard and R. Hayduk, 290–97. London: Verso.

Omi, Michael, and Howard Winant. 1994. *Racial Formation in the United States: From the 1960s to the 1990s.* 2nd ed. London: Routledge.

Pascoe, C. J. 2007. *Dude, You're a Fag!: Masculinity and Sexuality in High School.* Berkeley: University of California Press.

Pattillo-McCoy, Mary. 1999. *Black Picket Fences: Privilege and Peril Among the Black Middle Class.* Chicago: University of Chicago Press.

Perry, Imani. 2004. *Prophets of the 'Hood: Politics and Poetics in Hip-Hop.* Durham: Duke University Press.

Phillips, Susan A. 1999. *Wallbangin': Graffiti and Gangs in L.A.* Chicago: University of Chicago Press.

Pough, Gwendolyn. 2004. *Check It While I Wreck It: Black Women, Hip-Hop and the Public Sphere.* Boston: Northeastern University Press.

Rage Against the Machine. 1992. "Wake Up." *Rage Against the Machine.* Epic Records.

———. 1992. "Take the Power Back." *Rage Against the Machine.* Epic Records.

Reddy, Chandan. 1998. "Home, Houses, Nonidentity: Paris is Burning." In *Burning Down the House: Recycling Domesticity,* edited by R. M. George. Boulder, CO: Westview Press.

Rhomberg, Christopher. 2004. *No There There: Race, Class, and Political Community in Oakland.* Berkeley: University of California Press.

Rios, Victor. 2006. "The Hyper-Criminalization of Black and Latino Male Youth in theEra of Mass Incarceration." *Souls: A Critical Journal of Black Politics, Culture, and Society* 8, no. 2: 40–54.

Robnett, Belinda. 1997. *How Long? How Long?: African American Women in the Struggle for Civil Rights*. Oxford: Oxford University Press.

Rodríguez, Juana María. 2003. *Queer Latinidad: Identity Practices, Discursive Spaces*. New York: NYU Press.

Román, David. 1998. *Acts of Intervention: Performance, Gay Culture, and AIDS*. Bloomington: Indiana University Press.

Rose, Tricia. 1994. *Black Noise: Rap Music and Black Culture in Contemporary America*. Middletown, CT: Wesleyan University Press.

———. 2008. *The Hip-Hop Wars: What We Talk About When We Talk About Hip-Hop and Why It Matters*. New York: Basic Books.

Russell, Stephen, Anna Muraco, Aarti Subramaniam, and Carolyn Laub. 2009. "Youth Empowerment and High School Gay-Straight Alliances." *Journal of Youth Adolescence* 38:891–903.

Russo, Vito, and Rob Epstein. 2005. *The Celluloid Closet*. Sony Pictures Classic.

Sawyers, Traci M., and David S. Meyer. 1999. "Missed Opportunities: Social Movement Abeyance and Public Policy." *Social Problems* 46, no. 2: 187–206.

Schloss, Joseph Glenn. 2004. *Making Beats: The Art of Sample Based Hip-Hop*. Middletown, CT: Wesleyan University Press.

Sedgwick, Eve. K. 1991. *Epistemology of the Closet*. Berkeley, CA: University of California Press.

Self, Robert O. 2005. *American Babylon: Race and the Struggle for Postwar Oakland*. Oxford: Oxford University Press.

Shakur, Tupac. 1998. "Changes." *Greatest Hits*. Death Row/Interscope/Amaru.

———. 2002. *The Rose That Grew From Concrete*. New York: Simon and Schuster.

Sharpley-Whiting, T. Denean. 2007. *Pimps Up! Ho's Down!: Hip Hop's Hold on Young Black Women* New York: NYU Press.

Shepard, Benjamin, and Ronald Hayduk. 2002. "Urban Protest and Community Building in the Era of Globalization." In *From ACT UP to the WTO: Urban Protest and Community Building in the Era of Globalization*, edited by B. Shepard and R. Hayduk, 1–9. London: Verso.

Smelser, Neil J. 1963. *Theory of Collective Behavior*. New York: Free Press of Glencoe.

Springer, Kimberly. 2005. *Living for the Revolution: Black Feminist Organizations, 1968–1980*. Durham: Duke University Press.

Steinhauer, Jennifer. 2008. "Road to November: The Youth Vote in Pennsylvania." *New York Times*, October 13.

Sturken, Marita. 1997. *Tangled Memories: The Vietnam War, the AIDS Epidemic, and the Politics of Remembering*. Berkeley: University of California Press.

Strauss, Anselm, and Juliet Corbin. 1990. *Basics of Qualitative Research: Grounded Theory Procedures and Techniques*. Newbury Park, CA: Sage Publications.

Swidler, Ann. 1986 "Culture in Action: Symbols and Strategies." *American Sociological Review* 41, no. 2 (April): 273–86.

Taft, Jessica Karen. 2007. "Racing Age: Reflections on Antiracist Research with Teenage Girls." In *Representing Youth: Methodological Issues in Critical Youth Studies*, edited by A. L. Best: 203–25. New York: NYU Press.

Tarrow, Sidney. 1998. *Power in Movement: Social Movements and Contentious Politics.* New York: Cambridge University Press.

Taylor, Verta A. 1996. *Rock-a-By Baby: Feminism, Self-Help, and Postpartum Depression.* New York: Routledge.

Taylor, Verta, and Nicole C. Raeburn. 1995. "Identity Politics as High-Risk Activism: Career Consequences for Lesbian, Gay, and Bisexual Sociologists." *Social Problems* 42:252–73.

Taylor, Verta, and Nancy Whittier. 1992. "Collective Identity in Social Movement Communities." In *Frontiers in Social Movement Theory*, edited by A. Morris and C. M. Mueller. New Haven: Yale University Press.

Tomlinson, Lori. 1998. "'This Ain't No Disco' . . . or Is it? Youth Culture and the Rave Phenomenon." In *Youth Culture: Identity in a Postmodern World*, edited by J. Epstein, 195–211. Walnut Creek, CA: Blackwell Publishing.

Venkatesh, Sudhir Alladi. 1997. "The Social Organizations of Street Gang Activity in an Urban Ghetto." *American Journal of Sociology* 103, no. 1 (July): 82–111.

———. 1998. "Gender and Outlaw Capitalism: A Historical Account of the Black Sisters United 'Girl Gang.'" *Signs: Journal of Women in Culture and Society* 23, no. 31: 683–709.

Visweswaran, Kamala. 1994. *Fictions of Feminist Ethnography.* Minneapolis: University of Minnesota Press.

Warner, Judith. 2009. "Dude, You've Got Problems." *New York Times*, April 16.

Watkins, S. Craig. 1998. *Representing: Hip-Hop Culture and the Production of Black Cinema.* Chicago: University of Chicago Press.

———. 2006. *Hip Hop Matters: Politics, Pop Culture, and the Struggle for Soul.* New York: Beacon Press.

Weston, Kevin. 1999. "Youth Work Together to Address Racism," *Jinn Magazine.* <http://pacificnewscenter.org/jinn>.

Wheeler, Wendy (with Carolyn Edlebeck). 2006. "Leading, Learning, and Unleashing Potential: Youth Leadership and Civic Engagement." *New Directions for Youth Development* 109 (April): 89–97.

Willis, Paul. 1978. *Profane Culture.* London: Routledge and Kegan Paul.

Wilson, William J. 1996. *When Work Disappears: The World of the New Urban Poor.* New York: Knopf.

———. 1980. *The Declining Significance on Race: Blacks and Changing American Institutions*, 2nd ed. Chicago: University of Chicago Press.

Wimsatt, William Upski. 1994. *Bomb the Suburbs.* Chicago: Subway & Elevated Press.

———. 2002. "My Generation: A Young Visionary Sizes Up the Emerging Youth Movement." *Utne Reader* 113 (September/October).

Wood, Lesley J., and Kelly Moore. 2002. "Target Practice: Community Activism in a Global Era." In *From ACT UP to the WTO: Urban Protest and Community Building in the Era of Globalization*, edited by B. Shepard and R. Hayduk, 21–34. London: Verso.

Zald, Mayer N., and John D. McCarthy. 1987. *Social Movements in an Organizational Society: Collected Essays.* New Brunswick: Transaction Books.

INDEX

ABOUT THE AUTHOR

ANDREANA CLAY is Associate Professor of Sociology at San Francisco State University.